Your Money Vehicle

Financial Literacy for Beginners

Second Edition
Jedidiah Collins CFP®

DEDICATION

This book is dedicated to the **three most incredible women in my life—Kira, who has been my partner in all things, and my daughters, who have filled my world with love, laughter, and meaning.**

To my bride, Kira,

No one prepared us for the journey Money Vehicle has taken us on but knowing that you are willing to venture down this path with me has no doubt been the only reason I could continue. Only with you by my side did I find the confidence to try and do the impossible.

To my first students, Palmer & Perri,

My hope is that you see what daddy has done, chased a dream and made it become a reality, and that it encourages you to dream big! You have witnessed all that I have poured into this venture and seen the blueprint of what accomplishing those dreams will require.

Thank you for always lighting up my days and giving me the love needed to keep going.

May our journey together continue to be filled with love, adventure, and countless

Your loving husband and father."

TABLE OF CONTENTS

TABLE OF CONTENTS

MONEY VEHICLE

THE FIRST TEN STEPS FOR YOUR PAYCHECK

We welcome you to the Money Vehicle program and the beginning of your financial literacy journey. Throughout this blended educational program, you will work online watching videos and interacting with content as well as working offline taking steps to build your own financial plan.

Money Vehicle is designed to challenge and direct you in multiple ways.

1. You may work through the course materials and content in this program in a traditional classroom with an instructor leading the way.
2. You may use this program on your own, navigating the content and the interactive textbook, and accessing all the resources that come with the program.

COURSE OVERVIEW

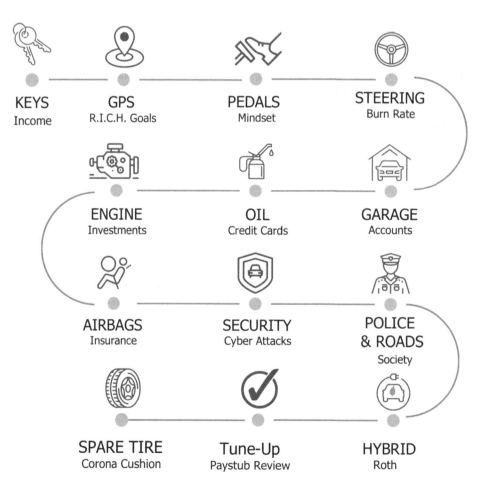

| KEYS | GPS | PEDALS | STEERING |
| Income | R.I.C.H. Goals | Mindset | Burn Rate |

| ENGINE | OIL | GARAGE |
| Investments | Credit Cards | Accounts |

| AIRBAGS | SECURITY | POLICE & ROADS |
| Insurance | Cyber Attacks | Society |

| SPARE TIRE | Tune-Up | HYBRID |
| Corona Cushion | Paystub Review | Roth |

A MESSAGE FROM MONEY VEHICLE FOUNDER:

Are you fed up with feeling like money is using you instead of you using it?

For so many this feeling can bring a sense of helplessness, like there is no breaking free from the cycle. In fact, most people are not confident in their finances at all and that is exactly how I felt before I went on my journey to become financially literate.

To understand why I started on this journey 15 years ago, I want to take you back to where it all began. Back in 2008 I was a rookie in the NFL and received my first large 'game check' from the Cleveland Browns. Despite being an Accounting Major in college the money was handled as you can expect, it came and went very fast!

My story is that I bought an engagement ring with this money and 15 years later it continues to be a very wise investment, but the reality is it was a poor financial habit. Habits are something we will be discussing a lot, but at this point, my understanding of financial habits was simple – make money, then spend it.

I, like so many other young professionals, had never been introduced to how money works and, as a result, I was "financially illiterate". This check humbled me and shocked me into realizing how unprepared I was for the financial opportunity of the NFL. This realization forced me to ask, "Why was I never taught how to handle money in school?"

Out of fear I would go broke, I decided to empower myself to begin speaking this foreign language of money. This journey began by walking through a Border's bookstore and learning from some of the guru's but really came to a vision of my path when a mentor challenged me to start studying for the CFP® (Certification in Financial Planning) during my NFL off seasons.

As my knowledge grew and I became a CFP®, I began to see this was not an NFL or even football problem, I began to see how little most people knew about money. I began to translate this language to teammates and friends, writing out analogies or stories that would become the beginning of "Your Money Vehicle."

Publishing the book was an amazing accomplishment and its intention was to be a stand-alone guide to help individuals, like me, learn the language of money. However, the question remained, "How is it that we don't teach the fundamentals of money in school, when we know that every student, regardless of career choice, is guaranteed to encounter one subject - money!"

Let me be clear, Money Vehicle is NOT a course about the NFL or really have anything to do with football. That is just where my journey began. This program is about where your journey begins and about what you are willing to do to learn the language of money.

MONEY VEHICLE MISSION:
BUILDING THE BEST HIGH SCHOOL FINANCIAL LITERACY CURRICULUM IN AMERICA!

Money Vehicle is designed for anyone who is about to receive their first paycheck or anyone who wants to learn how to U.S.E. their next paycheck. This course is for anyone who wants to speak the language of money and take control of their financial future by starting a plan.

To do this I knew we would have to move beyond just a textbook, I knew to keep your attention we would need to engage you through short stories on video and empower you through clear age-appropriate actions.

Together we can not only start the conversation around money, but we can also change the conversation all together. Through the stories and lessons found in Money Vehicle, we hope that you feel engaged, educated and empowered to change your future. This program will provide you with a skill to U.S.E. money throughout your life. When you can speak the language of money, you will begin to make money work for you and stop working for it.

I must point out that Money Vehicle is EDUCATION, NOT ADVICE. There is no conceivable way for anything in this program meant to give you the tools to make those decisions on your own. Money Vehicle does provide a certification that you can use to boost your resume and validate the start of your journey, but nothing is meant to be financial advice!

Remember, with anything you will get out what you put into Your Money Vehicle.

Thank you for your time and effort in this program. Welcome to the Money Vehicle Movement!

Jedidiah Collins

JEDIDIAH COLLINS CFP®;
NFL; AUTHOR; FOUNDER

MONEY VEHICLE CONTRIBUTORS:

 THERESA SEILER
Educator & Curriculum Designer

 KATIE MACDONALD CFP®
Financial Advisor & Financial Literacy Advocate

 MALCOLM JENKINS
2X Super Bowl Champion & Social Justice Advocate

 ELLIOT RIES
Investment Advisor & Money Vehicle Certificate

 NOAH BRUNE
Harvard Student Athlete and Money Vehicle Ambassador

 XAVIER LAGUNA
Money Vehicle Virtual Guide & Certificate

 VINCE HOLLERMAN
Financial Literacy Coach

 SAMUEL BECKER
Financial Writer and Industry Professional

 KRISTEN LOFARO
Curriculum design and brand

 MANISHA THAKOR MBA / CFA / CFP®
Founder of MoneyZen, Author, & Advocate of
Women's financial literacy

 FRAMEWORK CONSULTING: ANNA W. DAVIS
Curriculum Auditors & Superintendent of the Year

 SYNERGY COMPLIANCE SOLUTIONS
Curriculum Compliance and Audit

I N C O M E

INTRO

HOW CAN I INCREASE MY INCOME?

OVERVIEW

Part 1: Think like an Invest-OR

Part 2: What Money Is & What Money Is Not

Part 3: The Monster Eating Your Money: Inflation

Part 4: Earn Vs. Create Income

Part 5: Increase Income: Be a Pro

ACTION

Find a way to earn your first paycheck and turn Your Money Vehicle on.

DRIVING YOUR MONEY VEHICLE

Every road trip begins the same way, grabbing the car keys. In Your Money Vehicle, these car keys will be your income. They are vital to your journey because your vehicle will not go anywhere without them. An easy lesson is to not lose your keys, but a good plan has a spare set of keys too.

PART 1
INTRODUCE INCOME: THINK LIKE AN INVESTOR

TERMS

PRIORITIZED (DELAYED) GRATIFICATION: this is bit a sacrifice but is your ability to place what you want most over what you want now.

DESIRED LIFESTYLE: the life that you are building a plan to support in your future.

FUTURE YOU: the connection to your actions today impacting you in the future.

FINANCIALLY LITERATE: someone who can speak the language of money.

MONEY VEHICLE: the identification that money is a vehicle that will take you to your desired lifestyle, but money is not the destination.

OWNER'S MANUAL: the beginning of your financial plan and workbook you will create through your Money Vehicle journey. You keep this!

ASSET: something that puts money into your pocket.

LIABILITY: something that takes money out of your pocket.

MOORE'S LAW: a law stating that technology capabilities will double every two years, providing evidence you need to invest in yourself, not your job.

THINK LIKE AN INVESTOR: Money Vehicle principle that forces us to start seeing money through a long-term time horizon.

This journey will begin and end with questions. Questions that only YOU can answer and with each answer, you will begin taking control of Your Money Vehicle. So, let's get started:

QUESTION 1:
WHAT LIFESTYLE DO YOU ULTIMATELY WANT TO LIVE?

In 1972, Stanford Psychology Professor Walter Mischel conducted a study on **PRIORITIZED (DELAYED) GRATIFICATION**. In the study, which is often called "the marshmallow test," a child was offered the choice between one marshmallow now, or two marshmallows 15 minutes later.

> ## PRIORITIZED GRATIFICATION MEANS YOU VALUE SOMETHING MORE, NOT SACRIFICE FOR.

Stop for a moment and put yourself in the child's shoes. It's a simple enough scenario, right? But what is your choice?

This will be the first time Money Vehicle challenges you in a thought experiment, but trust me, it certainly won't be the last. If we take a step back for a moment, you're probably wondering: What the heck do marshmallows have to do with money?

Well, let's consider the fallout from the marshmallow test — which are, of course, open to interpretation. After following the children in the study for years after, the Stanford researchers found a relationship between their choices and their success. There was something unique about those children who chose to prioritize the second marshmallow. Those children went on to succeed in many of life's challenges over the children who ate the one marshmallow right away.

This connection to their discipline and ability to prioritize gratification for what they want MOST over what they want right NOW was a critical skill to their overall success.

> Discipline is choosing between what you want now and what you want most.
>
> -Abraham Lincoln

Money Vehicle is designed to enlighten and empower you to make choices, each day, concerning money. But you alone are making the choices, you alone are in control, and you alone will handle the aftermath of your choices.

Before we get started with how to make or manage money, we should really identify what it is, that you want from this journey and from Your Money Vehicle.

Take a moment and picture yourself at age 25 and wonder what your life looks like. Do you see a future where you spend $2,000, $4,000 or $8,000 a month?

Do not get lost in the details of this future, or the idea that you are not making enough money at all at this point in your life, just think about how much you will need to spend each month to live a lifestyle you desire. What does your lifestyle consist of:

 You can choose to pursue a lifestyle of being in power.

 You can choose to pursue a lifestyle of fancy things.

 You can choose to pursue a lifestyle of a large family.

 You can choose to pursue a lifestyle of travel.

 You can choose to pursue a lifestyle of working less.

 You can choose to pursue a lifestyle of impacting others.

We begin with this vision of your **DESIRED LIFESTYLE** because it will begin to paint a picture of what you want out of money and the income you will need to support it. Once you know your lifestyle and the income that will support it, you can begin to identify careers that can provide that income and build a plan from that career choice.

> **THIS IS CRITICALLY IMPORTANT: THIS FIRST CHOICE IS YOUR DESIRED LIFESTYLE. BECAUSE IT WILL IMPACT YOUR CAREER, YOUR INCOME, YOUR FAMILY, AND YOUR FULFILLMENT.**

STEPS DEFINING SUCCESS IN YOUR MONEY VEHICLE:

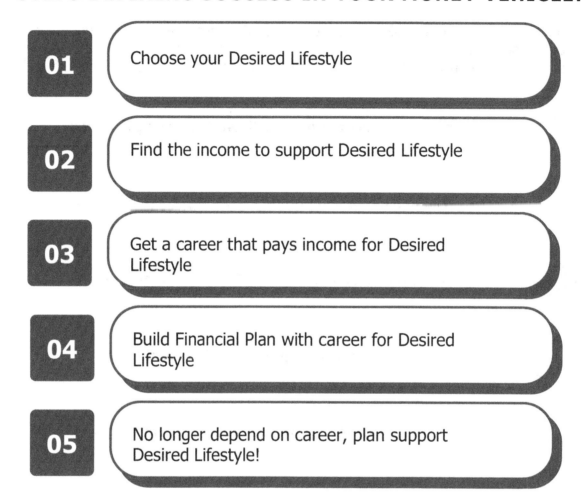

01 Choose your Desired Lifestyle

02 Find the income to support Desired Lifestyle

03 Get a career that pays income for Desired Lifestyle

04 Build Financial Plan with career for Desired Lifestyle

05 No longer depend on career, plan support Desired Lifestyle!

In Money Vehicle, we will assist you in establishing your money goals, money actions, and money plan, but remember throughout the program: **we make suggestions, you make decisions.**

WE MAKE
SUGGESTIONS  YOU MAKE
DECISIONS

The entire process begins with your decision around your desired lifestyle and what you want for **FUTURE YOU.** Introducing you to the idea of Future You may feel funny, but this program will begin laying out a path of actions to take between that person and where you are today.

Every decision and piece of this financial literacy puzzle will be about deciding if you want to reward Present You or Future You, and how to balance the two. The marshmallow test was a quick evaluation of how much you can look into the future and make decisions.

HOW DO I BEGIN CALCULATING A LIFESTYLE FOR MY FUTURE?

Your desired lifestyle will be determined, in large part by two decisions:

WHERE YOU CHOOSE TO LIVE  WHO (IF ANYONE) YOU CHOOSE TO LIVE WITH

WHERE DO YOU LIVE IN YOUR FUTURE:

There is a saying in real estate that goes: "The first three things that impact a home's price are location, location, location."

This means that if you choose to own a home, the area you choose to live in will significantly impact your home's value. What it does not say is that your location will also impact the lifestyle you will live and the income you will need to support it.

- Location will impact the cost of your rent or mortgage, the utilities to run your home, and the bills associated with maintaining your home.

- Location will impact your transportation to get around, the groceries at the local store, and prices at pretty much any business that offers goods or services near you.

When you look at your desired lifestyle, think through where you want to live and try to be specific as you can: country, state, city, street, size, floors, features, and what is around you.

- Do you want to live in Miami or Omaha?
- 2,000 or 4,000 square feet?
- In the city or in the suburbs?

If your Future holds a home worth $1 million, the corresponding lifestyle and income needed looks very different than someone living in a $400,000 or a $200,000 home.

WHO DO YOU LIVE WITH IN YOUR FUTURE:

Looking at your Desired Lifestyle, you will also need to look at who you will be supporting in that lifestyle. The first measurement is your friends as they will play a large role in defining a lifestyle. Then larger questions around any family members who will be depending on you to support? Will you start a family with children? Elderly parents?

- If your Future has your current friends, do they fore you to live beyond your means to keep up?

- If your Future has an income where you can support others, who would that be?

- If your Future has a family, what does that begin to look like?

WHAT IF I AM NOT STARTING WITH A LOT OF MONEY, DOES MONEY VEHICLE STILL MATTER?

That all depends on if you want Future You to be in a different place than Present You.

> If you want something you've never had, you must be willing to do something you've never done.
>
> -Thomas Jefferson

This quote seems straight forward but give it some serious thought as to what it means. Jefferson is saying if you feel you do not have a lot of money today, and desire to have more in the Future, than you must begin to act in a way you have never acted before. In other words, it's time to act.

If you see your income today and are comfortable seeing yourself next year, or in ten years, in the same situation as today, then you will not get much out of Money Vehicle. If, however, you start looking at things through the lens of Future You and your Desired Lifestyle, then we can get started with wherever you are today.

The truth is, we must change your mindset before we can change your behaviors and we will need to have both for success. If you think you will change either once more money begins to come in, you have not read the headlines of lottery winners, athletes, entertainers, or entrepreneurs who come into and out of money quickly.

It does not matter if you have $20 or $20,000 — when you become **FINANCIALLY LITERATE** and begin to speak the language of money, you will begin driving towards Future You!

WILL MY CHOICES TODAY REALLY HAVE A BIG IMPACT ON MY FUTURE?

Stop seeing Present You and Future You as separate, start seeing Present You and Future You as the same person. This is a difficult concept, so we will turn to someone who embodies this practice - Warren Buffett.

Warren Buffett is widely considered to be one of the greatest investors of our generation with a Net Worth of $113 Billion in 2023. What Buffett understood at an early age was that his Present financial decisions were connected to his Future financial situation. Once he understood this concept, he stopped treating the two as separate and began making decisions with both in mind. When Buffett made this discovery, it is partly what has led him to becoming such a great investor.

WARREN BUFFETT'S NET WORTH AS OF 2023[1]

$113,000,000,000

> The story goes that when Buffett was just eight years old, he calculated the total cost of haircuts over his lifetime. At the time, he could get his haircut for $8, but if he received 12 haircuts per year, over a 90-year time frame, that would amount to more than $50,000!

Buffett was not only calculating the cost of the haircut, but also measuring what else he could do with the $8 if not spent on a haircut - invest. Once he was able to see his financial decisions differently, he no longer separated them between the present and the future but instead began to treat all his financial decisions as if they impacted both.

This maybe a bit confusing, but the point is that every financial decision you make today in the present, will connect to the same person in 1, 5, or 50 years = YOU!

MONEY VEHICLE will not just introduce you to the language of money but will empower you to take the actions of a financially literate person.

GREAT! WHERE DO WE BEGIN?

The first action, and start of Your Money Vehicle journey, is getting the keys to your vehicle by earning your first paycheck. This paycheck will be connected to a job today, but as you begin to look at Future You, you will see how this paycheck connects to supporting your Desired Lifestyle.

We titled this program Money Vehicle because it is a message to see money differently. To begin, seeing money as the vehicle that will take you to the life and future you desire. We will provide you with an **OWNER'S MANUAL** a workbook that will assist you in learning how to drive and will document the beginning of your financial plan.

We want you to think of money as a vehicle which will take you to the life you want. Money Vehicle means money will take you to your destination, money is NOT the destination.

As you see this vehicle and the opportunity before you, take pride in the idea that upon completing this program, you will know the first 10 steps to take in your financial journey.

I AM DRIVING MY MONEY VEHICLE, BUT WHAT FEATURES OR RESOURCES DO I HAVE TO USE ON THE JOURNEY?

First off, congratulations on taking that first step in owning who is driving!

It may feel overwhelming, entering this new world and language but remember, Money Vehicle will introduce you to everything you need to know and define each of your first 10 actions. We are not going to try and teach you the entirety of money, we are going to focus on what you need to start. There will be plenty of time for you to dive into next level things after you take your first 10 steps.

Next, we need to introduce you to the resources you will use in Your Money Vehicle. In the financial world, these resources are called "assets."

Let's begin with an explanation of asset from a book that introduced me and millions to key terms in money: "Rich Dad Poor Dad" by author Robert Kiyosaki. In "Rich Dad Poor Dad," Kiyosaki uses a very simple analogy to introduce assets and their counterpart, liabilities, by framing it around what puts money into your pocket versus what takes money out of your pocket.

ASSET PUTS MONEY INTO YOUR POCKET

LIABILITY TAKES MONEY OUT OF YOUR POCKET

With this definition of assets in mind, what do you think will put the most amount of money in your pocket throughout your life?

WHAT IS MY GREATEST ASSET?

Most people think this is an easy answer, assuming their greatest asset will be a career or an investment. But the truth is the greatest asset that you have, and will ever have, is YOU.

Over your lifetime, the asset that will put the most money into your pocket is YOU. That includes the education you attain, the experience you garner, and the energy you can bring.

Read that again and say it out loud:

(YOUR NAME) IS MY GREATEST ASSET.

Warren Buffett's opinion on you being your greatest asset:

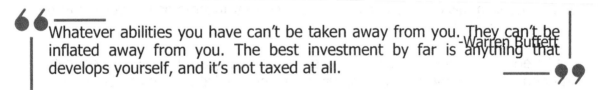

" Whatever abilities you have can't be taken away from you. They can't be inflated away from you. The best investment by far is anything that develops yourself, and it's not taxed at all.

-Warren Buffett

"

If you are starting to think about money differently, you should begin to think about yourself differently as well. Since you are an asset, you will need to invest time and money into maximizing you.

INVEST IN YOUR GREATEST ASSET: YOU!

IS INVESTING IN MY JOB THE SAME AS INVESTING IN ME?

This is where you will need to start mentally separating who you are from what you do. Money Vehicle is NOT saying that you should slack off at work or just slide by. We are saying that you should look at yourself independently from your current job, because your job is what you do, not who you are.

You may wash dishes, but that doesn't make you a dishwasher.

You may be a CEO, but you're still a person outside of that role, too.

You need to invest in you and not just your job because no one knows what the future holds, or what new careers and industries will develop over the next few decades. If you believe **MOORE'S LAW.** stating that technological capabilities tend to double every two years, then we know that we can't even conceive some of the careers you may have.

This uncertainty can be intimidating, but the best way to prepare for the unknown is to continuously develop ways to add more value to yourself. When you continually improve your greatest asset, then you will naturally bring more value to any job you have as well.

If you are more interested in developing knowledge or skills that do not pertain to or align with your current job, that should tell you a lot about where Future You wants to go. In this case, you can use your current income as the vehicle to get you to your next stop.

The three ways to add value to any asset or company are by bringing education, experience, or energy to it. We will dive into these attributes in the Be A Pro section shortly, but first, we need to identify what money is and what money is not to each of us.

PART 1

RECAP

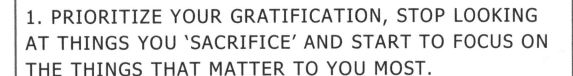

1. PRIORITIZE YOUR GRATIFICATION, STOP LOOKING AT THINGS YOU 'SACRIFICE' AND START TO FOCUS ON THE THINGS THAT MATTER TO YOU MOST.

2. YOU ARE YOUR GREATEST ASSET, CONTINUE TO INVEST IN YOURSELF TO PREPARE FOR AN UNKNOWN FUTURE.

3. MONEY VEHICLE MAKES SUGGESTIONS, YOU MAKE DECISIONS!

PART 2
WHAT MONEY IS,
AND WHAT MONEY IS NOT

TERMS

MONEY SUPPLY: the total amount of money circulating in an economy at one time, the USA is dollars.

GOLD STANDARD: an economic system where the currency is backed by a tangible resource of Gold being held by the government.

BRETTON WOODS AGREEMENT: an agreement stating you can exchange an ounce of gold for $35 cash.

MONETARY POLICY: a set of actions to control a nation's overall money supply and achieve economic growth.[3]

FIAT SYSTEM: an economic system where the currency is backed by an intangible concept such as confidence or trust in the country's economy.

TANGIBLE: something you can touch.

INTANGIBLE: something you cannot touch.

MONEY VALUES: a reflection of who you are and what money is to you.

FINISH THIS SENTENCE: MONEY IS...

MONEY IS POWER

MONEY IS FREEDOM

MONEY IS OVERWHELMING

MONEY IS EVIL

Money means something different to each of us, depending on where we grew up, who we grew up around, what we have used it for, our age, and why we are using it. It is amazing to see the different perspectives we can each have while looking at the same concept, but our own individual ideas of money are unique to each of us.

Too often, people confuse the value of money with a value based in time. For instance, we look at an hourly wage or an annual salary and see the connection of money to our time and are confused into thinking that money is connected to the amount of time we give it.

The old saying "time is money" leads us to believe that if we just put in more time, we will receive more money. This may be true in some cases — you get an extra shift or put in some overtime, you will (hopefully) earn more money. But you are still not being paid for your time.

Imagine you need to complete Project X, and have two employees: Employee A and Employee B. You ask each employee to work on Project X, and you know Project X's total value is $100.

- Employee A completes Project X in four hours
- Employee B completes Project X in one hour

In this scenario, Employee A would be paid $25 per hour, and Employee B would be paid $100 per hour. It is the same hour, but Employee B is receiving four times more money in the same amount of time.

This is because you, as the boss, are not paying the employees for the time they put into your business. You are paying your employees based on the value they add to your business.

YOU ARE NOT PAID FOR YOUR TIME; YOU ARE PAID FOR YOUR MARKET VALUE!

Even when you look at being paid $50,000 for a year's worth of work — an employer is not paying you for the time you will work in the year, they are paying you on the value they believe you will add in that year.

Think of it this way: That one year is the same amount of time it takes for anyone else to earn $100,000, $40,000, etc.

Today, people can make $1,000,000 in a single hour, it's not common of course, but possible. It's not because their hour is necessarily special or unique, but because their business or employer deems the value added to the business in that hour at that price.

HOW CAN PEOPLE ADD SO MUCH MORE VALUE IN LESS TIME TODAY?

Today, it seems as though dollar figures are limitless — think about the billions and trillions of dollars floating around out there. But there is a limit to the amount of U.S. Dollars (USD) in circulation around the world, and that limit is known as the **MONEY SUPPLY.** The money supply is the total amount of money (USD) circulating in our economy at one time.

MONEY SUPPLY

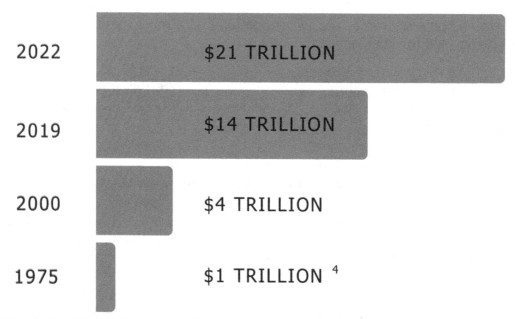

- Why is the Unites States' money supply growing so quickly?

- How is it growing so quickly?

- When will that growth impact us as individuals?

- To answer these questions, we need to travel back to 1970.

In 1970, the average American made $9,967 per year, the average home sold for less than $30,000, a car cost around $2,000, a McDonald's burger was $.20, the largest company was IBM (International Business Machines), and the total U.S. money supply was $500,000,000,000.[5]

For comparison: As of 2022, the average American earned $56,000, the average home price is more than $400,000, a McDonald's cheeseburger costs $3.49, the largest company (by revenue) is Walmart, and the total U.S. money supply was $21,000,000,000,000.

Another important fact about 1970 is that the U.S. used the **"GOLD STANDARD"** for its **MONETARY POLICY** which we will discuss deeper as we work through the program. But for now, just know it was a tool used to control the money supply. In 1970, there was an agreement in the U.S. in which you could go and exchange an ounce of gold for $35 cash — this was part of an agreement that was called the "**BRETTON WOODS AGREEMENT**." The gold standard meant that every dollar in circulation was equal to a standard amount of gold held by the United States government.

> **1970 GOLD STANDARD: YOUR DOLLARS ($) WERE BACKED BY GOLD (METAL).**

There were strengths and simplicity in having our nation's money tied to a tangible resource, like gold. However, one of the issues with the gold standard was that it could not support the demands of the Unites States' growing population, or its ever-changing economic needs.

When there was a high increase in spending or loans were needed because a war broke out, the dependency on gold would limit the country's ability to meet the financial need.

This challenged the flexibility of the gold standard to the point that, on August 15th, 1971, President Richard Nixon announced that the backing of the U.S. Dollar would change to be backed by the "confidence in one's economy."[6]

On that day, the U.S. would no longer be limited to the confines of its physical gold supply and, instead, the money supply would be as abundant as the confidence we had in our nation's economy. This shifted our economic system into what is called a **FIAT SYSTEM**, where the value of the dollar is not backed by a **TANGIBLE** asset, but instead, is backed by an **INTANGIBLE** concept — like one's trust in the economy.

> ## FIAT MEANS THE DOLLAR IS BACKED BY OUR CONFIDENCE IN AMERICA.

As such, no longer would $1 be equal to .35 ounces of gold, but instead $1 was equal to one note of trust in the United States economy. This monumental shift changed money from a tangible resource to an intangible resource, and with it, changed how our country views money as well.

> ## MONEY IS NO LONGER GOLD OR EVEN A TANGIBLE THING!

With this change, when the economy was in demand for more dollars, the money supply could be raised to meet the need without having to mine for more gold. This new fiat system was, again, based on confidence, and that confidence would provide the flexibility our economy would need to grow.

President Nixon challenged our country and economy to see money differently:

- Stop seeing money as gold, a tangible object.
- Start seeing money as confidence, an intangible idea.

We will continue to shift how we see money through this Money Vehicle journey, but it starts with the idea that money is NOT a physical thing anymore. Money is not time, and it is no longer gold either. One of Money Vehicle's Missions is to get you to U.S.E. money. This acronym plays into seeing money as a verb and not a noun, forcing you to see money as something you control and not something that controls you.

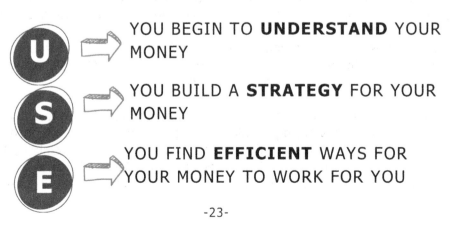

U → YOU BEGIN TO **UNDERSTAND** YOUR MONEY

S → YOU BUILD A **STRATEGY** FOR YOUR MONEY

E → YOU FIND **EFFICIENT** WAYS FOR YOUR MONEY TO WORK FOR YOU

HOW DOES THE GOLD STANDARD CONNECT TO BEING PAID FOR OUR VALUE?

Zoney is no longer limited by the amount of gold in a safe, and instead, it is limited only to the confidence we have in our country. With this concept in mind, you will see the limits of money differently. You will see that your income is not limited to time or gold, your income is abundant to the value you can add to a business.

Money is not simple but managing it can be broken down into simple steps – How to U.S.E. money, which we will work through as we drive on. But, before we can move on, you must identify what money is to you today, and what your core Money Values are going to be.

Your **MONEY VALUES** can only be determined by you and the principles you are going to U.S.E. to direct your money choices. These values will become a reflection of who you are and the things you want to prioritize on your financial journey. You can begin to see your Money Values like a mirror, a reflection of what you value and a guide to keep your choices on the right path.

These Money Values will be a co-pilot on your journey and continue to provide that compass to confirm if your choices reflect your core beliefs. In Chapter 1 we will set R.I.C.H. Goals and set some destinations for your plan, but you must continue to understand that money is NOT your destination. Money is a vehicle you will U.S.E. to show your values and move you to your next stop!

MONEY IS...A REFLECTION OF YOUR VALUES.

TYPES OF MONEY VALUES	
SECURITY	wanting money to meet your needs
FREEDOM	wanting money to provide your wants
STATUS	wanting money to show people who you are
POWER	wanting money to give you control over others or things
WORSHIP	wanting money over everything else
VIGILANCE	wanting money to guide your every decision
AVOIDANCE	wanting money to go away and ignore it
FAITH	wanting money to impact a higher purpose
SOCIETY	wanting money to impact the world or community
FAMILY	wanting money to take care of your loved ones

Warning: There is a monster out there who eats away at the power of your money. You must begin to fight the monster eating your money!

PART 2
RECAP

1. YOU ARE NOT PAID FOR YOUR TIME; YOU ARE PAID FOR YOUR MARKET VALUE.

2. AMERICA HAS MOVED AWAY FROM THE GOLD STANDARD INTO A FIAT SYSTEM BACKED BY CONFIDENCE.

3. MONEY IS... A REFLECTION OF THE VALUES YOU PRIORITIZE.

PART 3

THE MONSTER
EATING YOUR
MONEY:
INFLATION

TERMS

INFLATION: the future purchasing power of $1 will be less than today or things in the future will feel more expensive.

PURCHASING POWER: how much $1 can buy today.

BUREAU OF LABOR STATISTICS (BLS): the government agency responsible for measuring inflation.

CONSUMER PRICE INDEX (CPI): CPI is a theoretical basket of over 80,000 goods and services that consumers will purchase, and this basket can be used to compare prices of those purchases from one year to another year.

FEDERAL RESERVE (COMMONLY CALLED THE FED OR FED): a central bank for the United States that was created by the Federal Reserve Act back in 1913 as a response to financial panics occurring in the United States.

FEDERAL OPEN MARKET COMMITTEE (FOMC): the branch of the FED who is responsible for managing the money supply and attempting to achieve the FOMC mandate. That mandate is a goal of 2% inflation annually, and to keep unemployment low.

CONSUMER CREDIT PROTECTION ACT OF 1968: a statute that mandates that the total cost and calculation of a loan be disclosed, along with any fees.

FAIR CREDIT REPORTING ACT OF 1970: a statute that aims to promote accuracy, fairness, and privacy of consumer information obtained by a reporting agency.

FAIR DEBT COLLECTION PRACTICES ACT OF 1977: a statute that aims to eliminate abusive practice in the collection of consumer debt.

EQUAL CREDIT OPPORTUNITY ACT OF 1974: a statute that aims to require banks, credit card companies, and any other lenders to make credit equally available to all creditworthy customers.

CONSUMER FINANCIAL PROTECTION BUREAU (CFPB): a government agency dedicated to making sure you are treated fairly by banks, lenders, and other financial institutions as well as enforce consumer protection laws.

Now you know money is not backed by gold (or anything physical, really), you can begin to understand how prices can increase even when there's no real change to a product or service to cause it.

Let me ask you a question:

Do you remember the first time you noticed the price of something you wanted to buy had increased?

 Example: One day something was $5, and then a few weeks later, as if out of thin air, poof, it was $6?

Better yet, think of a toy you played with as a kid. Just ten years ago, this toy may have cost $20 but today kids are buying the same toy for $40!

What happened?

No matter if you have been conscious of the increase in prices or not, the reality is there is one strong likelihood we all face when it comes to money:

> **EVERYTHING IN YOUR LIFE IS GOING TO GET MORE EXPENSIVE AS TIME GOES ON.**

There is no better time to introduce you to one of the greatest challenges you will face in your personal finance journey, the monster who eats your money: **INFLATION**!

Inflation is a confusing concept, so we will introduce you to the dictionary definition, and then provide some Money Vehicle translation for you to better understand its meaning. The dictionary definition of inflation is "your future purchasing power of $1 will not be as high as the purchasing power of $1 today."

Your **PURCHASING POWER** is how much $1 can buy you today. When the future purchasing power of $1 is lower than today, it means that you will not be able to buy as much in the future with the same $1.

 With $20 today, you can go see a movie and get candy. But fast forward to the year 2030 and the SAME $20 will only get you into the movie, no candy.

2023 ⇒  **&**    **2030** ⇒

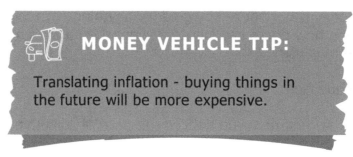

One of the only guarantees in money is that everything in your life, from the cost of soap in the bathroom all the way up to the cost of the house the bathroom is in, will cost more in the future. This can seem a little obvious when read straight forward, but very few take into consideration the mathematical impact inflation will have on their financial journey.

HOW MUCH WILL INFLATION IMPACT MY PLAN?

First, we need to understand that inflation is normal and natural in our economy. Economists see a small amount of inflation as necessary to grow the economy.

While inflation is natural it is also one of the biggest hurdles you will need to overcome for financial success. With inflation decreasing how much you can buy with your $1, you will need to look at your lifestyle and see the impact this monster will have on it. If you are living a lifestyle that is $2,000 a month today, you can see how that same lifestyle will cost you $3,000 a month as inflation increases prices each year.

Real Life Scenario: A family living off $1,000 in 1971 would need $7,649 a month to live in 2022 because the dollar lost 90% of its purchasing power.

This introduction to inflation is not meant to alarm you, but to warn you of why it is a necessity today to learn the language of money and to "Act like an Investor". We need to look no further than inflation to see that we must begin to make money work for us.

> **INFLATION IS MORE DEVASTATING THAN ANY TAX! 5% INFLATION IS EQUAL TO 120% INCOME TAX.**

BEFORE I FIGHT INFLATION, CAN YOU EXPLAIN HOW WE MEASURE OR TRY TO CONTROL IT?

In Economics, we learn that the **BUREAU OF LABOR STATISTICS (BLS)** measures inflation through the **CONSUMER PRICE INDEX (CPI).** CPI is a theoretical basket of over 80,000 goods and services that consumers will purchase, and this basket can be used to compare prices of those purchases from one year to another year.

 ## IN 2021 CPI ROSE NEARLY 9% AND GAS PRICES ALONE WENT UP 18%.

The measurement of CPI is the first step in trying to control inflation, the rest of the job falls to the entity responsible for controlling the economy's money supply, the Federal Reserve.

The **FEDERAL RESERVE (COMMONLY CALLED THE FED OR FED)** was created by the Federal Reserve Act back in 1913 as a response to financial panics occurring in the United States economy. Unites State citizens were concerned their bank deposits could become unsafe and began flooding the banking system in panic, demanding their money back. Money that was lent out to other people (Discuss in Chapter 4), and this caused a lot of problems for small, independent banks as they were not able to provide the demanded cash.

The FED was formed by the U.S. government as the central bank for the United States, but, the FED is INDEPENDENT from the United States government.

THE FED IS INDEPENDENT FROM GOVERNMENT TO ALLOW IT TO THINK LIKE AN INVESTOR!

That's right, the central bank of our economy and government is not part of the government. The reason for keeping the FED independent from the government was to ensure its decisions would always be made with an unbiased, long-term time horizon in mind, and not be influenced by short term political agendas.

This perspective and time-horizon epitomizes one of Money Vehicle's mindsets and allows the FED to Act like an Investor – Thinking Long-Term.

The FED works to protect you, the consumer, by overseeing the banking system and defending your consumer rights, such as the right to: basic needs, to be informed, to be safe, to be heard, and to consumer education. Overall, the FED wants to provide a healthy environment for the consumer to be able to stimulate the economy.

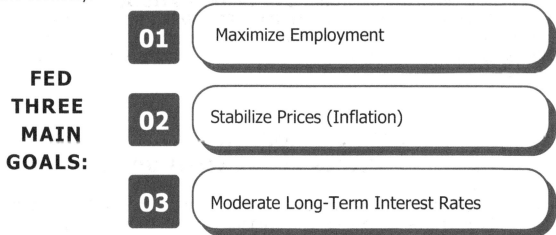

FED THREE MAIN GOALS:

01 Maximize Employment

02 Stabilize Prices (Inflation)

03 Moderate Long-Term Interest Rates

How most people learn or hear about what the FED is through the **FEDERAL OPEN MARKET COMMITTEE (FOMC)**, whose main responsibility is managing the money supply. The FOMC attempts to achieve their mandate of 2% average annual inflation and to keep 'maximum' employment.

That is right, the FED aims for and wants some amount of inflation to occur each year, because inflation is not necessarily all bad. Inflation increasing at a moderate level reflects a strong economy, without prices going up, it would be harder for companies to continue making a profit. Inflation also leads to a rise in wages and salaries, meaning people will make more money.

Inflation is such a massive concept that we will continue to address it throughout the Money Vehicle program:

CHAPTER 1.2	How does Inflation impact the Golden Rule?
CHAPTER 2.1	How does the FED control the Money Supply?
CHAPTER 3.3	How do you begin to outpace inflation?
CHAPTER 6.3	What investments will fight off inflation?

Consumer Protection Laws:

CONSUMER CREDIT PROTECTION ACT OF 1968	This statute aims to protect consumers and their financial records from banks, credit card companies, auto leasing companies, and other lenders by enforcing disclosure agreements. The Act mandates that the total cost and calculation of a loan be disclosed, along with any fees (Truth in Lending Act—Section 2.4). This Act also prohibits discrimination when considering loan applications.
FAIR CREDIT REPORTING ACT OF 1970	This statute aims to promote accuracy, fairness, and privacy of consumer (credit) information that is obtained by a consumer reporting agency such as credit bureaus, medical information, and tenant screening.
FAIR DEBT COLLECTION PRACTICES ACT OF 1977	This statute aims to eliminate abusive practice in the collection of consumer debt, amend inadequate laws, promote non-abusive debt collection, govern debt on interstate commerce and provide a consistent action of collecting debt.
EQUAL CREDIT OPPORTUNITY ACT OF 1974	This statute aims to require banks, credit card companies, and any other lenders to make credit equally available to all creditworthy customers. The ECOA prohibits discrimination based on race, color, religion, sex, marital status, age, or disability.
CONSUMER FINANCIAL PROTECTION BUREAU OF 2008	This government agency is dedicated to making sure you are treated fairly by banks, lenders, and other financial institutions as well as enforcing consumer protection laws.

PART 3
RECAP

OKAY, THE FED CONTROLS THE MONEY SUPPLY AND INTEREST RATES, BUT WHAT CAN I DO TO FIGHT INFLATION?

To fight off inflation, you must at the very least have your money working for you to outpace or grow faster than the rate of inflation. To outpace inflation, you will have to learn how to not just <u>earn</u> money, but also how to <u>create</u> money!

1. THE MONSTER EATING AWAY AT YOUR DOLLARS IS CALLED INFLATION.

2. CPI IS THE MEASUREMENT OF INFLATION, AND THE FED IS RESPONSIBLE FOR THE MANAGEMENT OF IT.

3. INFLATION WILL IMPACT EVERY ASPECT OF YOUR FINANCIAL PLAN, SO PREPARE TO FIGHT IT.

PART 4
EARN VS. CREATE INCOME

TERMS

MINDSET: the established attitudes and beliefs you hold.

EARNED INCOME: money you went to work for and represents your primary income.

CREATED INCOME: money that worked for you and represents secondary income sources.

TREATING MONEY LIKE AN EMPLOYEE: Money Vehicle term that means you need to treat each paycheck like it works for you, give it a job, and tell it what to do.

PRIMARY INCOME: the 'keys' for your Money Vehicle. This is the main source of income where you earn a wage or salary.

SECONDARY INCOME: the 'spare keys' for your Money Vehicle. These are the other income sources you create through business, property, debt, or talent.

WAGE: income for which you will be paid your market value at an hourly rate.

SALARY: income for which you will be paid your market value at an annual rate.

ENTREPRENEUR: someone who creates a business that can function without them.

SELF-EMPLOYED: someone who creates an income working for themselves.

INTELLECTUAL PROPERTY: a creative piece of work or invention that someone can claim ownership of.

NAME, IMAGE, & LIKENESS (NIL): the ability to get paid for who you are, what you look like, or what you represent for marketing or promotional use.

E-COMMERCE: buying or selling things online.

GIG-ECONOMY: a labor market primarily used for short-term contracts.

THE AVERAGE AMERICAN HAS A HIGHER INCOME TODAY BUT THAT DOES NOT ALWAYS EQUAL A HIGHER SPENDING POWER, THIS IS PARTLY DUE TO INFLATION, BUT ALSO DUE TO THE CHANGE IN ONE THING: THEIR MINDSET.

Throughout Money Vehicle, we will use character scenarios to help bring lessons to life. Today, let's look at how Adrian is using Money Vehicle to change his **MINDSET** on how money can work differently.

Adrian picks up odd jobs here and there, and at the end of each project, is given $10. With this $10, Adrian goes to a chicken farmer down the road and spends $2 buying an egg and toast for breakfast.

Adrian begins to question this spending cycle he is in. It feels as though he's earning his money only to spend it the next morning on food. He wonders how he can ever get ahead with this earn and spend cycle.

One day, Adrian asks the chicken farmer how much one of her chicken's costs - the answer: $40.

Adrian thinks about this for a moment. He had always thought his $10 was destined to buy food the next day. That is what his parents did with their money, and no one had ever introduced him to another option.

But now, Adrian has an idea! He sees an opportunity that could not only help him every day but also could change the spending cycle he is in. If he can just have toast one morning a week, he would be able to save up enough to buy his own chicken.

For the next several weeks, Adrian saves $5 per week. He doesn't let the week where he needed to replace a window for the house, or the week where his sister needed to borrow $2, derail him. He prioritized what he wanted, a chicken, and after some time, he saved up the $40.

With this $40 Adrian returns to the chicken farmer and asks to buy a chicken.

Now, each morning Adrian looks to see if his chicken has laid an egg for breakfast. Each morning that it has, Adrian takes the extra $1 and begins saving up to buy another chicken. Adrian believes he can buy several chickens and start to sell the eggs alongside his farmer friend.

Adrian knew how to work for money, and working hard is an essential part of your plan. But what he discovered is that if he learned to U.S.E. money differently, buying things that could put money into his pocket (Asset), then money would begin working for him.

Money Vehicle defines money that you earn through working as **EARNED INCOME**, and money that works for us as **CREATED INCOME**.

EARNED INCOME **MONEY YOU WENT TO WORK TO EARN**

CREATED INCOME **MONEY THAT WORKED FOR YOU**

There are many ways to earn an income, but the biggest reason people today have more income is because they have changed their mindset to look for ways of creating money. When you begin to search out ways to make money work for you, you start the process of creating money. We discussed assets earlier, now you can see that assets can create more money by making money work for you and putting that money in your pocket.

TREAT MONEY LIKE AN EMPLOYEE, PUT IT TO WORK!

This shift in mindset, from earning an income to creating an income, led people to stop being an employee for money and start making money an employee for you. **TREATING MONEY LIKE AN EMPLOYEE** means your money will be working for you even when you're not working, when you're asleep, or otherwise not paying attention. You have officially begun creating money.

This practice of putting money into assets for the future, instead of spending it on something today, is an example of "Prioritizing Gratification".

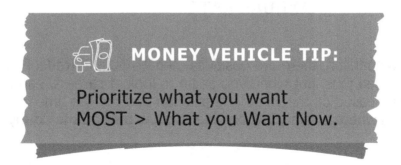

MONEY VEHICLE TIP:

Prioritize what you want
MOST > What you Want Now.

People today have a higher income because they are resisting the natural pull to earn and spend for something in their future that is worth prioritizing over today. Choosing to place money into assets, which will help them create their financial goals.

In Chapter 2 we will answer and dive deeper into the question How does money create money? For now, we want to focus on how earning money and creating money are different income sources in your financial plan.

That plan and everything in Your Money Vehicle begins with earning a "primary" source of income. This **PRIMARY INCOME** will come from you taking a Job, In which you earn a **WAGE** or a **SALARY**.

WHICH IS BETTER PRIMARY SOURCE OF INCOME: A WAGE OR A SALARY?

A big question when it comes to earning a paycheck is if you will be paid a wage or a salary. The distinction between the two will be how long your employer measures your market value, by the hour or by the year?

YOU WILL BE PAID YOUR MARKET VALUE ON AN HOURLY RATE

YOU WILL BE PAID YOUR MARKET VALUE ON AN ANNUAL RATE

As with any comparison, there are positives, negatives, and tradeoffs between hourly and salaried jobs. But when you begin to look at careers, earnings potential will be based on the value of a position and not the time in that position. This is where a salary will be able to grow beyond the hourly wage.

WAGE	SALARY
Will only be paid for time clocked	Consistency in being paid through the year no matter of business fluctuations
Minimum Wage set by state or federal whichever is higher	Minimum of $684 per week but no maximum of what you can earn
Autonomy to choose when you want to work	No control over the hours you work if your job or boss demands
Paid overtime, 1.5 times hourly wage, above 40 hours regular wage	Paid bonus, commissions, stipends, or reimbursements above salary
Can be offered benefits but not mandatory	Offered company benefits such as health insurance and retirement plan
No vacation pay	Typically, 2 weeks paid vacation
More project based or entry level	More senior positions
Taxed as ordinary income	Taxed as ordinary income
Harder to create financial plan due to uncertainty of income	Easier to create a financial plan due to certainty of income

I AM GREAT AT MY JOB, WHY DO I NEED TO WORRY ABOUT A SECOND INCOME?

The reality is that a primary source of income can disappear. A company makes layoffs, your parents get sick back home, you make a mistake at work, or your boss just doesn't understand you. There are endless ways for your primary income to vanish. Odds are that you will lose your primary income at some point in your career, which is why you need a Corona Cushion (Chapter 4).

To build your plan to not be solely dependent on your primary income, you want to start creating "secondary" sources of income. If, for some reason, your primary paycheck is taken away, there is a tremendous amount of security in knowing that you'll still have some money coming in through other income sources.

This may be the first time you hear the term other income sources, because many of us, growing up, were told to "get an education and then get a job." This mindset forces us to put our entire financial plan solely on that primary income source. Then, one day, for matters usually outside of our control, that one income is taken away and your plan with it.

What people have discovered is that when it comes to income, two is better than one. A "**SECONDARY**" source of income can be created by owning a business, owning a property, owning a loan, or owning your talent. This second source of income is like having a 'spare' set of keys for Your Money Vehicle.

> **SECONDARY INCOME SOURCES ARE 'SPARE' SETS OF KEYS!**

THREE WAYS TO CREATE A SECOND INCOME THROUGH OWNING A BUSINESS:

01

Earn it

This is an arrangement where a company will forgo paying you a salary and instead pay you in partial ownership of the company. You, as the employee, believe the company will grow and your share of the company with it.

WARNING: You will not receive any income until you sell your shares.

02

Invest in it

This occurs when you want to U.S.E. money you have earned to purchase a part of a company, via stocks or shares. You, as the investor, believe your dollars will grow with the company's growth.

WARNING: You will not receive any income until you sell your shares.

03

Start it

When you become an **ENTREPRENEUR**, you start your own business. No doubt, this is the hardest way to create a secondary source of income, and in fact, will not even be an income source until you start making money beyond your expenses. You, as the owner, believe the company will grow, and provide value beyond an income. We need to clarify that an entrepreneur is different than someone who is **SELF-EMPLOYED**. Self-employed people create a primary income for themselves, where an entrepreneur builds a business that can function without them in it. This is why entrepreneurs create an income and self-employed earn an income. Both are admirable!

TWO WAYS TO CREATE A SECOND INCOME THROUGH OWNING A PROPERTY:

01

Rental Property

When you purchase a home to rent it out to other people. Depending on how you purchased the home, you will have bills and payments, but the belief is that the rent paid to you will cover those expenses and leave you a second income source.

02

Selling or Flipping Property

When you purchase a home to resell it for more than you bought it. You believe you can increase the value of the home by fixing the place up, making additions, or waiting for the demand for the location to increase.

WARNING: You will not receive any income until you sell the home.

Owning a primary residence is intentionally left off this list. While owning your home can be a solid investment for your financial plan, it can NOT be seen as a secondary source of income. If homeowners can agree on anything it is that their home costs them more money after they own it.

ONE WAY TO CREATE A SECOND INCOME THROUGH OWNING DEBT:

01

Lending Money

When you allow someone else to U.S.E. your money for a fee. Of course, you must have money to lend to make this one work, but there are many forms of lending money to people, banks, and businesses.

FOUR WAYS TO CREATE A SECOND INCOME THROUGH OWNING YOUR TALENTS:

01

Your Skill

When you have a unique skill that others will pay to watch or use. Think of an athlete or entertainer, this skillset may not make you a professional, but you could be able to create a second income from utilizing this talent.

02

Your Idea

When you have a unique idea that others will pay you to U.S.E. Think of that entrepreneur who does not want to start the business themselves but does have a valuable idea. In the legal world this is called **INTELLECTUAL PROPERTY.**

03

Your Brand

When you have a unique **NAME, IMAGE, OR LIKENESS (NIL)** that others will pay to use. This form of income has become ordinary in the artist and athletic space as both college and high school students are able to be paid on their brand. It is also very common in Social Media influencers who have a 'following' that companies want to market to.

04

Your Idea

When you have extra time that you are willing to exchange for payment. This could include getting involved in an **E-COMMERCE** operation or using the **GIG ECONOMY** to find odd jobs.

PART 4
RECAP

You cannot begin to create money until you have earned money, so focus first on developing your primary source of income. But, if you see the importance of earning a primary source of income, and then securing your plan by creating other sources of income, you are starting to see how to U.S.E. your paycheck to its fullest!

Don't worry — we will discuss the actions and habits you need to find success in Your Money Vehicle throughout the program. For now, let's focus on how you can become more employable by using the mindset - BE A PRO!

1. PEOPLE CAN MAKE MORE MONEY TODAY BECAUSE THEY HAVE STOPPED JUST EARNING AN INCOME AND BEGUN CREATING INCOME SOURCES.

2. EARNED INCOME IS MONEY YOU WENT TO WORK FOR, CREATED INCOME IS MONEY THAT WENT TO WORK FOR YOU.

3. ALWAYS BEST TO HAVE A 'SPARE' SET OF KEYS OR MULTIPLE SOURCES OF INCOME FOR YOUR MONEY VEHICLE.

PART 5
INCREASE INCOME: BE A PRO

TERMS

PRO (PROFESSIONAL): a paid occupation that involves prolonged training and qualification.

BE A PRO: Money Vehicle mindset that brings employability through finding confidence, building trust, and adding value.

UNDERSTAND: the first step in how to U.S.E. money and means you know the definitions of money.

COCKINESS: an external voice that tells others how good you are.

CONFIDENCE: an internal voice that tells you how good you are. This can come from getting an education about your job both in and out of traditional school.

TRUST: a firm belief in the reliability or ability of someone or something.
- **TRUST TAX:** where trust takes away something in a relationship.
- **TRUST DIVIDEND:** where trust adds something to a relationship.

FIDUCIARY: someone who is legally obligated to put your financial interest above their own.

STRATEGY: the second step in how to U.S.E. money and means you have a plan for your money. This can come from getting experience in your job.

PRO BOWL: the best football player at their position in the world.

EFFICIENT: the third step in how to U.S.E. money and means you are finding ways to add value to your plan. This is achieving the maximum productivity with minimum wasted effort and will be found by bringing energy to your job.

ACT LIKE AN INVESTOR: Money Vehicle term meaning you will not just become educated in money but will implement your learnings into actions.

HOW DO I INCREASE MY INCOME?

We mentioned Moore's Law earlier, which discusses the increase in technology and the monumental shifts in our world that are occurring right before our eyes. Accepting that the world will continue to change, the question becomes how do you protect your income in a world that is changing as you grow into it?

You continue to invest in your greatest asset = YOU.

You are, and will always be, your greatest asset. Once you truly begin to accept this, you will begin to understand what it is to be a PRO.

A **PRO (PROFESSIONAL)** in any industry is confident in what they know about their job, builds trust in how they do their job, and adds value when they do their job. Choosing to spend your time today to increase any of those areas – confidence, trust, or value — will make your asset more valuable.

THESE PRINCIPLES CAN BE SUMMARIZED BY A MINDSET MONEY VEHICLE CALLS THE "BE A PRO" MINDSET:

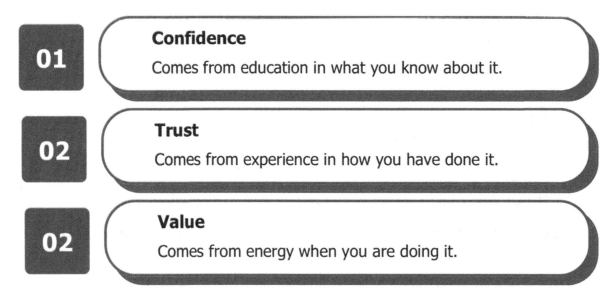

01

Confidence

Comes from education in what you know about it.

02

Trust

Comes from experience in how you have done it.

02

Value

Comes from energy when you are doing it.

Income is often determined by how a company views the market value you can add, and Money Vehicle wants to find ways for you to invest in yourself so that you can add value to any company you want to work for, including your own. Once you accept this **BE A PRO** mindset as a daily practice of investing in yourself, you will see that this investment increases your income and employment opportunities in the future.

To start thinking like a PRO and prepare you to earn an income, Money Vehicle will take you into a world that many people hope to make, but few get to experience: The National Football League (NFL).

Do not worry if you are not a football fan, these same concepts will transition into any career you choose to pursue. Focus on the concepts that the game showed me and not the story of how I was taught.

WHAT DOES IT TAKE TO "BE A PRO" IN THE NFL?

This saying "Be a Pro" is heard in many locker rooms and becomes more of a mindset than a saying. What "Be A Pro" means is that in the NFL, there is little room for excuses or errors, anytime you mess up, the response is simple: "Be a Pro!" This means you must take ownership of your mistakes and fix your issues before the guy behind you comes in and fixes it for you.

> **BE A PRO MEANS DO NOT MAKE AN EXCUSE, ACT LIKE A PROFESSIONAL AND GET IT DONE!**

Now, as you look at the employment opportunity before you, you may not find yourself in a professional locker room, but it will be an environment where your mindset will play a significant role in deciding your income. Let's break down the Be A Pro mindset into three areas and see how each will benefit you as you venture into the unknown career before you.

1. A PRO IS CONFIDENT IN WHAT THEIR JOB IS.

Every offseason, a new set of rookies show up, many of them fortunate enough to have been chosen by a team in the NFL Draft. These young players come into their new place of work and begin to tell everyone how good they were in college or how much they plan to earn during their playing careers.

This external voice where they go around and tell everyone how good they are is called cockiness. No surprise as cockiness is never received with the welcome the rookie had hoped for. Rookies are naïve to think the older veteran players will listen and believe they can play at this level. What rookies overlook is that their internal voice, the one in between their ears, the one that is loudest when no one is around, is much more important. This internal voice is confidence.

- **COCKINESS**: an external voice that tells others how good you are.
- **CONFIDENCE**: an internal voice that tells you how good you are.

Confidence is an ability to believe in yourself and say, "I am a Pro. I deserve to be here." It's the first factor in becoming a professional in anything, including the NFL. You begin to see that your external voice is cocky and leads nowhere positive. Your internal voice is confidence and becomes the foundational belief that you belong. This first step in becoming a professional is often the hardest, but the first person that must be confident you can do anything, is you.

HOW DO I BEGIN TO BUILD MY CONFIDENCE?

Confidence can come from many places, but often, it is confidence in what you know. That confidence grows through education. No, that does not mean you need to go to school for years to be educated enough to gain confidence. But you do need to understand the field you are entering and build a knowledge base of what you will need to succeed in it.

We began talking about a Desired Lifestyle you want to achieve and the type of job that can provide an income to support it. This should direct your educational endeavors. If you dream of earning a lot of money, there is a higher likelihood that you will need more education for that career.

 -VS-

WOMEN WITH A BACHELOR'S DEGREE EARN $630,000 MORE AND MEN WITH A BACHELOR'S DEGREE EARN $900,000 MORE OVER THEIR WORKING LIFE THAN THEIR COUNTERPARTS WITHOUT ONE.

Look at the career you want to have and ask yourself if you need college or graduate school to pursue that career, if the answer is no then you have clarity around your decision. The reality is the financial cost of college is not an opportunity that everyone should pursue. There are some career choices that you must go to college and graduate school for, while there are many career choices that will not require this form of education. With no right or wrong answer about college, you have to measure what desired lifestyle you want and what career can afford that lifestyle. How you measure this opportunity will be discussed in Chapter 3.1.

> ## A PRO KNOWS THE FIRST PERSON WHO MUST BE CONFIDENT IN YOU, IS YOU!

No matter what your career, find ways to continue improving your education in the industry. Look for books, courses, or materials where you can study this career. The more you can learn from others, the more confidence you will have.

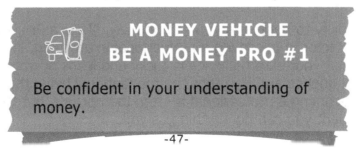

MONEY VEHICLE
BE A MONEY PRO #1

Be confident in your understanding of money.

If you have not been introduced to money, it can feel like a foreign language. However, you can begin to educate yourself on how to speak this new language. As you learn the concepts and terms in Money Vehicle, you will begin to **UNDERSTAND** the language of money and you will see your confidence grow with this new education.

Each chapter and section will outline terms that you will need to understand. Keep USE-ing these terms and keep speaking the language but your external cocky voice is not the one you should use. Build your confidence internally and remember, the first person to be confident you can speak the language of money, is you!

> **MONEY VEHICLE U.S.E. MISSION: U – UNDERSTAND = YOU WILL BE CONFIDENT YOU UNDERSTAND THE LANGUAGE OF MONEY.**

2. A PRO BUILDS <u>TRUST</u> IN HOW THEY DO THEIR JOB.

As a Philadelphia Eagle my rookie year, I was so excited to put on the jersey, so honored to put on the helmet, and just in awe of walking out onto the field the first time as an Eagle. This excitement transferred over to my performance and not in a good way.

I lined up for my first play as an Eagle — first play as a Pro — eager to prove that I belonged. Hopeful that on this very play I can make the team. But my excitement got the best of me, and I couldn't wait for the ball to be snapped. In football, if an offensive player moves before the ball, it is called a "false start" and results in a penalty. This play I moved too early and the first rep for Collins #48, would go down as an "ME" — or a mental error. Not a good first impression.

There is an endless line of people waiting to get into the largest football league in the country and for this reason, the game waits for no one. Before I knew it, the whistle blew, and my replacement was running in from the sideline, with a big smile on his face. I had lost my rep and had missed my first opportunity.

Jogging over to the sideline our head coach, Andy Reid, said to me "son, we can't beat ourselves out there."

"We can't beat ourselves."

In football or life, when someone doesn't know your name, they will use terms like 'son' or 'buddy'. I was an "undrafted" player, meaning I went through the NFL Draft, but did not hear my name called. This meant that I was a long shot to make the Eagles roster and that most people in the building didn't even really know who I was. With 90 players on the team, Coach Reid had never even spoken directly to me, and this was not a good first impression.

With a short sentence 'we can't beat ourselves'; Coach Reid shined a light on the second principle it takes to Be A Pro: Trust.

> **TRUST: THE ABILITY TO DEPEND ON OR RELY ON SOMEONE OR SOMETHING YOU HAVE PLACED YOUR CONFIDENCE IN. SEE WHY WE STARTED WITH CONFIDENCE?**

In football, the coaches, the team, and the entire organization must trust you on the field. Trust that you will help the cause (winning games), and not hurt it. When you do not know your assignment or commit a ME, you do not build trust from your team and in the professional world, trust is everything.

Stephen Covey, the author of "The 7 Habits of Highly Effective People" and "Speed of Trust", compares every relationship you have to financial concepts – a tax, and a dividend. A tax represents a toll that is taken away from you, and a dividend represents an extra payment that is made to you. With a "**TRUST TAX**" and a "**TRUST DIVIDEND**" Mr. Covey was able to look at each relationship and see if trust was adding or taking away from the relationship.

- Trust Tax: Trust in a relationship takes something away from it
- Trust Dividend: Trust in a relationship adds something more to it

Look around at the relationships you have and measure your trust in them using the tax or dividend concepts.

- If you were to do a project together, would it take more time or less time?
- If you were to give an assignment to someone, would you trust it will get done or continually check on their progress?
- If you needed help, would they help without question or pick at your reasoning?

Professionals do not beat themselves and they trust that the person next to them will not either.

HOW DO I BUILD TRUST?

The best way to build trust is by gaining experience. Getting the repetitions of practice in. We can pull from the Malcolm Gladwell book "Outliers" where he claims that it takes 10,000 hours of intensive practice to master a skill.

Too many get the concept of practice wrong — they believe you practice until you get something right, and then stop. A professional will practice until they cannot get something wrong, and the truth is they will continue to practice until they forget they are practicing, until it becomes a habit (Chapter 3.2).

Looking at Gladwell's definition, you can also see the word 'intensive' placed before practice, this is to call out the idea that you cannot simply go through the motions. You must drill as if it were in a game, performance, or test.

> **MOST PRACTICE UNTIL THEY GET IT RIGHT, A PRO WILL PRACTICE UNTIL THEY CAN'T GET IT WRONG.**

Experience comes with time, sometimes 10,000 hours of time and one thing you will see throughout Money Vehicle is that time is your ally. As a young professional, young investor, and young person, time is on your side. Whatever skill or talent you want to pursue, go start getting reps in, and start to build trust through your experience. Repetition after repetition is how a professional becomes an expert.

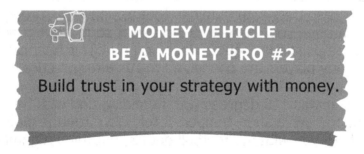

MONEY VEHICLE
BE A MONEY PRO #2

Build trust in your strategy with money.

Trust is a two-way street. Whether it's a tax or dividend depends on your point of view, so make sure to keep the people you trust with money a tight group.

When you go out into the world, understand that most financial products or services are sold — not bought. This means someone is trying to get you to do something, regardless of whether it is in your best interest. To protect yourself, you must be confident that you understand the language, and then you must trust the strategy this person is presenting is in your best interest.

One way to assure the person you are talking to about money will put your best interest first is asking if they are a **FIDUCIARY**. This will come into play as you talk to financial advisors and is a little beyond the scope of this class, but for now define Fiduciary as someone who is legally obligated to put your best interest first!

Begin to measure the trust you have in your relationships and confirm the strategy you are practicing will add to your plan, not take away from it.

> **MONEY VEHICLE U.S.E. MISSION: S — STRATEGY: YOU WILL TRUST THE STRATEGY OF YOUR PLAN.**

3. A PRO ADDS <u>VALUE</u> WHEN THEY DO THEIR JOB.

"I am from Missouri son, the Show-Me state."

This was a common quote from an old running back coach, and an introduction to the most important principle in the Be A PRO mindset: Professionals make plays! "Show me" means that you must make a play worth watching, that play does something irreplaceable on a team — it adds value.

I learned this lesson while playing for the New Orleans Saints. If you have never been to New Orleans, Louisiana in August, you know it is a different type of atmosphere. The air is so thick with humidity that as you walk through it, you can almost feel it move around your body. You will sweat so much in practice that your shoes will fill up to the point they squish when you run. This heat can dehydrate you so much that many players are connected to IVs after practice.

On this summer day, it was 118 degrees with humidity, and with heat like that everyone was going to have a short temper. It felt like a routine play for me at fullback; I will not bore you with the football details, but my assignment was called a "chip block."

This meant that I would throw my elbow into the ribs of the defensive end, helping my offensive linemen teammate, and then run out a little ways and hope to maybe have the ball thrown to me, it wasn't. On the Saints, I was a weapon, but not one that got the ball, my job was to solidify the chip block, which I did before running to the area I was assigned.

On my 'chip' I could feel the defensive player crunch as I hit him, and could only imagine how aggravated he must be, battling the heat, the player in front of him, and now me.

As I jogged back to the huddle after the play, the defensive end, who was a 315 lbs. **PRO-BOWL** player came and grabbed me by the facemask. He was obviously upset with my assignment and began laying a barrage of insults at me that are commonplace on a football field, but not necessary to share here. In this barrage, he did say something that I will never forget:

 I don't know you; I don't even know your name!

The insult was meant for an undrafted player, a no-name like me. While this player was a returning starter and sure in for the 53-man roster, in all reality I wouldn't find my name on the final 53-man roster. The obscenities didn't bother me, this message struck me like a punch.

With this comment I had a choice:

- I could use my external (cocky) voice and yell back at this man. Screaming at him and even telling him my name. Or I could practice my internal, confident voice.
- I could break the trust of practice and fight him, trying to prove my toughness or bravado that way. But then I would show that I had a short fuse, and that I could not be trusted to keep my cool during the chaos of a game.
- I could get back in the huddle and make a play!

One of the things I love about sports and football is that there is almost always another chance, a next play. This chance allows someone like me, a no-name, an opportunity to make a play. The very next play, my assignment was to go one-on-one with my new friend, the 315-pound Pro Bowl defensive end.

On the snap of the ball, I came down the line and put my facemask into the chest of this behemoth, knocking him backwards and onto the ground. Walking up to him after that play, he held up his hand for me to help him up. Instead, I hit his hand away and tilted my helmet down, pointing to the tape across the front of my helmet that read "Collins."

Without saying a word, I made a play, added value, and that night when we watched the film everyone would know my name.

A PRO MAKES PLAYS AND MAKES PEOPLE LEARN THEIR NAME BY ADDING VALUE.

HOW DO I ADD VALUE?

In business and life, it is not always clear if you are adding value or how to add it in the first place. Money Vehicle encourages you to see your name as an indication of your value.

In the professional world, anything that is being delivered with your name on it means you are taking ownership of that document and are responsible for the value or lack of value in that document. Whether it is an email, project, or an interaction with a customer, if your name is on it, then you are expected to add value. Each week, make sure your name is on something and make sure you are adding value to it.

When offered an opportunity to take on new responsibility or to even do a task that seems simple, raising your hand and having your name be seen adds value.

If you are wondering if your value is being recognized, then ask yourself if the people above you in your organization know your name or feel the energy you bring into the building. Too many people overlook the simplest way to be seen and it is by showing up with an energy to get better.

Many will tell you to chase your passion, but the truth is few get the pleasure of aligning their passion to their profession. What you must create is curiosity. Having curiosity to learn about your industry, giving effort in each task that you complete, and just coming to work each day with an energy that is not only seen, but felt.

This curiosity and energy can and will lead to passion once you are confident in what you are doing and trusted in how you are doing it. Passion then is not something you chase, but something that is found in your commitment.

Show up each day with a curiosity on how to improve and the energy to pursue what you find, and people will begin to know your name.

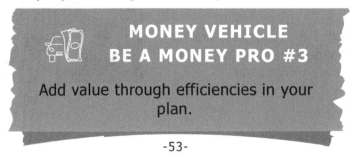

**MONEY VEHICLE
BE A MONEY PRO #3**

Add value through efficiencies in your plan.

One of the key concepts in Money Vehicle will be to Employ Your Money. We will work through the details of efficiency throughout the program, but for now see that this means you understand how money works, are beginning to build a strategy for your money, and you continually look for ways to add value to your plan.

Efficiency will come when you make money work for you in Chapter 2, give each dollar a job in Chapter 3, set-up automations in Chapter 4, use other people's money in Chapter 5, and of course, begin to invest in Chapter 6.

MONEY VEHICLE U.S.E. MISSION: E — EFFICIENT: YOU WILL ADD VALUE AND EFFICIENCY TO YOUR PLAN.

HOW THE BE A PRO MINDSET WILL INCREASE YOUR EMPLOYABILITY:

CONFIDENCE	You know what the job is. The more confidence you can have from the knowledge you bring to your job, the more employable you are.	Example: Someone who has studied three different ways to attack a problem is more employable than the person hearing the problem for the first time.
TRUST	You know how to do the job. The more trust you can build from the experiences you bring to your job, the more employable you are.	Example: Someone who has done this 100 times is more employable than the person doing it for the second time.
VALUE	You know where you can add efficiency to the job. The more curious and energetic you are about your job, the more employable you are.	Example: Someone who brings curiosity and energy to a problem is more employable than the person who shows up late and tells everyone which part of the project was "not their job."

PART 5
RECAP

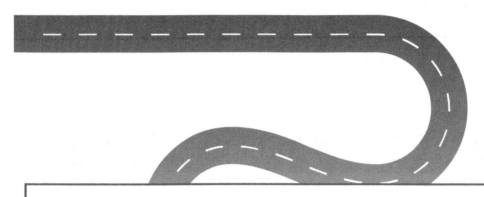

1. A PROFESSIONAL BRINGS CONFIDENCE THROUGH THEIR EDUCATION.

2. A PROFESSIONAL CREATES TRUST THROUGH THEIR EXPERIENCE.

3. A PROFESSIONAL ADDS VALUE THROUGH THEIR ENERGY.

REVIEW

THE RULE: ACT LIKE AN INVESTOR

Think of your income as the keys to Your Money Vehicle. No different than with an actual car, you cannot get very far without your keys.

For now, and probably for some time, your lifestyle and plan will depend on your primary income, so you do not do anything to jeopardize it. This will require you to evaluate the people and the situations that you put yourself in. Anything that puts your income at risk is something that you should avoid. There is no difference between a rookie football player or your rookie year on a job, the most important thing is to not let anyone, or anything, take your opportunity away.

Do not lose the keys to Your Money Vehicle!

The Money Vehicle program will take you on a financial journey, covering the first TEN actions you will take with this paycheck. We will build up your confidence in this language, your trust in how your strategy is unfolding, and continue to add value to different areas of your plan.

But Your Money Vehicle begins with your actions. We make suggestions, you make decisions!! The emphasis needs to be on ACTIONS.

In Part 1 of this chapter, we discussed how to "Think like an investor." But if all this program does is get you to think, then we have FAILED. The Money Vehicle program is designed to get you to ACT LIKE AN INVESTOR. With each chapter you will take action, and with each action, you begin your financial plan.

Here are five things to remember as you begin to ACT LIKE AN INVESTOR:
1. You are your greatest asset: Your talents and abilities will put the most amount of money in your pocket, so you must continue to invest in YOU!
2. Money is not gold; money is a reflection of your market value: The United States no longer ties its money supply to gold, and you should not continue to think of money as a physical thing. Money reflects your values and priorities in your plan.
3. The monster eating your money: Inflation is a real thing and will be a huge hurdle on your financial journey. You can fight it by investing in yourself and then making your money go to work for you like an employee.
4. Create an income: When you go to work for money, you earn it. Now you appreciate the beauty of and strength in creating new income streams that do not require – you! Freedom begins when your created income covers your desired lifestyle.
5. Be A PRO!: Be confident you can do the job. Build trust in your team. Start to add value through curiosity and energy.

REVIEW

ACTION

Find a way to earn your first paycheck and turn Your Money Vehicle on.

- Once you have a paycheck begin to think like an investor and identify how inflation will impact your desired lifestyle.
- Be A Pro and continue to invest in you!
- Act like an investor and start your financial plan by driving Your Money Vehicle.

GOAL SETTING

CHAPTER 1

WHY SHOULD I CARE ABOUT MONEY?

OVERVIEW

1.1: The New Money Vehicle

1.2: The Golden Rule of Money

1.3: Begin with the End in Mind

1.4: How to Set R.I.C.H. Goals

ACTION

Start driving Your Money Vehicle by beginning with the END in mind and setting a one-week, one-month, one-year R.I.C.H. goal for your money.

DRIVING YOUR MONEY VEHICLE

There is no question that receiving your keys (income) to Your Money Vehicle is vitally important. But now that you have your keys, you will need to establish why you are the driver and what the Golden Rule of the road will be. Once you understand these two things, you will lay out some destinations of where you are trying to go. This is where your Money Vehicle GPS will come into play.

SECTION 1.1
THE NEW MONEY VEHICLE

TERMS

PENSIONS: a retirement plan where your company will pay you an income stream after you retire for life. Example of the 'Train' financial industry.

SOCIAL SECURITY: a retirement plan where the government will pay you an income and provide insurance benefits later in life. Example of the 'Train' financial industry.

MEDICARE: a form of health insurance provided by the government that is meant to provide benefits later in life.

AUTONOMY: the freedom to choose. To decide what you believe will be best for your plan.

Personal finance is a hot topic these days, and everyone seems to be throwing money options in your face. What's all the fuss about lately? Well, the vehicle many of us expected to ride throughout our careers and into financial freedom has changed.

What do I mean? Let me ask you, when was the last time you heard about someone planning a cross-country trip by train? It was not so long ago that trains traveling across America were the primary source of transportation. It took a while to build all the cars and tracks, but once they were complete, all a passenger had to do was get a ticket, climb aboard, and ride—but the key was that they could travel only to the destinations to which the company train had built tracks.

This method used to be how people planned their financial freedom, as well. They would spend their entire careers building "train tracks," trusting that when it was time, they'd get a seat and their company would take them where they planned to go.

Those financial train tracks were called **PENSIONS**, which are benefits that pay an income stream after you retire. Yes, that is right, a pension will pay you even when you stop working.

Another train or pension-like retirement benefit is **SOCIAL SECURITY**, which was designed by the government after the Great Depression to support American workers entering the age of retirement.

The Social Security program has two main features:

Income: This is the replacement of your earnings after you stop working.

Insurance: This is the medical coverage known as '**MEDICARE**' for after you stop working or if you become disabled.

HOW DOES SOCIAL SECURITY WORK?

Throughout your career you will have a fixed payment deducted automatically from your paycheck for the Social Security system. Each year you can earn up to 4 credits in the system and upon reaching 40 credits, you will become eligible for benefits. While you may not appreciate this now, for many people Social Security becomes a primary source of income and key insurance plan after they are done working. In fact, as of 2022 over 66 million Americans are receiving Social Security with an average monthly benefit of $1,550.

Unfortunately,[8] Social Security can no longer be depended on as a sole provider of financial freedom. The Social Security system itself has challenges maintaining enough of a balance to cover current and future payments, but you also must look at the replacement of lifestyle. For lower earners, the monthly $2,000 can be sufficient, but for higher earners, $2,000 will not cover their lifestyle. Add in the impact of inflation on your lifestyle and the fact that we are living much longer lives, you can see that Social Security is a good system for our society but should not be your sole plan for Future You.

With or without social security, the old retirement system was simple and straightforward:

Step 1: Get a good job.
Step 2: Don't get fired.
Step 3: Retire with a pension.

GET A JOB.   RETIRE WITH A PENSION.

DON'T GET FIRED.

For workers today, both that advice and the pension system resemble the old train industry—outdated and not very helpful.

SO WHAT HAPPENED?

Companies began to shift away from pensions for three reasons.

- First off, employees seldom stay at a company for the ten to twenty years it takes to build up a pension.
- Second, people are living much longer, and that increases the amount of payout a company needed to make once an employee retired.
- Third, companies no longer want to hold the investment risk of their workforce's retirement.

Let us explain that last one. Under the pension system, your company had to contribute a certain amount to the pension fund each month for each employee, no matter how much money the company made or what the pension fund investments returned. Those large expenses became too much of a burden for companies to take on through the volatility of markets and the cycles of business.

AUTONOMY

The question became: how could companies transfer the risk of your retirement future onto you, the employee, and not on the company?

Enter WHY personal finance is such a trending topic and how employees began owning their own individual "Money (retirement) Vehicles." No longer would employees be taking their seats on the company train and riding into the designated pension sunset.

The system changed and the new system resembles the automobile industry more than the train industry. Instead of riding a train on predetermined tracks, you can drive your Money Vehicle down the road of your choice. This new system will give you the greatest gift in the world: **AUTONOMY** or complete control over your destination.

Your freedom is no longer determined by the company you work for or the governmental systems that can support you. Instead, you sit down in the driver's seat and decide your own future.

YOU MUST DRIVE YOUR MONEY VEHICLE

This new Money Vehicle can be exciting, but it does require that you read the Owner's Manual.

OWNER'S MANUAL
FOR YOUR MONEY VEHICLE:

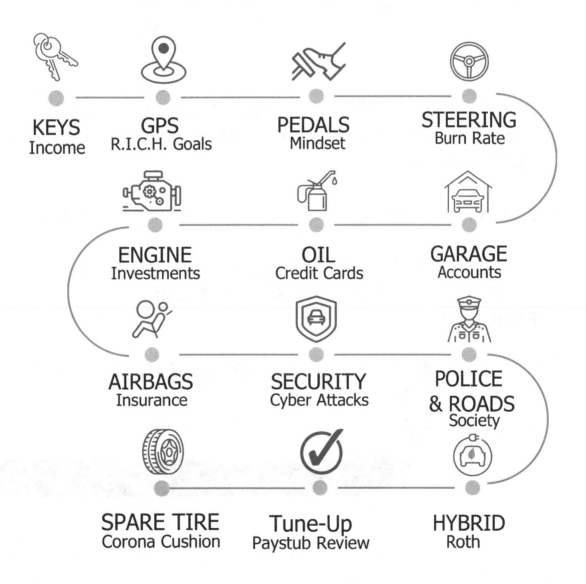

KEYS
Income

GPS
R.I.C.H. Goals

PEDALS
Mindset

STEERING
Burn Rate

ENGINE
Investments

OIL
Credit Cards

GARAGE
Accounts

AIRBAGS
Insurance

SECURITY
Cyber Attacks

**POLICE
& ROADS**
Society

SPARE TIRE
Corona Cushion

Tune-Up
Paystub Review

HYBRID
Roth

SECTION 1.1
RECAP

1. THE PENSION SYSTEM IS GOING EXTINCT, WITH IT THE FINANCIAL WORLD AND YOUR FINANCIAL FUTURE HAVE CHANGED.

2. YOU MUST BEGIN DRIVING YOUR MONEY VEHICLE!

3. MONEY VEHICLE WANTS TO EMPOWER YOU TO U.S.E. MONEY: UNDERSTAND, STRATEGIZE, EFFICIENT.

SECTION 1.2
THE GOLDEN RULE OF MONEY

Imagine that you lived in a log cabin in the woods with only a wood-burning stove to provide you warmth through a long winter. When the first cold night comes and you start putting logs into the fire, you will look at your wood supply and think either "We are going to burn through the supply too fast," or "We have enough stacked to make it through winter."

FINANCIAL FREEDOM begins with an education around controlling what is coming in and what is going out each month. This is like the wood supply in our cabin example where:

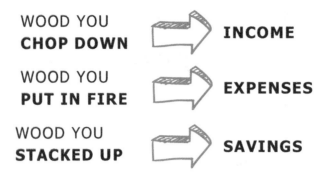

WOOD YOU **CHOP DOWN** ➡ **INCOME**

WOOD YOU **PUT IN FIRE** ➡ **EXPENSES**

WOOD YOU **STACKED UP** ➡ **SAVINGS**

The "**GOLDEN RULE**" in any financial plan is:
'Do not spend more than you make and focus on what you keep!'

THE GOLDEN RULE

DO NOT SPEND MORE THAN YOU MAKE AND FOCUS ON WHAT YOU KEEP!

If you understand how to chop more wood than you burn, and you begin to keep the excess, your wood supply will grow. This wood supply will allow you to start enjoying the warmth of the fire, and maybe even a s'more , instead of constantly worrying about chopping more wood.

Understanding the Golden Rule can feel simple but following it will be anything but simple. As you begin to follow the Golden Rule, there are four hurdles Money Vehicle wants to callout:

#1

HOW MUCH WOOD YOU CHOP = HOW MUCH MONEY YOU MAKE (INCOME)

It doesn't matter how much you make; if you only look at the number at the top of your paystub called the 'gross' amount, you will end up breaking the Golden Rule.

GROSS INCOME is the number you see at the top of your paycheck before things like taxes and automatic deductions are taken out. Spending based on the gross amount shows that you do not have a clear understanding of the many things that will impact how much money you will take home. Later in Chapter 9 of the Money Vehicle program, we will cover how you go from 'gross' to 'net' income. But for now realize that however much you signed on to receive as a wage or salary is NOT how much you will take home. Plan your spending on 75% of whatever your wage or salary is .

GROSS INCOME IS THE
MONEY YOU MAKE

NET INCOME IS THE
MONEY YOU TAKE

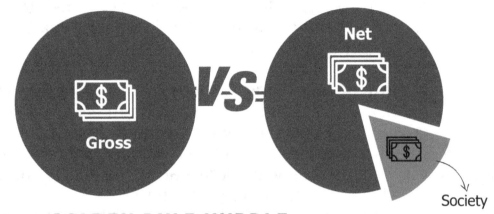

Society

GOLDEN RULE HURDLE
PEOPLE BEGIN TO SPEND ON WHAT THEY THINK
THEY WILL MAKE AND NOT ON WHAT THEY
ACTUALLY TAKE HOME.

#2

HOW MUCH WOOD YOU BURN = HOW MUCH MONEY YOU SPEND (BURN RATE)

Money can be spent in endless ways, and each expense can be categorized into buckets. To live Golden you must begin to take note of how much money is going out each month and then begin to manage where it is going. This overview of your spending will show you which 'Money Bucket' (preview of Chapter 3) you are filling and which you are leaving empty each time you spend money. Once you have an overview, you can begin to prioritize which bucket you want to fill first.

WHY IS THE BURN RATE SO IMPORTANT?

Your **BURN RATE** becomes the most important number in your financial plan because it reflects the lifestyle YOU choose. When you think about what money is meant to do, covering your lifestyle today and in the future should be one of your goals. What your Burn Rate should be able to show you is how to invest, how long to work, and what your **FREEDOM YEARS** will look like.

1. Shows how to invest. In Chapter 6 we will discuss the risk associated with investing and the time you need for investments to work, but for now just see a goal of your saving and investing is to protect your lifestyle. To do this you will have to both take on higher risk to protect your lifestyle of the future as well as lower risk to protect your lifestyle of the present.

2. Shows how long to work. This is based on how much you can contribute to your future each year and the goal you have set for your freedom. Your burn rate is essential because once you know your after-tax income, you subtract out your Burn Rate to find how much you have left to contribute to your future
(After-tax Income − Burn Rate = Future contribution). Then, you just need to look at how many years it will take you to achieve your Freedom Number based on how much you can contribute each year.

3. Shows how freedom years will look. Understanding your Burn Rate today and the plan you have set for yourself will also shine a light on what you want your freedom years to look like. You can choose to have a larger number and work longer to achieve a larger freedom or you can choose to have a lower Burn Rate in freedom and achieve this goal much sooner.

HOW CAN WE BEGIN TO UNDERSTAND
WHAT GOES INTO OUR 'BURN RATE'?

Again, we will add details to this process as the program unfolds, for now what is important is tracking where all the money is going and adding up the total amount being spent.

For this, let's use Darrel as an example:

DARREL'S EXPENSE TRACKER

DESCRIPTION	AMOUNT	DESCRIPTION	AMOUNT
RENT/MORTGAGE	$2,250	PARKING	$50
FOOD (MAIN MEALS)	$750	CAR PAYMENT	$400
FOOD (SNACKS)	$255	CAR INSURANCE	$120
HEALTH INSURANCE	$0	GAS	$250
MEDICAL EXPENSES	$50	UTILITIES	$250
CLUBS/ ORGANIZATIONS	$100	CELL PHONE	$150
CLOTHES	$50	CABLE	$50
ENTERTAINMENT	$150	INTERNET	$125
HYGIENE	$20	GYM MEMBERSHIP	$80
HAIRCUT ETC.	$100	EMERGENCY $	$300
		TOTAL	$5,500

As you can see Darrel spends **$5,500** each month. This number reflects the lifestyle Darrel has chosen for himself and can be quantified as his Burn Rate.

- When Darrel begins to invest, he will need to make sure he has a few months if not years of this Burn Rate protected.

- When Darrel starts his Freedom Plan, he will be able to see how much he can contribute to this choice based on his Burn Rate.

- When Darrel begins to think about his Freedom years, he will be able to use the current Burn Rate as a measure for what he wants to do later in life.

GOLDEN RULE HURDLE

 PEOPLE SPEND WITHOUT ANY UNDERSTANDING OF HOW MUCH IS GOING OUT THE DOOR. AN IMPORTANT STEP IN NOT BREAKING THE GOLDEN RULE IS KNOWING HOW MUCH YOUR BURN RATE IS.

#3
HOW MUCH WOOD YOU STACK = HOW MUCH MONEY YOU KEEP (EMPLOYEES)

Now, it's important to realize that you should always have a stack of wood on hand, or money that you don't spend. A stack of wood provides warmth and security all through the winter, and the money you have saved provides financial security, something we all need to reach Financial Freedom.

Understanding how much you make and how much you spend each month is the first step in achieving your financial goals. When your stack of wood grows large enough that it is protecting your Burn Rate today, you can begin to strategize ways to use the excess lumber. With the wood this will come from building something or selling the extra wood at the market, with money this will come from different forms of saving or investing.

GOLDEN RULE HURDLE

 PEOPLE DO NOT HAVE A WOOD SUPPLY READY TO HELP THEM WHEN EMERGENCIES OR OPPORTUNITIES ARISE AND THEN BREAK THE GOLDEN RULE WHEN THEY DO OCCUR.

#4

HOW MUCH WOOD YOU NEED TO STAY WARM = HOW MUCH THE COST OF THINGS GOES UP (INFLATION)

Throughout the winter you will need to put wood on the fire to stay warm, but as the winter goes on and the wood begins to dampen with moisture, you will need more wood to create the same warmth. This can resemble the impact inflation will have on your Burn Rate. Whatever lifestyle you choose today will no doubt increase in price as time goes by, because inflation will raise the cost of everything.

To fight off inflation and this rise in cost, you would need to increase your income, decrease your expenses, or create new income sources through investing.

GOLDEN RULE HURDLE
PEOPLE BEGIN TO UNKNOWINGLY BREAK THE GOLDEN RULE BECAUSE THEY DO NOT ACCOUNT FOR THE MONSTER EATING THEIR DOLLARS – INFLATION.

WHY START WITH THE GOLDEN RULE?

The Golden Rule comes as the first real financial lesson in the Money Vehicle program and the first behavior you must begin to follow because if you spend more than you make, you will never have anything left over to invest.

Do not see your Burn Rate as a negative, just as the fire needs more wood to keep burning, spending money today is a necessary part of your plan. But how big of a fire
begin to ask yourself how you could U.S.E. that extra stack of wood? This question and perspective are how you begin to speak the language of money.

When you follow the Golden Rule and you will begin to have excess money leftover that you did not spend. This is like the 'wood supply' and gives you options for how to U.S.E. the extra money.

HOW DO I DECIDE THE DIFFERENCE BETWEEN WANTS & NEEDS

This age-old question of what a want is versus what a need is, will come down to your individual choices and lifestyle. At a high level you can see 'Needs' as things like shelter, food, clothes, medical care and 'Wants' as things that can improve a need or add a level of enjoyment to your lifestyle.

But even within these categories you will have the option for 'Wants'.

Example: You need to eat dinner, but you want to try the new steakhouse.

You need to have shelter, but you want to have a spare bedroom for guests.

This can be hard to determine which is which, but when it boils down to it, the question is – Do I need this for my life, or do I want this for my lifestyle?

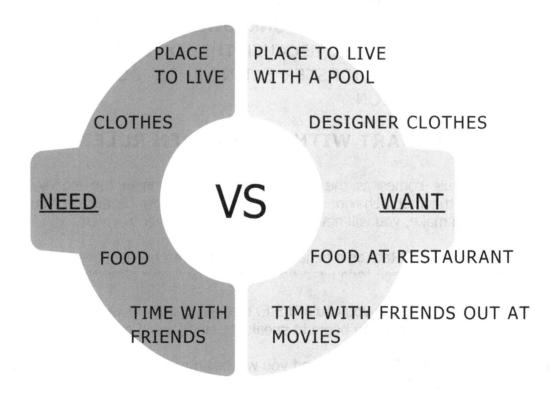

NEED VS WANT

NEED	WANT
PLACE TO LIVE	PLACE TO LIVE WITH A POOL
CLOTHES	DESIGNER CLOTHES
FOOD	FOOD AT RESTAURANT
TIME WITH FRIENDS	TIME WITH FRIENDS OUT AT MOVIES

SECTION 1.2
RECAP

As you can see from the chart above, every need has a similar "want". The trick is to separate what you need for your life and what you want for your lifestyle. You need a place to live, and as nice as it is to float around your swimming pool in the summer, this is a lifestyle want. Be conscious of the difference in your choices.

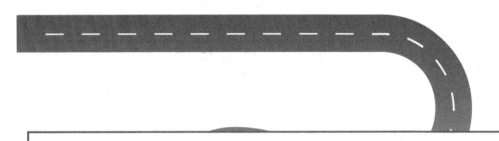

1. GOLDEN RULE OF MONEY: DO NOT SPEND MORE THAN YOU MAKE, AND FOCUS ON WHAT YOU KEEP.

2. DO NOT OVERLOOK THE RISE IN PRICES KNOWN AS INFLATION.

3. YOUR LIFESTYLE SPEND 'BURN RATE' IS AN IMPORTANT NUMBER ON YOUR FINANCIAL JOURNEY.

SECTION 1.3

BEGIN WITH THE
END IN MIND

TERMS

R.I.C.H. GOALS: reachable, individual, controllable, and happy goals you set for your plan in a week, month, or year time frame.

Arriving at my third off season in the NFL I was ready to make the team, I was in the best shape of my life, and I was hungry to prove my value. But looking around I couldn't help noticing some of the veteran players didn't exactly show up in their best shape.

'Hey, Bow, why don't the older guys come back in the off-season ready to go?' I asked one of the veteran wide outs.
His response came in the form of a question that was cryptic at first but ended up being poetic, "What did you eat for dinner last night?"

I had no idea where this was going but responded with 'I grilled some chicken and whipped up minute mashed potatoes. Why?'

"See last night I had a Big Mac, I love McDonald's and last night was my last McDonald's trip until we reach our goal in January." Bow's response was pointing to the Super Bowl which every NFL player and team strives for. I think he saw the confusion on my face and asked, "When do you want to be at your 'Most'? Be in your best shape possible?"

I thought about it for a moment and thought I knew the answer 'In August, I want to be my best to make the team'.

With a likeable and confident smile, he knew his point would be made, "You are still just trying to survive. Vets, we want to be at our 'Most' in December and January, when championships are won, and money is made."

This mindset is the discipline of every successful person in the world, the ability to set a goal and prioritize what they want 'Most' over what they want 'Now'.

Goals prioritize what you want MOST over what you want NOW.

When we set a destination in our GPS, our car shows us the best way to arrive at that destination. To know the best way to drive your Money Vehicle we must first know where it is you want to go and what you will be plugging into your GPS.

How will you ever know if you got to where you want to go unless you laid out the destination first.

> "Would you tell me, please, which way I ought to go from here?" asked Alice.
>
> "That depends a good deal on where you want to get to," said the Cat.
>
> "I don't much care where—" said Alice.
>
> "Then it doesn't matter which way you go," said the Cat.
>
> —Alice's Adventures in Wonderland
> by Lewis Carroll

When you set out to accomplish something—winning a championship game, acing a final exam, or buying a home—you must have a clear vision of what it is you want to achieve. Knowing where you would ultimately like to land is the beginning of any journey. The sad reality is most people never set a destination with their money, never set goals. They get stuck in Money Dreams and therefore cannot find a route to achieve what they desire.

WHAT IS THE DIFFERENCE BETWEEN A DREAM AND A GOAL?

 A dream is something that you create in your mind about a future state you hope to achieve without doing a single thing.

 A goal on the other hand will take focused effort and attention to the actions you must take to become this future state.

One is an idea and the other is an action. You can imagine that with Money Vehicle's mission of empowering you to take action, we will be focusing on setting goals.

Your goals will reflect your values and your priorities in life, we may focus on financial goals in Money Vehicle, but make no mistake your goals are a mirror to who you are in life. These goals will push you out of your comfort zone and give you the ability to define what 'success' means. Your goals will provide a measuring stick for you as you pursue your dream while also holding you accountable to the actions you committed to taking. Put simply, goals will allow you to track your progress and perhaps most importantly to celebrate your progress.

Setting a goal is a massive step forward for many, but if you really want to increase your chances of arriving at this destination, then you should also write them down!

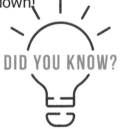 Did you know that only 17% of people have their goals written down and people who write their goals down are 50% more likely to achieve them?

This statistic may shock you, but that means that 1 in 20 of your classmates has goals written down. Do you think they are more or less likely to achieve them?

 By recording your dreams and goals on paper, you set in motion the process of becoming the person you most want to be. Put your future in good hands—your own.

—Mark Victor Hansen

SETTING R.I.C.H. GOALS

WHAT CAN I ACHIEVE?

The only way you will carry on is if the first person convinced that you can achieve your goal, is **you**.

WHAT DO I WANT?

Your goal must be what you truly desire, and it must be your response to the challenges you'll face along the way.

WHAT DO I CONTROL?

It is amazing. how things take care of themselves when you take control of what you can control.

WHAT MAKES ME SMILE?

What's most important is that your goal makes you smile at the end of a long day.

1 WEEK. 1 MONTH. 1 YEAR.

People define all kinds of goals around personal finance, from getting out from under credit card debt to planning a trip to Italy. Before any action is possible, you must create a solid goal and purpose for why you are embarking out on this journey.

These goals become the destinations for Your Money Vehicle and provide the answer as to why you will delay gratification and keep going!

Money Vehicle defines

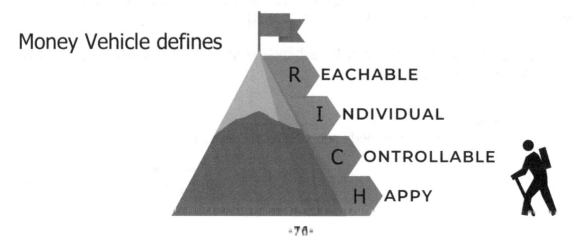

R EACHABLE

I NDIVIDUAL

C ONTROLLABLE

H APPY

REACHABLE:
WHAT CAN I ACHIEVE THIS WEEK, MONTH, YEAR?

 Everyone wants an ideal outcome, a dream that they have in their head of their world absolutely turning upside down and becoming something so far off that it feels almost impossible. This is a good place for your dream to start, but it is just the start of the process.

Now that you can see the dream-case scenario, you need to take a step or two back and think about what is achievable over the next week, month, and year from where you are today.

Money Vehicle will never tell you to stop dreaming, but Denzel Washington is quoted in saying 'A dream without goals, are just dreams'. This means that you can keep your dream but must begin to set reachable goals for you to achieve along the way. Your goals must be things that you can achieve with the resources available to you today.

 Example, "I want to have $1 million" becomes "I want to have $1,000 saved by the end of the year."

Setting out on a dream journey, you will run into obstacles that will try to persuade you that the path is too difficult or too long, and you should give up. Often, the first obstacle you will face is that you set an unrealistic goal. Setting reachable goals will build your confidence as you begin to see your ability to achieve these goals. No different than the confidence you need at work, the first person who must believe you will achieve, is YOU!

Now that you see your goals must be achievable in a week, month, or year time frame you can set better goals.

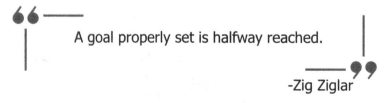

A goal properly set is halfway reached.

-Zig Ziglar

INDIVIDUAL:
WHAT DO I WANT TO ACHIEVE?

You do not get told this very often, but this is the time to be selfish! The time where you need to begin to really visualize why YOU are going to change your habits in pursuit of something, that something is what you need to identify. What exactly is it you want to have more of, or want to do less of?

This is not the time to take your parents, coaches, friends, or celebrities' idea of a goal, this is the time to really review what it is you want to achieve.

To find your individual goal, you will need to peel off some layers and dive into finding the true purpose behind your goal. Money Vehicle recommends a technique called the "5 Why's" that was first used by Sakichi Toyoda in the Toyota car production systems. The concept is simple, state the problem you are facing and ask yourself 'Why is that' 5 times. While it can sound simple, it will force you to truly dig into your individual desires.

Example:
- **Step 1: State the problem:** I want to save $1,000
- **Step 2: Why is that?** Because I want to have more money
- **Step 3: Why is that?** Because then I can buy more things
- **Step 4: Why is that?** Because Kim got a new computer for school, and I want one
- **Step 5: Why is that?** Because I think it will help me do better in school
- **Step 6: Why is that?** Because I want to graduate

This is an interesting turn of events, where a financial goal becomes an academic goal, but you can see as you dive into the 5 WHY process how it will lead you to understanding more about yourself and your goals.

Your goal must be what you truly desire and will become your response to challenges along your journey. Whatever your goal—concert, car, or Caribbean Cruise—it must be your purpose, your priority, and your goal.

Make sure to align the goals you have with your individual values as well. This alignment will ensure that your goals are truly yours.

> " It is better to be at the bottom of the ladder you want to climb than at the top of the one you don't. "
>
> -Stephen Kellogg

CONTROLLABLE:
WHAT DO I CONTROL?

If you are not in the driver's seat, the car won't go where you want it to go. Different factors and people outside of your control will always affect your life, but the trick is to focus on what you can control.

We have all heard the saying 'the grass is always greener, on the other side of the fence', this is speaking to our ability to look around at what everyone else has and see why it is better. A phrase Money Vehicle wants to introduce you to is "Mow Your Grass". This is a change from focusing on your neighbor's yard, to focusing on your own yard.

No, you do not need an actual yard or grass for this concept to make sense. Think about this as identifying what you do control and what you do not control. The grass on the other side of the fence is out of your control, so stop wasting your time with it, start spending your time thinking about what you do control, the grass in front of you.

Begin to ask yourself what you are willing and what you are not willing to do to achieve your goals. This will allow you to achieve your goals by creating actions that are within your control. Listing out the things that you are willing to give up and things that you are not willing to give up.

It is amazing how things take care of themselves when you take care of what you can control.

> Grant me the serenity to accept the things I cannot control, courage to change the things I can, and wisdom to know the difference.
> -Reinhold Niebuhr

HAPPY:
WHAT MAKES ME HAPPY?

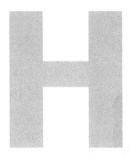 Perhaps what's most important about your goal is that it makes you smile at the end of a long day. When you close your eyes and visualize achieving your goal, you should feel a sense of satisfaction.

Remember these destinations you are setting for your plan are meant to inspire and motivate you, so make sure that achieving this goal will bring with it a sense fulfillment or purpose. That purpose is arriving at the next destination in your journey and the warm feeling within that you have achieved this goal.

If your path leads to a destination you have set and you take enjoyment in achieving it, you will be able to enjoy every step of the journey.

Whatever you choose as a goal must bring joy into your life—if it doesn't, why are you chasing it?

> " ——
> Your goals are the roadmaps that guide you and show you what is possible for your life.
> —— "
>
> -Les Brown

R.I.C.H. Goals are going to be set with a reachable time frame of one week, one month, and one year. Start to visualize what you want to accomplish in that time frame. To get you started, here is a list of common financial goals:

☑ EARN MY 1ST PAYCHECK   ☑ GET OUT OF DEBIT

☑ TRACK WHERE MY MONEY IS GOING   ☑ CREATE A FINANCIAL PLAN

☑ IDENTIFY WHERE SPENDING CUES OR TRIGGERS ARE   ☑ SET UP CASH MANAGEMENT SYSTEM

☑ START TO SAVE MONEY   ☑ START YOUR CREDIT HISTORY

☑ FOLLOW THE GOLDEN RULE   ☑ INCREASE YOUR INCOME

FOR DIRECTION, BEGIN TO SEE THESE GOALS AND THEIR INTENDED FOCUS BELOW:

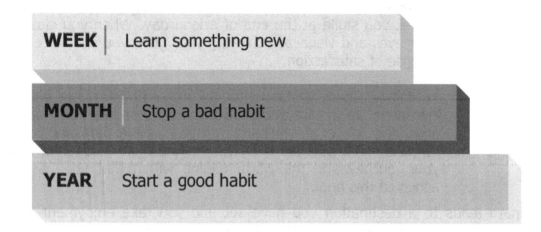

WEEK | Learn something new

MONTH | Stop a bad habit

YEAR | Start a good habit

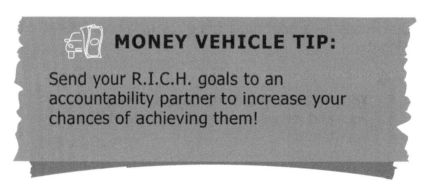

🖐💵 MONEY VEHICLE TIP:

Send your R.I.C.H. goals to an accountability partner to increase your chances of achieving them!

Every NFL facility has a picture of the Lombardi Trophy displayed in their building, it is meant to symbolize the entire team's MOST and goal they are all after. This picture is a reminder every day that you must continue to choose, your Goals over your now. It is a natural thought to place what you want right now in this moment over what you want most, but now you appreciate the idea of prioritizing your goals over everything.

SECTION 1.3
RECAP

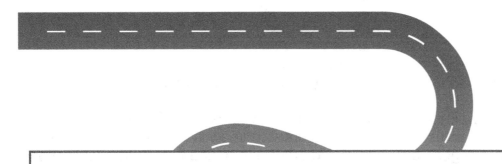

1. EVERY SUCCESSFUL JOURNEY BEGINS WITH THE END IN MIND: MOST > NOW.

2. THE DIFFERENCE BETWEEN A DREAM AND A GOAL IS FOUND IN THE ACTIONS YOU TAKE.

3. SET WEEKLY, MONTHLY, YEARLY R.I.C.H. GOALS = REACHABLE, INDIVIDUAL, CONTROLLABLE, HAPPY.

SECTION 1.4
HOW TO SET R.I.C.H. GOALS

Malcolm Jenkins said it best 'Make sure your goals align with your values!'

As we look to develop our goals, we must begin to measure our values as well. What is important to us in money and in life. We know a plan is only as good as its destination, the goal, but we also are beginning to see that if that destination does not align with your individual values, then there is a higher chance we will end up not prioritizing it.

LET'S START TO BUILD A PLAN FOR OUR R.I.C.H. GOALS

1. WRITE DOWN YOUR R.I.C.H. GOALS

This is the action you took in Section 1.3 and now you have your goals in place.

2. CREATE A PLAN FOR YOUR R.I.C.H. GOALS

The first thing about setting goals many people struggle with is the feeling of being overwhelmed. It is like getting your syllabus the first day of class and wondering 'how on Earth am I going to do all of this?' Effective goals will be broken down into small and manageable steps. You know the R.I.C.H. goals are broken into weekly, monthly and yearly time horizons, but can you break down the goal even further from there?

 If your goal is to go to the gym 4 times a week, then your goal for tomorrow can be to go to the gym for an hour.

 If your goal is eat healthier this month, then your goal for this week can be to set up a meal plan.

 If your goal is to improve your college application by next year, then your goal can be to meet with your counselor once a month or take an extracurricular activity next month.

 If your goal is to ask that special someone on a date this week, then your goal can be to find something that they are interested in today.

 If your goal is to save $1,000 by the end of this year, then your weekly goal can be to save $20.

Setting your R.I.C.H. goal into the week, month, year timeframe puts a solid date of when you want to accomplish, but breaking the goal down even further into small steps will allow you to focus on your progress and not be overwhelmed. This will allow you to build motivation as you accomplish each step.

3. IDENTIFY OBSTACLES FOR YOUR R.I.C.H. GOALS

With a goal and a plan in place, you are ready to start attacking your R.I.C.H. Goals. The other key to planning ahead is the ability to identify obstacles and then prepare a strategy to not let the hurdle knock you off track.

With the R.I.C.H. technique you should not have the obstacles of losing sight of your WHY, having no timetable, or having undefined goals, but you should start to look at your plan and Identify what your obstacles will be.

- Is this time in your life going to be your obstacle?
- Is peer pressure or naysayers going to be your obstacle?
- Is overlooking the effort it will take your obstacle?
- Is having too many goals and things on your plate your obstacle?
- Is the fear of failure going to be your obstacle?
- Is procrastination going to be your obstacle?

Allow yourself some leeway in your goals, you cannot expect to be perfect every day! You also need to expect things like tests, sports, vacations, or celebrations to derail you at times. But with any obstacle the point is to see it and even if it knocks you off course, to get back on track.

4. STAY FOCUSED ON YOUR R.I.C.H GOALS

Focus comes from the confidence you can and will achieve this goal. Most New Year's resolutions do not even make it to February and that is because people did not identify their obstacles (#3), nor did they stay focused on why they wanted their goal. A great way to stay focused is to search out and find more resources or support that will help you.

There is also great evidence of having an accountability partner with you to help keep you focused. Someone who is going to not just encourage but also push you to focus on what you shared with them was important to you.

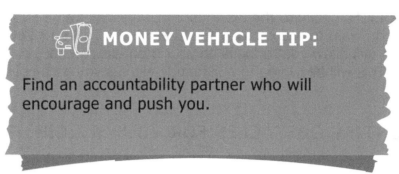

MONEY VEHICLE TIP:

Find an accountability partner who will encourage and push you.

Persistence is a necessity for success. Many lose focus and allow a small setback to derail them. They simply gave up too soon because they lost focus of their goal. There is a Japanese Proverb that says 'fall down seven times, stand up eight. When you are fighting for your goal, you will get knocked down, your ability to focus on the goal and stand up will be a measurement of if you achieve or not.

New Year's Goals end in January because people lose focus!

5. TRACK AND CELEBRATE PROGRESS IN YOUR R.I.C.H. GOALS

You broke your goal down into smaller more actionable steps and now you need to keep track of the progress you are making. This progress will bring more confidence and show you how far you have come. Too often we get caught looking up at what we have left to do and forget how far we have come to be here.

Tracking your progress will also provide feedback on how you are doing in relation to achieving your goal. This review will shine light on if there needs to be any adjustments to your plan. Do not be dismayed by correcting your course, think of a pilot flying a plane, the wind moving the plane, and the pilot corrects the course to make sure they land at the desired destination.

Review your plan monthly (12) at first and then you will be able to drop to quarterly (4). Once your systems are in place and you understand your measurements, you will not need to be consumed by this process. Money is not meant to consume your life; we learn about it to be able to better control it. You can use an excel template, free APP on your phones or a variety of other ways to track your R.I.C.H. Goals, but the important thing is that you are tracking them.

SECTION 1.4
RECAP

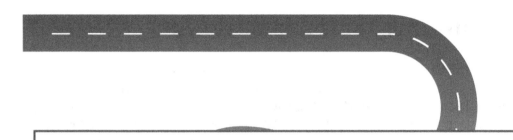

1. SETTING SOLID R.I.C.H. GOALS MEAN YOU HAVE ALSO SET A COURSE OF ACTIONS.

2. YOU MUST IDENTIFY YOUR OBSTACLES AND THEN FIND RESOURCES TO HELP YOU OVERCOME THEM.

3. WHEN YOU MEASURE AND TRACK YOUR PROGRESS YOU WILL INCREASE YOUR CHANCES OF SUCCESS.

REVIEW

THE RULE: YOU ARE DRIVING

Why should you begin your financial education or even care about money? You are in the driver's seat of Your Money Vehicle and your future is in your hands. Begin with the end in mind and set R.I.C.H. goals as the destinations of your financial journey. Your first step should be following the Golden Rule! No doubt you will take a wrong turn or hit a pothole, but if you align your values with your R.I.C.H. goals, you will be heading in the right direction.

ACTION

Set your R.I.C.H. Goals:

- **Week:** Learn a new skill, subject, or something interesting related to your R.I.C.H Goals
- **Month:** Stop doing something that is distracting from your R.I.C.H Goals
- **Year:** Start something today that will come to fruition in a year for your R.I.C.H Goals

OWNER'S MANUAL
FOR YOUR MONEY VEHICLE:

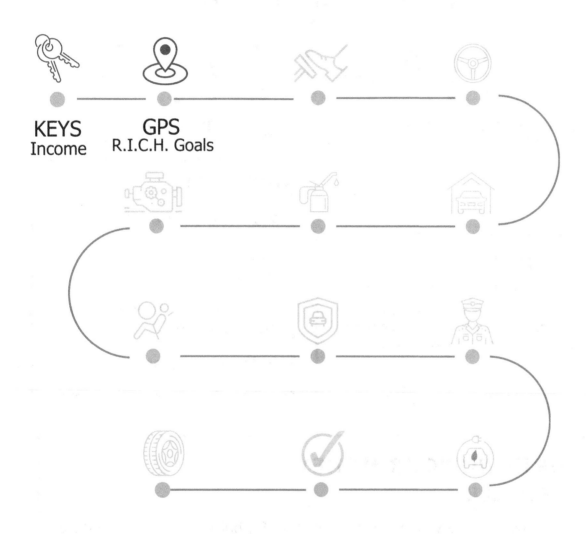

KEYS
Income

GPS
R.I.C.H. Goals

TIME VALUE OF MONEY

CHAPTER 2

HOW DOES MONEY CREATE MONEY?

OVERVIEW

2.1: The Cost of Money

2.2: The 8th Wonder of the World

2.3: Treat Your Money Like an Employee

2.4: How a Loan Works

ACTION

Start thinking and acting like an invest-OR, by employing a percentage of your paycheck to start working for future you!

DRIVING YOUR MONEY VEHICLE

Knowing where you are going is vital (GPS), but when learning to drive a car, one of the first things you need to know is how to speed up and slow down. This is where the pedals come into play. On the left – the brake and on the right – the gas. Your Money Vehicle cannot just sit in one place, you must begin to move it in the direction of your goals. Knowing how to press down on the brake or gas pedal is critical to driving.

SECTION 2.1
THE COST OF MONEY

TERMS

LOAN: an amount of money that is borrowed with the expectation that when it is paid back, there will be interest paid as well.

INTEREST: money you must pay for the U.S.E. of someone else's money.

PRINCIPAL: the original amount of money borrowed in a loan.

COLLATERAL: something pledged as security in a loan that will be forfeited if the borrower does not pay.

MONETARY POLICY: decisions made by the FED to expand or contract the economy.

QUANTITATIVE EASING AND TIGHTENING: the practice of the FED to buy (easing) or sell (tightening) loans held by the United States government to either increase or decrease the available cash in the economy.

FEDERAL FUNDS RATE: this is the benchmark interest rate that financial institutions will lend their money reserves held at the FED to one another.

ECONOMIC EXPANSION: the economy is growing.

ECONOMIC CONTRACTION: the economy is shrinking.

Can I borrow $5?"
This question has been asked amongst friends for ages, but have you ever wondered what happens when the answer is Yes? When the response is yes, a new relationship forms: borrower and lender. This borrower and lender relationship is the same relationship that develops when you walk into a bank and ask for a loan or even deposit your money. We will discuss more about this in Chapter 4.

The difference in the borrower/ lender relationship can be seen in how people U.S.E. money. Is the person U.S.E.-ing money as the means or as a means to an end?

To better understand this relationship, answer this question: What does it take to borrow money?

The answer is more money!

Despite the fairytales and the crazy stories of riches appearing overnight, money is never free. If someone is willing to lend you money, it is because they are using money as a tool to make more money, the means to an end.

When your friend says 'Yes' to letting you borrow $5, does she mention that she not only wants the $5 back, but also an extra $1? Or even an extra $5?

This expectation comes from the formation of a LOAN and the fundamental principle of charging **INTEREST** to U.S.E. someone else's money. In a loan, the amount of money you borrow is called the **PRINCIPAL**, and anything you pay back on top of the principal is the value of using the money, or the interest.

 You ask for $5 (the principal) and your friend says, 'Yes but I want $6 back', the $1 is the interest.

 To borrow money, it takes MORE MONEY!

WHY DO PEOPLE CHARGE YOU INTEREST?

People can charge you interest to use their money because of two reasons, first it is a privilege to U.S.E. their money and second, they will not be able to U.S.E. the money while you have it.

Any lender has a choice of who they want to loan their money to, the person receiving it is receiving a favor of sorts. Not a free favor, but a generosity or kindness to allow you the privilege of doing what you desire with the money. The other reason there is interest is because of the choice the lender makes to no longer U.S.E. the money while it is in your possession.

Now, if your friend says 'Yes' to lending you the money but tells you to pay her $10 next week, you should really consider getting a new friend. That would be charging 100% interest on the $5 principal. If she says you owe $6 next week, it is because she understands the value in letting you U.S.E. her money and thinks the privilege is worth $1. Again, that $1 value is called interest.

Borrower question:

What price am I willing to pay to U.S.E. other people's money?

Lender question:

What price am I willing to accept to allow someone to U.S.E. my money?

WHAT ARE SOME EXAMPLES OF COMMON BORROWER AND LENDER RELATIONSHIPS?

Borrowing and Lending money is a common practice in everyday life. Here are some examples of real-life lender and borrower relationships:

AUTO LOANS

Auto loans are a very common form of a lender-borrower relationship. In this case, a person looking to buy a car (borrower) takes out a loan from a lender (such as a bank or auto finance company) to purchase a vehicle. The lender provides the borrower with the funds needed to buy the vehicle, and the borrower agrees to repay the loan with interest over a set period of time.

The vehicle serves as **COLLATERAL** for the loan, which means that the lender can take back possession of the vehicle if the borrower fails to make their loan payments.

LENDER **BANK OR AUTO FINANCE COMPANY**

BORROWER **CAR BUYER**

6-10% **AVERAGE INTEREST RATE IN 2023 IS 6% FOR NEW CARS AND 10% FOR USED CARS** 10

STUDENT LOANS

Student loans are another example of a lender-borrower relationship. In this case, a student (borrower) takes out a loan from a lender (such as a bank or the US Government) to pay tuition or student expenses. The lender provides the borrower with the funds needed to pay for school and the borrower agrees to repay the loan with interest over a set period of time.

LENDER ➡ **BANK OR US GOVERNMENT**

BORROWER ➡ **STUDENT**

5-8%

AVERAGE INTEREST RATE IN 2023 IS 5% FOR FEDERAL LOANS AND 8% FOR PRIVATE LOANS [10]

MORTGAGES

A mortgage is another very common example of a lender-borrower relationship. In this case, a homebuyer (borrower) takes out a loan from a lender (such as a bank or mortgage company) to purchase a property. The lender provides the borrower with the funds needed to buy the property, and the borrower agrees to repay the loan with interest over a set period of time.

The house serves as collateral for the loan, which means that the lender can take back possession of the house if the borrower fails to make their loan payments.

LENDER ➡ **BANK OR MORTGAGE COMPANY**

BORROWER ➡ **HOMEBUYER**

6.75%

AVERAGE INTEREST RATE IN 2023 FOR A 30-YEAR FIXED MORTGAGE IS 6.75% [11]

HOW DOES THE FED CONTROL LENDING MONEY AND THE MONEY SUPPLY?

We learned in the Income Chapter that the FED controls the money supply and the decisions the FED makes to expand or contract the money supply is called the **MONETARY POLICY**. The monetary policy will shift, and change depending on the FED's intention to expand or contract current economic activity. The two primary ways the FED can impact the monetary policy are:

Federal Funds Rate: Financial institutions hold their 'reserves' at the Federal Reserve (the FED) and this is the benchmark interest rate that those institutions will lend money to one another.

1.

2.

QUANTITATIVE EASING OR TIGHTENING: This is the practice of the Federal Reserve buying or selling loans held by the United States government.

WAIT A MINUTE, BANKS LEND MONEY TO ONE ANOTHER?

Yes. Remember there is not an amount of gold anymore representing the money supply. Banks are allowed to loan out money beyond their reserve requirement and can do so to one another at the Federal Funds Rate. We will dive more into 'reserve requirements' in Chapter 4, but for now continue to remember that money is always working for someone, you are taking Money Vehicle to make that someone – You.

The question you should be asking: Is the Fed trying to grow or reduce the economy?

In economics, when your economy is growing it is called **EXPANSION** and when your economy is shrinking, it is called **CONTRACTION**.

WHEN TRYING TO EXPAND THE ECONOMY, THE FED CAN:

Lower Federal Funds Rate:

This will make it less expensive to borrow money and therefore will increase the money being used by people and businesses.

Quantitative Easing:

The FED will purchase loans from the United States government and put more money into the economy.

These actions will increase spending behavior of consumers; in doing so increase the demand, raising prices, and eventually raising inflation.

In August of 2021, the FED took extraordinary measures to stabilize the country by practicing quantitative easing and increasing its total assets from $4.17 trillion to $8.33 trillion in response to the Covid-19 epidemic.

WHEN TRYING TO CONTRACT THE ECONOMY, THE FED CAN:

Raise the Federal Funds Rate:

This will make it more expensive to borrow money and therefore will decrease the money being used by people and businesses.

Quantitative Tightening:

The FED will sell loans back to the United States government and take money out of the economy.

SECTION 2.1
RECAP

These actions will decrease spending behavior of consumers and in doing so decrease demand, lowering prices, and eventually lowering inflation.

When we think about the economy at large, we can begin to see a large line of dominos, each measurement or action taken will set off an impact to the next domino. With how connected our economic system is, you will see that each action is not inherently a good or a bad thing, it is how it impacts the next domino that is the indicator.

1. MONEY IS NEVER FREE, THERE IS ALWAYS INTEREST WHEN YOU U.S.E. OTHER PEOPLE'S MONEY.

2. PRINCIPAL IS HOW MUCH YOU BORROW, AND INTEREST IS HOW MUCH IT COSTS TO BORROW.

3. THE FED CAN CONTROL SOME OF THE ECONOMY THROUGH THE FEDERAL FUNDS RATE.

SECTION 2.2
THE EIGHTH WONDER OF THE WORLD

TERMS

SIMPLE INTEREST: when you receive interest payments based solely on the principal amount you borrowed or invested.

COMPOUND INTEREST: the 8th wonder of the world and occurs when you receive interest payments based on the principal amount you invest plus the interest that has already been created.

TIME VALUE OF MONEY: states that money is worth more today than in the future because if you put the money to work, it can create more money!

Suzy and Ricky are both twenty-five and want to be financially free at sixty-five. Although their R.I.C.H. goals are similar, they have very different approaches to getting there.

Suzy got a good job out of school and wants to start investing right away. She is a musician at heart and knows when she turns 35, she is going to pursue her dream of playing guitar. Suzy wants to put as much money to work for her before then as possible.

Ricky on the other hand does not think he can start investing for a while as he has some student loans, rent, and enjoys going out with his friends. Ricky is going to enjoy working for a few years and around age 35 he will start investing.

Suzy starts investing $5,000 a year from twenty-five until she is thirty-five and then stops saving for freedom altogether.

Total invested by Suzy over 10 years = $50,000

Ricky is going to live it up in his twenties and won't start investing until he's thirty-five. Then he will save $5,000 every year until he reaches freedom.

Total invested by Ricky over 30 years = $150,000

OK, SO WHO ENDS UP WITH MORE AT RETIREMENT?

The answer depends on how well you understand the "eighth wonder of the world"—compound interest. Don't take our word for how important compound interest is, take the word of one of the smartest people who has ever lived.

Compound interest is the eighth wonder of the world. She who understands it, earns it...she who doesn't...pays it.

-Albert Einstein

WHAT IS THE DIFFERENCE BETWEEN SIMPLE AND COMPOUND INTEREST?

Interest can be calculated in one of two ways: Simply or Compounded. The difference can be exponential!

SIMPLE INTEREST is when you receive interest payments based solely on the principal amount you borrowed or invested. The money you have earned goes to work for you and creates new money.

Simple interest is the principal multiplied by the interest rate and periods of time.

Seen as a math formula:

$$I = P \times R \times T$$

Where (I) represents the interest being created, (P) represents the original amount or principal, (R) represents the interest rate per year, and (T) represents how many years it is creating.

SIMPLE INTEREST EXAMPLE, $100 AT 5% OVER 10 YEARS:

YEAR	PRINCIPAL	INTEREST EARNED	TOTAL AMOUNT
1	$100	$5	$105
2	$100	$5	$110
3	$100	$5	$115
4	$100	$5	$120
5	$100	$5	$125
6	$100	$5	$130
7	$100	$5	$135
8	$100	$5	$140
9	$100	$5	$145
10	$100	$5	$150

COMPOUND INTEREST is known as the 8th wonder of the world and occurs when you receive interest payments based on the principal amount you invested plus the interest that has already been created. Your money goes to work for you, creates new money, and then that money goes to work for you too!

Compound interest is the value of your money today, multiplied by the interest rate you believe you will receive, and then exponentially multiplied by the number of periods you will invest over. That is why we say the difference between simple and compound is exponential!

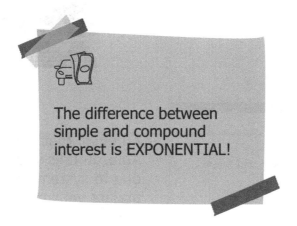

The difference between simple and compound interest is EXPONENTIAL!

Seen as a math formula:

$$FV = PV (1+R)^N$$

Where (FV) represents the future value of the dollars, (PV) represents the present value of the dollars, (r) represents the interest rate per year, and (n) represents the periods of time it is compounding.

We introduced phishing in our last section, but this is such a rampant issue today that we need to take a deep dive into what exactly it is and how you can begin to identify it when it happens. Before you skip ahead and think, 'I am not going to be hacked' ask yourself if you have received one of these kind of messages:

A message that appears to be from Netflix says, "Your membership has expired, click here to renew."

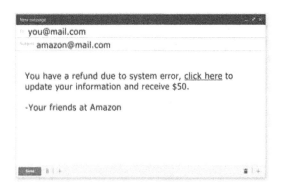

An email that looks like it's from Amazon tells you, "You have a refund due to system error, click here to update your information and receive $50."

What you think might be an electronic bill from your phone provider states, "You haven't paid last month's bill. Pay attached invoice as soon as possible to avoid penalties."

These are all imposter emails known as phishing. Phishing emails take advantage of our human makeup by creating a connection, lowering our guard, and then hooking us to give away personal information—usernames, passwords, or credit card information. This manipulation is accomplished by the impersonation of someone or something we trust, creation of a sense of urgency, and focus of our attention onto something we want or need.

The attackers will first build a connection by using stolen logos or common email templates to make their work look believable. Next, there will be an issue where you need to provide information of some sort to solve the problem. Typically, a deadline will be included to create a sense of urgency. Lastly, they include a call to action such as "Click Here" or "Log into Your Account" to provide an easy solution to the problem. Sadly, on the other side of that action is not a solution but instead, the attacker is waiting to steal your information and identity.

Most common brand names [31] used in phishing attacks:

- Microsoft: Office or OneDrive
- Amazon
- DocuSign
- Google
- Adobe

With an understanding of what phishing attacks are, let's move onto how these hackers will politely request information from you using different techniques.

TYPES OF PHISHING

ACCOUNT ACTIVITY: The company is reaching out to confirm your account information, to alert you that your account has been locked out, or to inform you that more information is needed for your account to be completed. This attack also may be alerting you that your account has been logged into from a "new browser." Creating a small ask to remedy a simple issue seems harmless and that is what they are counting on.

PAYPAL

PayPal account

What's going on ?.

We're concerned that someone is using your PayPal account without your knowledge. Recentactivity on your account seems to have occurred from a suspicious location or under circumstances that may be different than usual.

What to do ?

Log in to your PayPal account as soon as possible. We may ask you to confirm information you provided when you created your account to make sure you're the account holder. We'll then ask you to Confirm your password and security questions. You should also do the following for your own protection:

Confirm Your Account Now

Log in to confirm your account

MEMBERSHIP UPDATE: A company you may or may not have a membership with is contacting you about restarting or deactivating your service. They are trying to create a sense of urgency around your membership, to push you into logging in through their fake landing page.

CREDENTIALS PHISH: This is where you receive an email asking you to log into your account. Seems straightforward and harmless enough, but this attack is coming from a fraudulent source. Even though it appears as normal as any search engine, a company you do business with will not reach out to you and ask you to login, they spent a lot of money on their website. This ask for credentials is a productive scam because with a simple tweak to the HTML attachment that is commonly used by financial institutions, they can get by your antivirus software.

 For example, BankofAmrica.com—did you catch it? You may have because you were looking for it, but what if it is in the 'Sender' box on 1 of 40 emails you got this morning.

PACKAGING PHISH: A recognizable company that you have received packages from in the past wants you to verify your shipping address or confirm something on a missed delivery. With online shopping as prevalent as it is today, "A delivery attempt was made" is the second most clicked phishing campaign according to KnowBe4.

 For example, a message from UPS is alerting you that you missed a package delivery and need to click on the tracking number to locate it. You will then be taken to a different web page, where you are expected to hand over information about yourself or the delivery address.

UNEXPECTED MONEY PHISH: It's your lucky day! Somehow, the company you just had a transaction with, or even the IRS, made a mistake, and you are due for some money. Or, perhaps, a stranger wants to give you something for free—all you need to do is send a small amount of money or information first.

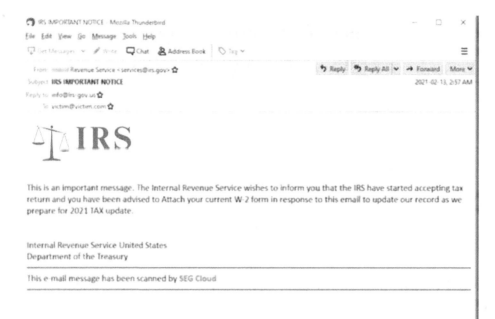

ARE PHISHING ATTACKS ONLY COMING THROUGH EMAIL?

Not anymore! A company called Lookout conducted a report on analytics from 210 million devices, 175 million apps, and 4 million URL's daily to see that email is not the only type of phish out there. 'Non-email-based phishing' is on the rise.

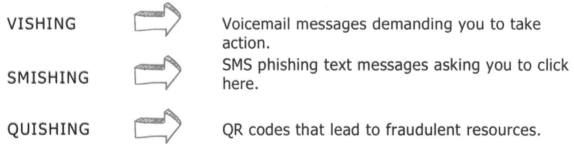

VISHING — Voicemail messages demanding you to take action.

SMISHING — SMS phishing text messages asking you to click here.

QUISHING — QR codes that lead to fraudulent resources.

Phishing scams are ever-changing, and with each successful new tactic, you can expect ten more to be created. The best way to defend yourself online is to know what you are looking for!

Money Vehicle wants you to begin to **THINK BEFORE YOU CLICK.** This means that when you receive a message from an email, text, or other you stop and think through a few things before you just respond and especially before you CLICK!

IF IT SMELLS PHISHY, ASK THESE 5 CYBERSECURITY QUESTIONS:

1. IS THIS FOR ME?

Who is the email addressed to, and where did it come from? Do you even have a connection to the source or the sender's address? Begin to ask if this message was actually meant for you or if it feels like something that could have been sent out to the masses. Check who the message was sent to and who it was sent from. Often the message will begin with something generic like "Dear Valued Customer", that does not sound like a company, that sounds like someone is buttering you up.

This sense of unfamiliarity should make you pause and question, is this even for me?

2. WHY WOULD THEY ASK ME FOR THAT?

No true company that you work with will ever reach out and ask you for your password and they will not ask you to change it through an email. If a company is asking you for information, question that company. When they reach out to you it is to get you to buy more things, not to help you with tasks like logging in, that is what automation is for. To change our password or confirm any information, you should initiate that process yourself after logging in to their website directly.

This sense of curiosity should make you pause and question, why would they ask me for that?

3. AM I REALLY THAT LUCKY?

No one has a rich cousin or is being contacted by a friendly Nigerian prince who wants to give them a pile of money. It may feel exciting, but unfortunately that just does not happen in life. This is also the case when a random email is telling you that there is unearned money waiting for you just on the other side of this click. We discussed earlier the idea of earned income, people work very hard to make money, no one is out there just giving it away. Also, if you think a company of any sort is going to make you aware of a mistake they made and offer to make you whole via email, you are sadly mistaken. If it feels too good to be true, it probably is.

This sense of unearned fortune should make you pause and question, am I really that lucky?

4. WHY DOES IT LOOK SO SLOPPY?

Professional organizations spend a lot of time and money on their brand, they have entire marketing departments and copy writers scouring every word that is being sent out. When you receive an email, begin to look for misspelled words, incorrect information, or a browser that doesn't match the one you use for your actual account. You will see this in the brand logos being blurry or words being off in the printing. Even having incorrect grammar is a giveaway, if when reading a sentence out loud you can almost hear a computer typing it, be on alert.

This sense of unprofessionalism should make you pause and question, why does this look so sloppy?

5. WHERE'S THE FIRE?

Any email that is trying to create a sense of urgency by putting you on a clock is simply using a scare tactic to disarm you. Why are they trying to get you to act so quickly? A real company has an entire customer service department to help with your questions.

This sense of urgency should make you pause and question, where is the fire?

SECTION 8.2
RECAP

'THINK BEFORE YOU CLICK':

1. IS THIS FOR ME?

2. WHY WOULD THEY ASK ME THAT?

3. AM I THAT LUCKY?

4. WHY SO SLOPPY?

5. WHERE'S THE FIRE?

SECTION 8.3
FIGHT THE HACKERS

TERMS

FIGHT THE HACKERS: Money Vehicle's approach to defending yourself in the online cyber war.

HARD DRIVE: a data storage device that can be used even when the device is turned off.

THE CLOUD: a data storage device that is stored on the internet.

ANTIVIRUS SOFTWARE: a program designed to detect and remove viruses and other malware from your computer.

FIREWALL: a system designed to block unauthorized access while still allowing outward communication.

PASSWORD: a secret phrase used to gain admission into something.

STRONG PASSWORD: an unpredictable password made up of eight (8) or more characters and using a combination of uppercase letters, lowercase letters, symbols, and numbers.

In my rookie season, I was released by the Chicago Bears and activated by the Cleveland Browns. By this time, my fiancé and I had decided that moving furniture around the country was too much work and cost too much money, especially when we didn't know how long we would be at our next destination. Trying to be more frugal, we put the Tempur-Pedic® mattress I bought as a Philadelphia Eagle on Craigslist.

You read that correctly, I got cut a lot in the NFL, in my rookie year alone was: Eagles, Bears, Browns, and Chiefs.

Right away, we received an offer on the mattress and they were a motivated buyer:

> "I am very interested in buying your mattress and need it ASAP, because I move into my apartment this weekend. The bank I work with will only allow money orders to be sent in denominations of $500, so here is a money order. Can you please send the mattress to this address and just mail me back the difference in cash?"

Something smelled fishy, I had not heard of a bank with restrictions on amount, but we wanted to get rid of the mattress before the move to Cleveland, so we agreed.

Then the money order came. It was kind of fuzzy, the logo of the bank was tilted a little, and there were odd markings in the corners of the page. It looked to us as if it had been scanned before it was sent and it was not scanned very well. We quickly called the bank it had supposedly come from and, unsurprisingly, they had no knowledge of that money order!

Now we had confirmation it was fake and tore it up immediately! We were both happy to have caught this attacker, to have saved our money, and to each have a new sense of caution when dealing with people online. Long story short, we did sell the mattress in Chicago and good thing because I got cut again two weeks after arriving in Cleveland.

These types of experiences may seem obvious when selling a mattress online, but the truth is people are waiting around lots of virtual corners to defraud you into giving them your money. Remember 'can you send me back the difference?' Seemed innocent, but they were relying on me to just mail them the money, no threat or danger of any kind.

With these attacks growing each day and coming now through email, phone calls, text messages, and even social media messages, we need to start practicing ways to Fight the Hackers!!

Money Vehicle wants to arm you with some ways to take action in the battle against cybersecurity:

HOVER OVER THE LINK.

The easiest and best defense is just holding your curser arrow over the link. A bubble will appear that shows you exactly where the link will send you. If a destination pops up that you aren't trying to go to, don't click. Delete.

DO NOT HIT REPLY, LOG IN DIRECTLY.

- Do not click anywhere in the message to respond. Instead, close the email and go directly to the source it is supposed to have come from, such as your bank's actual website. Seriously, even if the email is legitimate, it is still a best practice to go to the site on your own. Follow the same rule when you receive fishy phone calls—hang up and call the business back from the number listed on their website.

- Even clicking "Cancel" or "Close Here" within the email can be hazardous. Always click on the X in the top right corner of the window to close it.

NEVER DOWNLOAD

If the website or email seems suspicious at all, do not download the attachment. Downloading items from any source allows an open door into your computers system. Remember the old malware attack when people try and hack into your system, they do not need to do that if you just let them in by downloading.

STOP POSTING.

Some personal information is not meant to be on social media, including your birth date, address, phone number, and vacation plans. These data points that you post unconsciously can be gathered and used against you. Seeing all this information online is also why your password should not be connected to a favorite sports team, jersey number, or other identifiable information from social media.

BACK UP YOUR FILES.
- This process has gotten easier and easier with technology. Now all you must do is go to the 'Start' menu and type in backup, from there all you need to do is point where you want to send the files. Typically, you will store this backup either on an external **HARD DRIVE** or to **THE CLOUD** which just means they are on internet servers and not a hard drive.

- It is best practice to back up your files in case you ever lose your computer but also in the event of a cyberattack. If the hacker locks you out of your computer and holds your content for ransom, you will be comforted knowing you have a backup.

UPDATE AND REMOVE SYSTEMS.
- Keep your operating system up to date, and make sure that your ANTIVIRUS SOFTWARE and FIREWALL (system designed to prevent unauthorized access to your desktop and network) are enabled. These systems will be your second line of defense as hackers try to get into your system.

- Install protective tools like an anti-phishing toolbar that will alert you when you stumble onto malicious sites. Also set your systems to have an automatic update so they do not get out of date. Try to automate your updates. Lastly, remove any old systems that you are no longer using to clear up space but also to close loose ends.

ALWAYS LOG OUT.
Throughout the day we will open dozens of windows while searching around online. This amazing ability to dive in so many directions sometimes leave opportunities for foul play. Attacks can happen when you move from one site to another and the attacker maybe able to get onto your internet server and access to the accounts that you have open. Logging out completely and closing the account you are in will close these open doors. If you do want to remain in the account while you are searching, then open a new browser session instead of just a new window.

AVOID PUBLIC ACCESS.

- Beginning with your home wireless network and mobile phone, assign a passcode to log in. This will prevent people you do not want on your system from having access to it. If you are going to public places, turn off Bluetooth® when you are not using it. Bluetooth offers amazing connectivity, but if you are not looking to connect, it should not be looking either.

- You should also be very conscious of public wi-fi. Whether you are sitting on a bus, walking through an airport, or just at a local coffee shop, connecting to the public internet opens a lot of windows for people to tap into your system. Being on the public internet is like being at a public pool, everyone has the same access. If you need to jump online with your computer, try accessing your phone's mobile device through a hotspot.

BE AWARE OF SLOPPINESS.

- Be on alert when messages come through sloppily, if there are misspellings, or the text is filled with poor grammar. Poorly written, badly designed, and/or vague emails did not come from a professional company with a marketing department.

- Verify that the URL begins with http and has a closed-lock icon in the address bar!

CREATE A SECURE PASSWORD.

- PASSWORDS are your first line of defense when it comes to cyberattacks. With so many accounts and logins today, people are struggling to create strong passwords and even more so in managing what their passwords are. We must see passwords as a gate protecting our personal information and make sure the gate is closed with a lock.

- A STRONG PASSWORD should be eight (8) or more characters in length and use a combination of uppercase letters, lowercase letters, symbols, and numbers.

- Ex. H7&3DD1!

- With passwords, you do not want to be predictable. Things like your birthday, pet's name, or favorite soccer player are all easily identified through social media. The same can be said for answers to your security questions. Create unique passwords for different types of accounts such as casual accounts, financial accounts, or work accounts. Having different passwords will help prevent you from a global breach, where an attacker gets one password and then gets access to anything.

- There are tools, such as 1Password or LastPass, that were devised to make password creation and management easier. I will not speak to their quality, but if you are interested in having unique passwords for each of your accounts, you should check them out.

SECTION 8.3
RECAP

1. HOVER OVER LINK AND NEVER REPLY; ALWAYS GO DIRECT TO THE SOURCE.

2. NEVER DOWNLOAD AND SECURE YOUR PROPERTY BY BACKING UP YOUR FILES.

3. TRY TO AVOID PUBLIC ACCESS AND ALWAYS LOG OUT.

4. CREATE A SECURED PASSWORD AND UPDATE TWICE A YEAR.

REVIEW

THE RULE: THINK BEFORE YOU CLICK

Where is the new phishing hole? Unfortunately, it is not a place where you can catch real fish. Cyberattacks began with intense codes and hacking, but as antivirus software improved, the hackers adopted a new approach—social engineering. This scam tries to trick you into handing over sensitive personal information. Attacks happen every day through the mimicking of a person or company that you are familiar with. It's important for you to recognize certain red flags or warning signs of phishy emails. Always remember to Fight the Hackers and continue to think before you click!

ACTION

Setup your first line of cyber defense with a strong password that has 8+ characters and is not predictable based on your information.

- Have a list of passwords somewhere or use a password manager.
- Backup your computer and stop posting personal info.
- Stay off public Wi-Fi .

OWNER'S MANUAL
FOR YOUR MONEY VEHICLE:

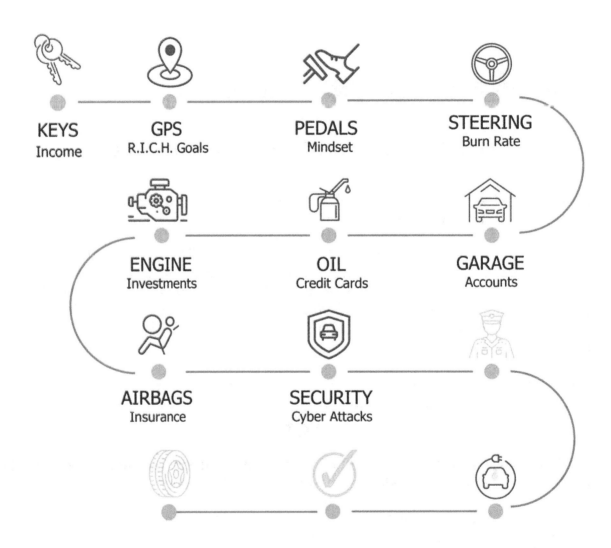

KEYS
Income

GPS
R.I.C.H. Goals

PEDALS
Mindset

STEERING
Burn Rate

ENGINE
Investments

OIL
Credit Cards

GARAGE
Accounts

AIRBAGS
Insurance

SECURITY
Cyber Attacks

SOCIETY CHOICE (TAXES)

CHAPTER 9

IS ALL MY MONEY TAXED THE SAME?

OVERVIEW
9.1: Why We Need Taxes

9.2: Net Income: Your Biggest Expense

9.3: How Your Income is Taxed

9.4: Filing Your Taxes

ACTION

Plan for your Society Choice, understanding that 25% of your Gross Income will be contributed to this choice.

DRIVING YOUR MONEY VEHICLE

There will be many overlooked resources on your journey—the first is often right at the end of your driveway—a paved road! This resource is frequently taken for granted, but once you've hit a few potholes, you'll learn to appreciate it. Other valuable resources that are a part of our society are frontline workers who throw caution to the wind in serving us. These oversights for services that we need are like our relationship with taxes. People have positive and negative relationships with taxes, but no matter what, the resources they provide are essential to your journey and our Society.

SECTION 9.1
WHY WE NEED TAXES

TERMS

TAXES: a law stating how much of your earned income or business profits can be contributed and how much additional charge can be added to goods or services in order to support our Society.
- **Tassein:** to fix (Greek)
- **Taxare:** to charge (Latin)

SUPPLEMENTAL HOUSING SNAP: the nation's most important anti-hunger program. Formerly known as the 'Food Stamp Program', SNAP is helping over 41 million people afford a nutritionally adequate diet each month.

STATE CHILDREN'S HEALTH INSURANCE PROGRAM (SCHIP): provides insurance coverage for children whose families earn too much to afford Medicaid (another Society benefit), but who cannot afford private coverage.

HOUSING AND URBAN DEVELOPMENT (HUD): a Federal agency responsible for national policy and programs that address America's housing needs, that improve and develop the Nation's communities, and enforce fair housing laws.

INTERNAL REVENUE SERVICE (IRS): the revenue service for the United States responsible for collecting the U.S. federal taxes and administering the Internal Revenue Code.

SALES TAX: a tax paid for the sales of certain goods or services.

HERE IS A WACKY WEDNESDAY:

On your morning drive to class, you turn onto the road your school is on and your tire hits a pothole. That same pothole has been there for months, and you begin to wonder why no one has come to fix it?

Next, you arrive at school to find that there are no teachers in any of the classrooms! You are excited at first, but then start to wonder how you will ever get your grades or graduate without them.

At the end of the school day, you get changed and ready to head out to your soccer practice, only to realize that the practice field has been cleared to make way for some new apartment buildings.

WHAT IS GOING ON?

This Wacky Wednesday is an example of what would happen if we didn't have to pay into supporting our society, better known as "paying taxes".

TAXES are laws stating how much of your earned income or business profits can be contributed and how much additional charge can be added to goods or services to support our Society. The word "tax" originally comes from the Greek work **TASSEIN**, which means 'to fix' and the Latin word **TAXARE**, which means 'to charge'. Seeing it through the historical lens, tax translates to mean 'a charge to fix'.

No matter one's stance on how the tax dollars should be spent, we all identify the benefits it could provide and the beauty in the Society it creates.

So, why is there such a negative response to the idea of taxes?

There is a saying, "The only two guarantees in life are death and taxes."

The only two guarantees in life are death and taxes.

This mindset paints a negative view of taxes, and we need to start seeing taxes in a new light. Of course, in America everyone is entitled to an opinion on how much we should pay in taxes and how those taxes are spent, but before you complain too much, appreciate what those taxes provide.

Look no further than a public high school to see how far taxes truly reach.

 The salary of the teachers/staff.

 The funded programs that we study, such as NASA.

 The books or tablets students use.

 The fields we practice on and the playgrounds we play on.

 The buses to and from school.

 The library and all its content.

 The lunches for those in need.

 The public court system that enforces the school laws.

 The security guards on campus.

 The school buildings themselves.

This list of things supported by taxes at a local high school is just the beginning of the amazing society we belong to. Look around town at the public service sector and our frontline workers—firefighters, police officers, public hospitals, and the military are all supported by taxes. The millions of people who take public transportation to get to work and the millions of families who get support for a member with special needs benefit from this society.

The entire United States government is run on our tax dollars!

SOCIETY CHOICE

Our taxes pay for everything in between what you own and what I own.

Other programs our taxes go to support in our society:

- **SUPPLEMENTAL HOUSING SNAP:** the nation's most important anti-hunger program. Formerly known as the 'Food Stamp Program', SNAP is helping over 41 million people afford a nutritionally adequate diet each month.

- **STATE CHILDREN'S HEALTH INSURANCE PROGRAM (SCHIP):** provides insurance coverage for children whose families earn too much to afford Medicaid (another Society benefit), but who cannot afford private coverage.

- **HOUSING AND URBAN DEVELOPMENT (HUD):** a Federal agency responsible for national policy and programs that address America's housing needs, that improve and develop the Nation's communities, and enforce fair housing laws.

WHO IS COLLECTING ALL THE TAXES?

That is a logical question after we said this is a positive thing to pay, who you are paying it to?

The **INTERNAL REVENUE SERVICE** or better known simply as the IRS is who will be collecting all the taxes for the United States government. The IRS was founded in 1862 to be the revenue service for the government and is tasked with collecting taxes to pay all the government's budgetary needs. They are also responsible for enforcing the tax codes and tax laws that Congress enacts with 'integrity and fairness for all'.

OK, WE KNOW WHY AND WHO, BUT WHAT IS THE FIRST TAX YOU WILL ENCOUNTER?

SALES TAX

Most people like buying things, so the ability to buy something is a positive event. **SALES TAX** is a tax on sales and is charged when you buy something. So, if we connect sales tax to a positive event like buying something, you can see that taxes are not connected to negative events, but positive events. Much like it helps to understand why we need taxes in general, seeing sales taxes through this positive lens removes the negative connection most often associated with them.

When you go to purchase goods or services, there will be a tax associated, the sales tax. This tax is imposed by state and local governments to generate revenue and support their local communities.

So, when you go out to dinner and your meal costs $20, but the bill comes back saying you owe $21, the additional $1.00 is the tax associated with the sale of your dinner.

- Go out to dinner with friends $20 with a 5% sales tax: total meal cost $21.

- New pair of $100 shoes with 6% sales tax: total cost of shoes $106.

This is a big problem with consumers as their cash management strategy does not always account for this added cost. Sure, when you look at $1 a meal it doesn't amount to much, but when you start adding 5% to all the things you buy, it does add up.

Remember discussing how people break the Golden Rule back in Chapter 1? We showed how Income Tax is a common way people start to spend more than they make, but now you can see that Sales Tax should also be included in that list.

WHERE DOES SALES TAX COME FROM?

There are over 10,000 different jurisdictions that can charge a sales tax. Counties or large cities, such as Seattle Washington or Chicago Illinois, will have their own sales tax on top of their state's sales tax.

Let's say you were to buy that same $20 dinner but instead of 5% sales tax, you went to dinner in downtown Chicago where the state of Illinois charges 6.25% and the city charges another 4%, to make a total of 10.25%. Now the $20 dinner would cost $22.05.

DOES EVERY STATE HAVE SALES TAX?

No. There are five states—Alaska, Delaware, Montana, New Hampshire, and Oregon—that do not charge a state sales tax.

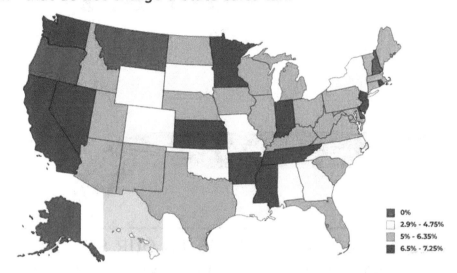

0%
2.9% - 4.75%
5% - 6.35%
6.5% - 7.25%

WHAT IF I BUY SOMETHING ONLINE?

As of a Supreme Court ruling in 2018, you are charged a sales tax based on your state of residence, no matter where you make a purchase—in a store or online. Don't worry, your Amazon purchases won't go up; Amazon has paid these taxes voluntarily since 2016.[37]

DO I PAY SALES TAX ON DISCOUNTED ITEMS?

Yes, but typically the sales tax will come into effect after the discount has been taken out.

While people may not enjoy seeing taxes taken out of their income or added to a purchase, this public duty provides protection of everything in between what you own and what I own. So, try to start seeing taxes as an investment in our society.

Paying taxes is never fun, but when you understand all that they support, it is a little easier to bear.

SECTION 9.1
RECAP

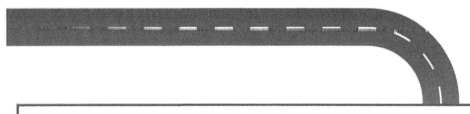

1. TAXES ARE CONTRIBUTIONS TO OUR SOCIETY, STOP TO LOOK AROUND AT ALL TAXES SUPPORT.

2. YOUR SOCIETY CHOICES SUPPORTS CHILDREN IN NEED AND HOMES TO MANY.

3. YOU WILL HAVE A CHARGE ON CERTAIN GOODS AND SERVICES CALLED SALES TAX.

SECTION 9.2
NET INCOME: YOUR BIGGEST EXPENSE

TERMS

INCOME TAX: the government charge placed on your earned income.

GROSS INCOME: the amount of money you 'make' before taxes and deductions.

NET INCOME: the amount of money you 'take' after taxes and deductions.

FEDERAL INCOME TAX: the progressive tax paid to the Federal Government from your earned income.

STATE INCOME TAX: the taxes paid to the State Government from your earned income and the amount will vary from state to state.

FICA TAX (FEDERAL INSURANCE CONTRIBUTIONS ACT): the tax deducted from your paycheck to go toward paying Social Security and Medicare Taxes. The amounts will be based on your income level and your employer will pay half of the cost.

SURTAXES: additional taxes paid by higher earners for certain programs.

SELF-EMPLOYED CONTRIBUTION ACT (SECA): a replacement for FICA on self-employed workers and states you will pay 15.3% to cover both employee and employer contributions.

FORM 1040: (Money Vehicle calls the tax table of contents). This form will hold all your taxable transactions for the year and be used to report the process from your Gross Income to your Net Income.

TAX AVOIDANCE: building a plan to U.S.E. taxes and reduce your tax liability.

TAX EVASION: attempting to trick or defraud the IRS into not paying your taxes.

FORM 1040X: a document that will amend your tax return to file the correct version.

TERMS

TAX DEDUCTION: a reduction of your taxable income.

TAXABLE INCOME: how much of your income will pass through the Gross to Net process and be used in calculating your income tax liability.

STANDARD DEDUCTION: an amount that every American taxpayer that does not itemize is allowed to take in reducing their taxable income. In 2023 this is $13,850.

TAX CUTS AND JOBS ACT: in 2018 this ruling changed the standard deduction and other tax items.

TAX REFUND: after filing your Form 1040, you are owed money in return.

ITEMIZED DEDUCTIONS: qualified expenses that can reduce your taxable income like the standard deduction. The catch is listing out and adding up your 'qualified expenses' to see if itemizing is even worth your time.

SCHEDULE A: the form you will need to file should you choose to itemize your deductions.

TAX CREDITS: a reduction of your tax liability.

TAX LIABILITY: after filing your form 1040, you owe more money.

Every year I played in the NFL, I looked forward to seeing a rookie open their first paycheck. Each year these young men were introduced to the largest expense they will incur in their lives – Income Taxes. We discussed in the last section all the positive things your tax dollars go towards, but now we must begin understanding how the Income Tax process works and how to go from your Gross Income to your Net Income.

INCOME TAX

We need money to do most things, so we all want to earn an income, so we have money. Earning an income is a positive event and **INCOME TAX** is charged when you earn an income.

Imagine for a moment that you are about to pop your Thanksgiving turkey into the oven. Your crazy cousin, Ficano, asks, "How many pounds of meat is that? Because I am so hungry, I could eat a pound to myself."

As you silently wish Ficano had made other holiday plans, you remember that the label on the turkey had said twenty pounds and you flippantly respond '20 pounds'. Even though the question and person may have bothered you, there is plenty of turkey for the family.

But just then you begin to think through the process. You waited in line for a 20-pound turkey, but does that mean all 20 pounds will be cooked and delivered to the table to eat?

Before you put that cooked turkey out on the table, you will have to remove the bones, giblets, and for some even the skin. Quickly you start to think about Ficano's question, and you realize maybe 12 pounds of turkey will end up on the table. Suddenly you need to tell Ficano to take it easy!

This concept of going from 20 pounds of turkey you bought down to 12 pounds of turkey you can eat is oddly like going from **GROSS INCOME** to **NET INCOME**. Only, with income, the pounds you lose are income taxes you pay.

Your gross income is how much money you earn BEFORE taxes, employee benefits, or other payroll deductions are taken out.

GROSS INCOME=

HOW MUCH
YOU <u>MAKE</u>

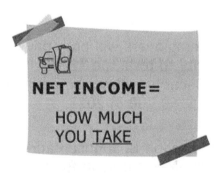

NET INCOME=

HOW MUCH
YOU <u>TAKE</u>

Your net income is how much money is left over AFTER taxes, employee benefits, and other payroll deductions are taken out.

Example: You earn $1,000 gross income and receive a paycheck for $700 as your net income.

THE PRIMARY SOURCE OF U.S. GOVERNMENT REVENUE IS INDIVIDUAL INCOME TAXES.

THE THREE MAJOR INCOME TAXES THAT ARE TAKEN OUT FROM GROSS TO NET:

FEDERAL INCOME TAX The amount of taxes paid to the Federal Government. This is a progressive tax which we will cover in 9.3.

STATE INCOME TAX The amount of taxes paid to the state you live and work in. The amount varies from state to state.

FICA TAX (FEDERAL INSURANCE CONTRIBUTION ACT) The amount that goes toward paying Social Security and Medicare Taxes. The amounts will be based on your income level and your employer will pay half of the cost. FICA is a federal payroll tax, which means it is automatically taken out of your paycheck to support the Social Security and Medicare systems in the United States.

Social Security was started in August 1935 by President Franklin Roosevelt and is meant to replace a portion of your pre-retirement income. How much of that income it replaces will depend on how much you earned throughout your career. The original purpose of Social Security was to establish economic security for workers coming out of the Great Depression. Today, it can be a beneficial resource for your 'Future You' years but will not be solely relied on to cover your lifestyle.

 Tax: Employees and employers will both pay 6.2% for social security to total the 12.4% requirement. Social Security will not be paid on income that exceeds $160,200 in 2023.

Medicare was started in July 1965 by President Lyndon B. Johnson and is meant to provide medical services for the elderly. Medicare can fund hospital, hospice, and nursing home expenses for older or disabled Americans.

 Tax: Employees and employers will both pay 1.45% for Medicare to total the 2.9% requirement.

There are **SURTAXES** or more taxes added onto higher earners regarding Medicare, but for the scope of Money Vehicle we will not confuse you with issues only pertaining to the top income earners.

7.65%

EMPLOYEES WILL PAY 7.65% OF INCOME TO SOCIAL SECURITY AND MEDICARE

If you are interested in becoming an entrepreneur, then you get the privilege of being both the employee and employer regarding Social Security and Medicare. This means under the **SELF-EMPLOYED CONTRIBUTION ACT (SECA)** you will pay all 15.3% of these taxes yourself.

15.3%

ENTREPRENEURS WILL PAY 15.3% OF INCOME TO SOCIAL SECURITY AND MEDICARE

WHAT OTHER PAYROLL DEDUCTIONS WILL THERE BE?

Two other common payroll deductions you will encounter are insurance policy deductions and retirement deductions. The good news is that these are not dollars you are paying to the government, instead they are dollars being designated for other parts of Your Money Vehicle.

Insurance: You learned about insurance in Chapter 7 and if you are a traditional employee working at a company, you will have the option of participating in the employer sponsored health, dental, and vision care plans. To participate you will have to pay premiums for the policies and these premiums will be automatically deducted from your paycheck. Typically, you will get better pricing for insurance policies through your employer.

Retirement: You are probably thinking, 'retirement'? I am way too young to be thinking about that! But what we learned in Chapter 2 around compound interest is that time is your greatest ally. If you choose to, and Money Vehicle is obviously recommending that you do, into an employer sponsored retirement plan for 'Future You,' then these dollars will also be automatically deducted from your paycheck and placed into your retirement account. You will get to choose how much you want to put into this account and we want to remind you Made a dollar, Saved a dime! Which account you should contribute to will be covered in Chapter 10.

HOW MUCH WILL I PAY THE IRS IN INCOME TAXES?

Understanding the big 3 taxes associated with your income – Federal, State, and FICA – should give you more confidence in knowing you will not take home all the money you make. But each person will pay a different amount of taxes based on their overall earnings as well as their individual circumstances.

Starting with FICA, you see now that you can expect to pay 7.65% if you are a traditional employee. With your state income tax, you will have to research what the rate is within your state as it varies from state to state. In Section 9.3 we will work to calculate your federal income tax rate and in Section 9.4 we will discuss more on how your individual circumstances will have an impact on your final tax liability.

For now, let's use a placeholder in your Money Buckets at 25%. Remember back in Chapter 3 when we created our Money Buckets Habits and on the 25th of each month we designated 25% to our Society Choice. This is a great place to start, some of you will owe less than that and some more than that but reserving $.25 of every $1.00 you make for Society is a sound strategy.

DOES EVERY STATE HAVE INCOME TAX?

No, nine states do not have income tax: Alaska, Florida, Nevada, New Hampshire, South Dakota, Tennessee, Texas, Washington and Wyoming

The other states each have a custom tax rate as well as an option of a flat or progressive tax.

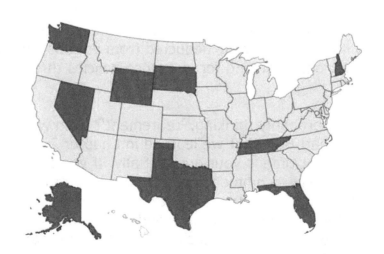

WHAT DO YOU ACTUALLY FILE WHEN PEOPLE SAY THEY ARE 'FILING TAXES'?

This is a perfect introduction to the FORM 1040 or what Money Vehicle calls the tax table of contents. This form will hold all your taxable transactions from the year. There are other forms and schedules, but if you look at your taxes as a book, Form 1040 would be at the start of the book and direct you through the other pages.

The 1040 will be used to report all your gross income and will show you how much of that gross income will be taxable to arrive at your net Income. No matter if you are self-employed or work at a company, most Americans will need to file a Form 1040. This document will report all your income from any source, claim your tax deductions or tax credits, and even calculate your tax liability. We will discuss filling out Form 1040 in Section 9.4.

WHAT DO PEOPLE MEAN WHEN THEY SAY THEY ARE AVOIDING OR EVADING TAXES?

Let us start with intention. When people say they are trying to 'avoid' or 'reduce' their taxes they mean they are intending to use a legal strategy to lessen their tax liability. This concept of **TAX AVOIDANCE** will be seen through deductions and other tax planning strategies coming up.

It is when your intent is to trick or defraud the IRS and United States Government where things get tricky. **TAX EVASION** is an illegal strategy where you fail to pay your tax liability, or you report less than your true taxable income. If you do not pay your tax liability in full by the filing deadline, the IRS will charge you interest on the amount outstanding.

On top of the interest, you could also receive failure to pay or failure to file penalties. If you do underpay your tax liability, you will be charged 0.5% of the underpayment each month you do not pay, up to a maximum 25% of the amount underpaid. If you do fail to file or report your income, the penalty is much more severe and will be 5% of the tax liability for each month up to a maximum 25% of the amount unreported.

Simply put, if you belong to our society, you must pay for your Society Choice.

MONEY VEHICLE MINDSET

Taxes happen in positive events and go to support positive things!

WHAT HAPPENS IF I MAKE A MISTAKE ON MY TAXES?

It's okay but own up to it. Send in the necessary corrections with another **FORM 1040X**. Form 1040X is a way to amend your tax return to file the correct version. The longer you wait, the more interest the IRS will charge you on the money you owe them.

"I am taxed on every dollar I make."

DEDUCTIONS: TAX AVOIDANCE STRATEGIES

Lucy heads out to grab some lunch at 'Pizza Premiums' because she was told they have $1 slices. But when she is handed a receipt for 10 slices, she asks in confusion 'I have to pay for the whole thing?!'

Sam the cashier at 'Pizza Premiums' politely smiles and points to the big sign that says '$10 for 10 slices'. The deal is to get an entire pizza and then each slice costs $1 each.

Lucy begins to explain that she doesn't plan on eating the entire pizza pie herself. She is going to give two slices to some of her employees that joined her and wanted to give one slice to the young man who looked hungry on the corner.

Sam punches a few numbers into the register and hands Lucy a receipt for $7! How did this happen?

Uncle Sam (the IRS) believes you shouldn't be charged for pizza you are using for specific things such as business expenses or charitable contributions. In our example, business expenses are the slices for employees and charitable contributions is the slice to the young man on the corner. This ability to not pay for specific things you spend your money on is called a **TAX DEDUCTION.**

The IRS allows you to 'deduct' or remove income that you have used for specific purposes to lower your **TAXABLE INCOME.** Your taxable income is how much of your income will pass through the gross to net process. By deducting taxable income, you are in effect lowering the amount of dollars you can be taxed on and reducing the tax liability you will end up owing when you arrive at net income.

Example: You have $1,000 of income and are in the 10% tax bracket. Removing $100 that you gave to charity will lower your taxable income to $900. This action will remove $100 from your tax calculation and if that $100 would have been taxed at 10% then you would save $10 in taxes. Do not be confused because you are still spending the $100, you will just get an advantage in taxes because of how you spent the money.

EXAMPLES OF COMMON TAX DEDUCTIONS:

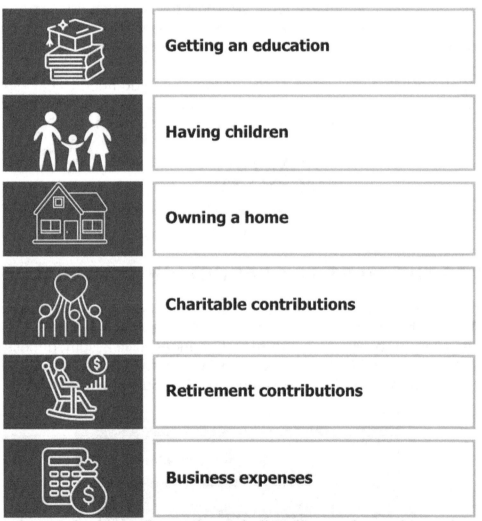

Getting an education

Having children

Owning a home

Charitable contributions

Retirement contributions

Business expenses

Lucy understands she really won't need all 7 slices today and intends to come back in a few days to eat the leftovers. She doesn't want to push her luck but is honest with Sam and asks, "I will really only be able to eat 5 slices today, is there a way I can leave 2 pieces in the refrigerator in the back?"

Sam smiles and goes back to his cash register, coming back now with a bill for $5!

Lucy is thrilled she asked, and in this example, the refrigerator is acting like a retirement account contribution. We will discuss 401(k)s and IRAs in Chapter 10.

Example: Lucy has $40,000 of income and decides to place $4,000 (Saved a Dime) of it into her company 401(k) to use later, like the refrigerator. Making this decision will remove the $4,000 401(k) contribution from her taxable income, lowering it from $40,000 down to $36,000. When Lucy comes back to the pizzeria for these 2 slices, she may even be able to get them at a cheaper price, but that is also a lesson for another day.

Tax avoidance is when you make legal strategic decisions on how you will U.S.E. your money to lower your tax liability. By taking deductions, you are removing taxable income and avoiding some of the taxes you owe.

The question becomes how many slices (income) do you need to eat (spend) today and what are your options with the extra slices? Begin reviewing your expenses and see if there are any ways to take tax deductions on where your money went.

WHAT IS THE FIRST TAX DEDUCTION I SHOULD TAKE?

The first deduction is basic, in fact it is called 'standard' the **STANDARD DEDUCTION**. The standard deduction is an amount that every American taxpayer is allowed to take and with recent changes, it is assumed most will take. In 2017 the **TAX CUTS AND JOBS ACT** nearly doubled the standard deduction amount and in 2023 the amount is $13,850 for single filers.

> **THE STANDARD DEDUCTION MEANS THAT THE FIRST $13,850 DOLLARS YOU MAKE WILL NOT BE TAXED!**

Example: If you make $20,000 of earned income and you take the standard deduction, your taxable income would be reduced to ($20,000 - $13,850) $6,150 and you would not be taxed on the $13,850.

 Example: If you make $2,500 of earned income and you take the standard deduction, your taxable income would be reduced to $0 and any taxes that were withheld at a company would be returned via a **TAX REFUND** (Section 9.4).

SHOULD I CHOOSE THE STANDARD DEDUCTION OR CHOOSE TO ITEMIZE MY DEDUCTIONS?

ITEMIZED DEDUCTIONS are qualified expenses that can reduce your taxable income like the standard deduction. The catch is listing out and adding up your 'qualified expenses' to see if itemizing is even worth your time.

QUALIFIED EXPENSES TO ITEMIZE INCLUDE:

- Money paid for state and local income or sales tax (SALT).

- Money paid for real estate and personal property taxes.

- Interest paid on a home mortgage.

- Contributions made to charitable organizations.

- Money paid for medical or dental expenses.

If you choose to itemize, you will need to file a form that will roll up to our tax table of contents (Form 1040), the Schedule A. **SCHEDULE A** is where you can elect to 'itemize' or list out how you spent money this year to see if you exceed the Standard Deduction.

To qualify for itemizing your deduction, your list of qualified expenses will need to total more than the $13,850 standard deduction. For most students and most Americans, they will not exceed the standard deduction and therefore will not choose to itemize their deduction. If you do not itemize your deductions, you do not need to file Schedule A.

WHAT IS THE DIFFERENCE BETWEEN A TAX DEDUCTION AND A TAX CREDIT?

We know that tax deductions lower your taxable income, the amount that is used to calculate your tax liability. **TAX CREDITS** on the other hand directly reduce your tax liability. This is a concept that is easier seen than read, so let's look at an example.

EXAMPLE OF $1,000 DEDUCTION AND $1,000 CREDIT IF BOTH FALL INTO 20% INCOME TAX:

	TAX DEDUCTION	TAX CREDIT
INCOME	$50,000	$50,000
DEDUCTION	$1,000	NO DEDUCTION
TAXABLE INCOME	$49,000	$50,000
TAX LIABILITY	($49,000 X 20%) = $9,800	($50,000 X 20%) = $10,000 TAX CREDIT = $1,000 FINAL TAX LIABILITY = ($10,000 - $1,000) = $9,000

MONEY MYTH

"I am taxed on every dollar I make."

Reality Check: You will have opportunities to lower your taxable income through actions like taking the Standard Deduction. These deductions show that you are not taxed on every dollar; you are taxed on every dollar in your 'Taxable Income'.

SECTION 9.2
RECAP

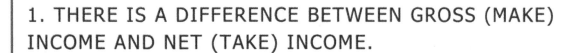

1. THERE IS A DIFFERENCE BETWEEN GROSS (MAKE) INCOME AND NET (TAKE) INCOME.

2. ELEMENTS OF YOUR INCOME TAXES: FEDERAL, STATE, CITY, FICA.

3. TAX DEDUCTION: MONEY THAT WILL NOT BE TAXED, IN 2023 THE STANDARD DEDUCTION IS $13,850.

SECTION 9.3
HOW YOUR INCOME IS TAXED

TERMS

'TAX BRACKETS: your income is divided into groups depending on how much income you earn and then taxed based on which group they are in.

PROGRESSIVE' INCOME TAX CODE: this means that people who earn a higher income will be placed in a higher tax bracket and pay more taxes.

MARGINAL TAX RATE (MTR): the rate at which your next dollar of earned income will be taxed.

EFFECTIVE TAX RATE (ETR): the average tax rate you pay on earned income.

CAPITAL GAIN: the amount your investment has gained in value and will be subject to tax.

CAPITAL LOSS: the amount your investment has lost in value and will be able to reduce taxable gains.

REALIZED TAX: investment gains and losses go up and down with the value of the investment, until you sell. Once you sell your investment, you realize or make real the taxable action.

SHORT TERM CAPITAL GAIN (STCG): asset bought and sold within one year and realizing a gain. STCG will be taxed as ordinary income and fall into the Marginal Tax Rate of your next dollar.

LONG TERM CAPITAL GAIN (LTCG): asset bought, held for longer than one year, then realizing a gain. LTCG will get a tax advantage by being placed in a different tax bracket than Earned Income, one specifically for Capital Gains.

DIVIDEND: a sum of money that is paid out regularly to shareholders of a certain stock.

Standing in line at Pike Place Ice Cream Parlor, you begin to plan out your order —rocky road looks good, but mint chocolate chip is calling your name. Vanilla never fails, and obviously, cookie dough is in the mix. So much to choose from, and now that it's summer, you feel you have earned a three-scoop celebration!

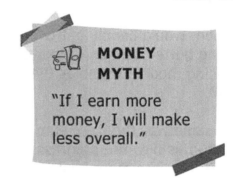

MONEY MYTH

"If I earn more money, I will make less overall."

As you get closer to the counter, you notice that Pike Place Ice Cream Parlor has changed their pricing per scoop. As any good ice cream store knows, you want to push the customers' incentive to buy more scoops of ice cream by having the price per scoop go down as the number of scoops go up. However, today, you see the price per scoop going up?!?

It makes sense that adding scoops should add to the total cost, but why would the second and third scoops cost more than the first?

When you ask the man behind the counter scooping the ice-cream, he shares that Pike Place Ice Cream Parlor believes the first scoop of ice-cream should cost the same for everyone, then if you are fortunate enough to get more, every scoop after the first will cost a little more. With their pricing model going up in this way, everyone pays the same amount for the first scoop, and there isn't an advantage for those lucky enough to get a second scoop as they will pay a little more.

Why, then, would people get two or three scoops? Well, they do say that "The only thing better than one scoop of ice cream is three scoops of ice cream!" This pricing model resembles the United States Tax Code - did you see that coming?

But the same way the ice-cream scoops are priced, meaning they increase with each scoop, is how the progressive tax bracket system works here in the United States. The more money you make (more scoops), the more taxes you will be charged (prices going up). This extra payment is not a penalty, but rather a system designed to ensure that everyone will pay the same level of tax on the same level of income (first scoop is equal).

In this system your money is divided up into **TAX BRACKETS** where a range of your income will be grouped together and taxed at the same rate. Like the ice-cream scoop prices, your money will fall into categories or brackets that will then be charged the same tax percentage.

> **PROGRESSIVE INCOME TAX CODE ENSURES PEOPLE PAY SAME TAX ON SAME LEVEL OF INCOME.**

Let's look at an example to understand how the **PROGRESSIVE TAX CODE** and the tax bracket system works:

Let's say we have our 3 characters Adrian, Kim, and Darrel. Adrian made $100, Kim made $160, and Darrel made $250. In this example, there will be a tax bracket for every $100 earned. Meaning dollars $1 - $100 will be taxed at 10%, then dollars $101 - $200 will be taxed at 20%, and dollars $201 - $300 will be taxed at 30%. The 3 characters want to know how much they will owe in this system.

ADRIAN

$100 at 10% = $10
TOTAL TAX LIABILITY: $10

KIM

$100 at 10% = $10
$60 at 20% = $12
TOTAL TAX LIABILITY: $22

DARREL

$100 at 10% = $10
$100 at 20% = $12
$50 at 30% = $15
TOTAL TAX LIABILITY: $45

This is just an example to introduce the progressive tax code and tax brackets. The real U.S. tax brackets for a single filer looked like this in 2022:

IF TAXABLE INCOME IS:	THE TAX DUE IS:
NOT OVER $10,275	10% OF THE TAXABLE INCOME
$10,275 - $41,775	$1,027.50 + 12% OF THE EXCESS OVER $10,275
$41,775 - $89,075	$4,807.50 + 22% OF THE EXCESS OVER $41,775
$89,075 - $170,050	$15,213.50 + 24% OF THE EXCESS OVER $89,075
$170,050 - $215,950	$34,647.50 + 32% OF THE EXCESS OVER $170,050
$215,950 - $539,900	$49,335.50 + 35% OF THE EXCESS OVER $215,950
OVER $539,900	$162,718 + 37% OF THE EXCESS OVER $539,900

EXAMPLE OF CALCULATING INCOME TAX ON $170,050 IN 2022:

10% RATE FOR DOLLARS BETWEEN ($0 -> $10,275) ➡️ **(10,275 − 0) = 10,275 * 10% = $1,027.50**

12% RATE FOR DOLLARS BETWEEN ($10,275 -> $41,775) ➡️ **(41,775 − 10,275) = 31,500 *12% = $3,780**

22% RATE FOR DOLLARS BETWEEN ($41,775 -> $89,075) ➡️ **(89,075 − 41,775) = 47,300 *22% = $10,406**

24% RATE FOR DOLLARS BETWEEN ($89,075 -> $170,050) ➡️ **(170,050 − 89,075) = 80,975 *24% = $19,434**

TOTAL TAX LIABILITY = $34,647.50

HOW DOES TAKING THE STANDARD DEDUCTION IMPACT THE TAXES I OWE?

Example of calculating Income Tax on $170,050 in 2022 AFTER Standard Deduction of $13,850:

Taxable Income = $170,050 − $13,850 = $156,200

10% RATE FOR DOLLARS BETWEEN ($0 -> $10,275)	⇒	(10,275 − 0) = 10,275 * 10% = $1,027.50
12% RATE FOR DOLLARS BETWEEN ($10,275 -> $41,775)	⇒	(41,775 − 10,275) = 31,500 *12% = $3,780
22% RATE FOR DOLLARS BETWEEN ($41,775 -> $89,075)	⇒	(89,075 − 41,775) = 47,300 *22% = $10,406
24% RATE FOR DOLLARS BETWEEN ($89,075 -> $170,050)	⇒	(156,200 − 89,075) = 67,125 *24% = $16,110

TOTAL TAX LIABILITY = $31,323.50

TAX SAVINGS FROM STANDARD DEDUCTION = $34,647.50 - $31,323.50 = $3,324

WHAT IS THE DIFFERENCE BETWEEN MARGINAL AND EFFECTIVE TAX RATES?

MARGINAL TAX RATE (MTR) is the rate at which your next dollar of earned income will be taxed. Meaning, if you were to make $1.00 more, what tax bracket would that next $1.00 fall into after you take deductions and find your taxable income?

TAXABLE INCOME + $1.00 ⇒ WHAT BRACKET?

EFFECTIVE TAX RATE (ETR) is the average tax rate you pay on your earned income overall. Meaning, if you were to take all your tax liability and divide it by all your income (Gross Income) what tax rate would you pay overall on average?

TAX LIABILITY / GROSS INCOME WHAT RATE?

For example, you made $170,050 this year and took the standard deduction of $13,850, your taxable income is $156,200:

- Your Marginal (Next) Rate: if you earn $1 more, with a Taxable Income of $156,201, that $1 would fall into the 24% tax bracket after the standard deduction because it is between (89,075 – 156,200) and you would be taxed $1.00 * 24% = $0.24 on this NEXT dollar you earned.

- Your Effective (Average) Rate: if your Gross Income is $170,050 your total tax liability is calculated at $31,323.50 (Found in previous after deduction calculation) than your average tax rate would be (31,323.50 / 170,050) = 18.42%

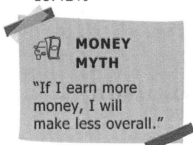

MONEY MYTH

"If I earn more money, I will make less overall."

Reality Check: We are all taxed the same on the same amount of money. Yes, as your income goes up, so will the taxes you owe, but a higher tax bracket on the last dollar you made this year does not impact the tax bracket on the first dollar you made.

INVESTMENT INCOME

IS THIS THE SAME WAY WE ARE TAXED FOR INVESTMENT INCOME THAT WE CREATE?

One of the missions of this program is to get you to think and act like an invest-OR, understanding not many of you are in this situation yet, we will discuss investment taxes but not in depth. As you complete the first 10 actions in driving Your Money Vehicle, there will be plenty more topics and steps to take, for now focus on getting started in the right direction and getting started!

With that said, let's look at how you will be taxed on 3 different ways to create income:

1. INTEREST PAID FROM A BANK OR A BOND: ORDINARY INCOME

This one is simple, any interest you are paid from the savings account you opened in Chapter 4 or from the bond you invested in back in Chapter 6, will be taxed as ordinary income. This means it will fall into your Marginal Tax Rate and be treated as your next dollar earned.

Example: You had $1,000 in a Savings Account earning 3% interest. At the end of the year you created $30 of interest, and it would be taxed as ordinary income and fall into your marginal tax bracket.

2. CAPITAL GAIN ON A STOCK:

We have discussed the difference between earned verse created income and now we will see the difference in how these two income types are taxes. When you invest, what you hope is that the value of the investment will go up and when it does you create a **CAPITAL GAIN.** If unfortunately, the value of the investment goes down, then you will create a **CAPITAL LOSS.** But you do not 'realize' or make the gain/loss real until you SELL the investment. You can have gains or losses pull forward from year to year and until you sell the investment it is not taxable.

- **REALIZED TAX:** Investment gains and losses go up and down with the value of the investment, until you sell. Once you sell your investment, you realize or make real the taxable action.

Let's focus on the positive for this section and look at how you will be taxed on a Capital Gain. You will still need to account for a 'Society Choice' with your created income, however you can receive an advantage in your tax bracket if you U.S.E. the right strategy. This brings in the question of 'how long' you held the investment and is it short or long term?

SHORT TERM CAPITAL GAIN (STCG): asset bought and sold within one year and realizing a gain. STCG will be taxed as ordinary income and fall into the Marginal Tax Rate of your next dollar.

 Example: You bought Amazon stock at $100 per share on August 1, 2023, and sold it for $200 per share on December 1, 2023. Since you only owned Amazon stock for less than a year before selling, it would be STCG, therefore it would be taxed as ordinary income and fall into your marginal tax bracket.

LONG TERM CAPITAL GAIN (LTCG): asset bought, held for longer than one year, then realizing a gain. LTCG will get a tax advantage by being placed in a different tax bracket than earned income, one specifically for Capital Gains. This new Capital Gain tax strategy has 3 brackets: 0%, 15%, 20%, and which you fall into depends on your income that you can see in the table below. Example: You bought Amazon stock at $100 per share on August 1, 2022, and sold it for $200 per share on August 2, 2023. You owned Amazon stock for more than a year before selling, it would be LTCG, therefore it would be taxed at Capital Gains rates.

HOW DO I KNOW WHICH CAPITAL GAIN RATE I FALL INTO?

2023 Tax Brackets for Long-Term Capital Gains and Qualified Dividends - Single Filer:

1. Income from $0 - $44,625 will pay 0% on Capital Gains
2. Income from $44,625 - $492,300 will pay 15% on Capital Gains
3. Income from $492,300 and up will pay 20% on Capital Gains

If you are a student making under $44,625 and you have a Capital Gain you will pay 0% in taxes. That's right, the United States wants to reward those who are changing their futures and investing by allowing them to avoid Capital Gains tax.

If you fall into the majority who make between $44,625 and $492,300 then you will pay 15% on all your Long-Term Capital Gains, which will most likely be lower than your ordinary income Marginal Tax Bracket.

Much more to be discussed around tax strategies when it comes to Capital Losses, but for now understand that the income you create through long-term investing will have a 15% Society Choice attached to it.

3. DIVIDEND PAID FROM A STOCK:

First let's discuss what a **DIVIDEND** is, a dividend is a sum of money that is paid out regularly to shareholders of a certain stock. When a company is profitable it may choose what to do with its profit, some companies reinvest that profit into the company to grow and some pay it out to their shareholders in the form of a dividend. These dividends will be taxed similarly to Capital Gains in that it depends on 'how long' you owned the investment.

- **ORDINARY DIVIDENDS:** If you held the stock for less than 60 days* before the dividend was paid out, it will be deemed an Ordinary Dividend and taxed as ordinary income. Meaning it will fall into your Marginal Tax Bracket.

QUALIFIED DIVIDENDS: If you held the stock for more than 60 days* before the dividend was paid out, it will be deemed as qualified dividend and taxed as Capital Gain and fall into the same tax brackets as Long-Term Capital Gains.

*The timing calculation around dividend payments is a little more complex than we will cover in this section.

Example: You bought Amazon stock at $100 per share on August 1, 2023. On September 1, 2023, there was a dividend paid on the Amazon stock of $3.00. Since you only owned Amazon stock for less than the 60-day requirement before the dividend was paid, it would be an 'ordinary' dividend, therefore taxed as ordinary income and fall into your marginal tax bracket.

You bought Amazon stock at $100 per share on August 1, 2022. On September 1, 2023, there was a dividend paid on the Amazon stock of $3.00. Since you owned Amazon stock for more than the 60-day requirement before the dividend was paid, it would be a 'qualified' dividend, therefore taxed in the capital gain brackets.

SECTION 9.3
RECAP

1. EARNED INCOME IS PLACED INTO TAX BRACKETS BASED ON HOW MUCH YOU EARN – REMEMBER YOUR ICE CREAM SCOOPS!

2. MARGINAL TAX RATE IS HOW MUCH YOUR NEXT DOLLAR WOULD BE TAXED AND EFFECTIVE TAX RATE IS HOW MUCH YOU PAID ON AVERAGE FOR YOUR EARNED INCOME.

3. THE LONGER YOU HOLD INVESTMENTS, THE MORE ADVANTAGEOUS TAX BRACKET YOU WILL FALL INTO.

SECTION 9.4

FILING YOUR TAXES

TERMS

W2 EMPLOYEE: you work for a company; they help you with taxes and benefits.

1099 CONTRACTOR: you work for yourself; you pay taxes and benefits for yourself.

W4: tax document an employer provides a W2 employee for tax information.

W2: tax document sent at the end of the year, summarizing what you were paid as an employee.

W9: tax document a company will provide a 1099 contractor for tax information.

1099 NEC 'NON-EMPLOYEE COMPENSATION': tax document sent at the end of the year, summarizing what you were paid as a contractor.

FILING STATUS: a tax election you will make around who you are filing taxes with: Single, Head of Household, Married Filing Jointly, Married Filing Separately, and Widow. Most students will choose SINGLE.

DEPENDENTS: a tax election you will make around who you are responsible for taking care of. You must also confirm if your parents claim you as dependent.

FORM 1095 A, B, C: tax documents relating to your Health insurance.

FORM 1098: tax document relating to your home mortgage.

FORM 1098 E: tax document relating to your student loan.

1099 INT: tax document relating to any interest you were paid.

1099 DIV: tax document relating to any dividends you were paid.

1099 K: tax document relating to any third-party income payments you were paid, for example PayPal, Venmo, Upwork.

STANDARD DEDUCTION: a tax deduction available to all tax filers who do NOT itemize and worth ¢13,850 (2023).

TERMS

AMERICAN OPPORTUNITY TAX CREDIT: a tax deduction relating to educational expenses such as tuition, books, and even some transportation costs.

E-FILE: ability to sign and file your taxes electronically and not have to physically mail it in.

PIN (PERSONAL IDENTIFICATION NUMBER): a number sequence used as a password and identification tool for your tax filing.

TAX REFUND: filing your Form 1040 will give you an official calculation of your Society Choice and if you overpaid taxes through the year, you are owed money back from the government.

TAX LIABILITY: filing your Form 1040 will give you an official calculation of your Society Choice and if you underpaid taxes through the year, you owe money to the government.

BANK ACCOUNT NUMBER: number sequence that identifies your account at a financial institution.

BANK ROUTING NUMBER: number sequence that identifies your financial institution.

CERTIFIED PUBLIC ACCOUNTANT (CPA): a professional license to provide accounting services to the public.

"FREE FILE ALLIANCE": a group of tax preparation companies who operate a public-private partnership with the Internal Revenue Service to provide free electronic tax filing services under the IRS 'free file' program to people with a straightforward return and income under $72,000.

VITA (VOLUNTEER INCOME TAX ASSISTANCE): an IRS and community sponsored program designed to assist low to moderate income taxpayers with preparation of their Form 1040 at no cost.

FORM 1040 SCHEDULES:
- **Schedule A:** Document if you are Itemizing your deductions.
- **Schedule B:** Document if you were paid interest or dividends.
- **Schedule C:** Document if you received self-employment income and deductions.
- **Schedule D:** Document if you realized any Capital Gains or Losses.
- **Schedule E:** Document if you received income from rental properties, royalties, partnerships, S-corporations, or trusts.
- **Schedule SE:** Document reporting any self-employment tax you paid.
- **Schedule 1:** Document if you had additional income from a business, rental property, or unemployment.
- **Schedule 2:** Document if you paid additional taxes.
- **Schedule 3:** Document if you received any additional tax credits.

I KNOW I FILE THE FORM 1040, BUT WHEN ARE MY TAXES DUE?

Typically, Tax Day is April 15. However, it can float a little if the fifteenth falls on a weekend or holiday. Just always be aware that it will be coming mid-April for individuals.

If you do start running your business one day, you will have to report taxes quarterly and you will have to file estimated tax payments on the 15th day of the fourth, sixth, ninth, and twelfth month of the year.

HOW DO I KNOW WHICH TYPE OF EMPLOYEE I AM?

Ultimately this boils down to who you work for. If you work for a company, then you are considered a **W2 EMPLOYEE.** If you work for yourself and contract with different companies, then you are considered a **1099 CONTRACTOR.** The biggest differences will be seen in how you are taxed and what benefits you are able to receive from the company.

As a W2 employee your company will help you manage your tax liability by withholding taxes from each of your paychecks. This is meant to help you prepare for your tax liability while also helping reduce tax evasion. Another benefit your company will provide is access to programs for insurance and retirement. These are massive advantages over being self-employed because you will get lower costs in insurance and more turn-key resources in retirement.

HOW DO I KNOW WHICH TYPE OF EMPLOYEE I AM?

W4: This document Is provided by the company you are beginning to work for to gain information on your tax situation. Your employer will withhold taxes from each paycheck, based on the elections you make on your W4.

W2: This document summarizes the wages your employer paid you, the benefits you received, and the taxes that were taken out of your income throughout the year. The W-2 is merely a reporting tool to inform the IRS of what you were paid and does not decide your taxes; it is more of an estimate until you file your Form 1040.

Example: On Kim's first day working at her new school, the school sent her a W4 form to fill out. Throughout the year the school withheld taxes, contributed to her retirement, and allowed her to participate in the group insurance policy, all this information was then sent to Kim on her W2 form.

As a 1099 contractor you will be responsible for all the things a company helps their employees with. No one will withhold any taxes from your paycheck, no one will help you buy insurance, and no one will offer your retirement benefits. There are pros and cons to being self-employed, the biggest everyone wants to point to is that 'you are your own boss', but the reality is there is a lot of responsibility that comes with being the boss.

1099 CONTRACTORS TAX FORMS:

 W9: This document replaces the W4 for 1099 contractors and is meant to provide the third party you are contracting with your tax information – Name, Address, and Taxpayer Identification Number. There are no elections because the third-party company you are contracting with will not assist you in making your tax payments or offer you any benefits, these responsibilities will fall solely on you.

 1099 NEC 'NON-EMPLOYEE COMPENSATION': This document summarizes the earnings you were paid throughout the year as a non-employee contractor. If you made over $600 working as a contractor for any company, they would send you a form 1099 NEC at the end of the year laying out the specifics of what you were paid. Again, there are NO taxes being withheld with a 1099 contractor.

 Example: Adrian is so excited that the smoothie shop on the corner wants to hire him for a marketing project. The job will not be full-time, instead it is a contract for a project building out social media deliverables. When they agreed on the deal, the smoothie shop sent Adrian a W9 form to get his information. At the end of the year the smoothie shop will send Adrian a 1099 NEC showing how much they paid Adrian for the project.

OK, SO I KNOW WHAT TYPE OF EMPLOYEE I AM, BUT HOW DO I START TO FILE MY TAXES?

1. STEP 1: BASIC INFORMATION

The IRS tax form 1040 is the standard federal income tax form used and what Money Vehicle calls 'The Tax Table of Contents' because everything else is outlined on this document. Use Form 1040 to answer questions around your filing status, identification, dependents, and contact information. If you have filed your taxes before, you will need a copy of last year's Form 1040.

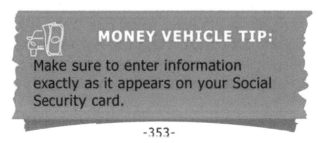
MONEY VEHICLE TIP:
Make sure to enter information exactly as it appears on your Social Security card.

FILING STATUS may seem a bit confusing with all the options – Single, Head of Household, Married Filing Jointly, Married Filing Separately, and Widow; but most students will choose Single.

DISCLAIMER: MONEY VEHICLE DOES NOT KNOW YOUR SITUATION, SO CONFIRM ALL THESE ELECTIONS,

ELECTION 1

If you are not married and do not have kids, single is your election.

DEPENDENTS can be a little tricky because most students will be claimed as a dependent on their parent's tax return. If this is the case, then you must check the box on page 1 of Form 1040 where it asks, 'Someone can claim'. The rules for your parents to claim you are that you are under age 19 or if a student aged 24 and your parents are providing you support.

If you have communicated with your parents that they cannot claim you and you do not have anyone who is dependent on you to support them then you can make these elections.

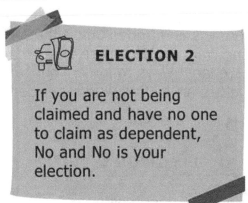

ELECTION 2

If you are not being claimed and have no one to claim as dependent, No and No is your election.

2. STEP 2: GET ORGANIZED – INCOME

On the first page of Form 1040, you will be required to document all the income you received from any source. This can include your primary income, interest, dividends, capital gains, third party payments, unemployment, and many other sources you can create an income stream from.

When you begin to outline your income, you should begin by looking through the tax documents you have received throughout the year. It is a good idea to have one physical and one digital folder where you will keep all your tax-related documents and transactions throughout the year. This organization will be helpful when you begin to file your taxes.

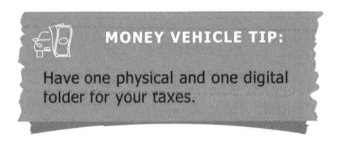

MONEY VEHICLE TIP:

Have one physical and one digital folder for your taxes.

Common Documents you should look out for:

- **W2 or 1099 NEC:** The wages you were paid throughout the year.
- **FORM 1095 A, B, C:** Health insurance related documents.
- **FORM 1098:** If you have a home Mortgage.
- **FORM 1098 E:** If you have a Student Loan.
- **1099 INT:** If you received interest payments.
- **1099 DIV:** If you received dividends payments.
- **1099 K:** If you received third party payments Ex. PayPal, Venmo, Upwork.

3. STEP 3: CLAIM TAX DEDUCTIONS

We all are proud to be Americans and understand that Society is a part of the choices we make, but no one wants to pay more taxes than they owe. We discussed how deductions are legal ways to lower your taxable income and will save you some money, so let's start to find where our deductions are hiding.

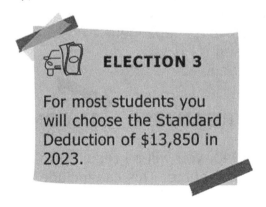

ELECTION 3

For most students you will choose the Standard Deduction of $13,850 in 2023.

Common Tax Deductions for students:

- **STANDARD DEDUCTION:** this is going to be a huge advantage as your first $13,850 is not taxed!
- **Education Expenses:** investigate the AMERICAN OPPORTUNITY TAX as well as other items like tuition, books, and even some transportation costs.
- **Business Expenses:** what you spend running your business or side-hustle. Ex. Marketing, travel, supplies. Charitable Donations: only if you itemize and are above the standard deduction.
- **Traditional Retirement Contributions:** this is NOT Roth accounts, but traditional 401(k) and IRA.

Once you have calculated your income and deductions, you can begin calculating your taxes on page 2 of Form 1040. This is where you will be able to get a more personalized percentage for your Money Bucket system. In Chapter 3 we placed a 25% hold, but now with your understanding of the tax system, that percentage may go down or even up if you are making more than you thought.

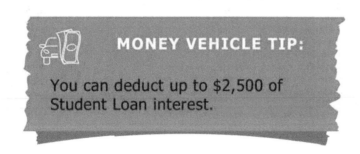

MONEY VEHICLE TIP:

You can deduct up to $2,500 of Student Loan interest.

① Form 1040 Department of the Treasury—Internal Revenue Service (99)
U.S. Individual Income Tax Return **2021** OMB No. 1545-0074 IRS Use Only—Do not write or staple in this space.

② Filing Status ☐ Single ☐ Married filing jointly ☐ Married filing separately (MFS) ☐ Head of household (HOH) ☐ Qualifying widow(er) (QW)
Check only one box. If you checked the MFS box, enter the name of your spouse. If you checked the HOH or QW box, enter the child's name if the qualifying person is a child but not your dependent ▶

③

Your first name and middle initial	Last name	Your social security number
If joint return, spouse's first name and middle initial	Last name	Spouse's social security number

Home address (number and street). If you have a P.O. box, see instructions.	Apt. no.	**Presidential Election Campaign**

City, town, or post office. If you have a foreign address, also complete spaces below.	State	ZIP code	Check here if you, or your spouse if filing jointly, want $3 to go to this fund. Checking a box below will not change your tax or refund.

Foreign country name	Foreign province/state/county	Foreign postal code	☐ You ☐ Spouse

At any time during 2021, did you receive, sell, exchange, or otherwise dispose of any financial interest in any virtual currency? ☐ Yes ☐ No

④ Standard Deduction
Someone can claim: ☐ You as a dependent ☐ Your spouse as a dependent
☐ Spouse itemizes on a separate return or you were a dual-status alien

Age/Blindness You: ☐ Were born before January 2, 1957 ☐ Are blind **Spouse:** ☐ Was born before January 2, 1957 ☐ Is blind

⑤ Dependents (see instructions):
If more than four dependents, see instructions and check here ▶ ☐

(1) First name Last name	(2) Social security number	(3) Relationship to you	(4) ✔ If qualifies for (see instructions):	
			Child tax credit	Credit for other dependents
			☐	☐
			☐	☐
			☐	☐
			☐	☐

Attach Sch. B if required.

1	Wages, salaries, tips, etc. Attach Form(s) W-2		**1**	**⑥**
2a	Tax-exempt interest	2a	b Taxable interest	**2b**
3a	Qualified dividends	3a	b Ordinary dividends	**3b**
4a	IRA distributions	4a	b Taxable amount	**4b**
5a	Pensions and annuities	5a	b Taxable amount	**5b**
6a	Social security benefits	6a	b Taxable amount	**6b**
7	Capital gain or (loss). Attach Schedule D if required. If not required, check here ▶ ☐		**7**	**⑦**
8	Other income from Schedule 1, line 10		**8**	
9	Add lines 1, 2b, 3b, 4b, 5b, 6b, 7, and 8. This is your **total income** ▶		**9**	
10	Adjustments to income from Schedule 1, line 26		**10**	
11	Subtract line 10 from line 9. This is your **adjusted gross income** ▶		**11**	
12a	Standard deduction or itemized deductions (from Schedule A)	12a		**⑧**
b	Charitable contributions if you take the standard deduction (see instructions)	12b		
c	Add lines 12a and 12b		**12c**	
13	Qualified business income deduction from Form 8995 or Form 8995-A		**13**	
14	Add lines 12c and 13		**14**	
15	**Taxable income.** Subtract line 14 from line 11. If zero or less, enter -0-		**15**	**⑨**

Standard Deduction for—
• Single or Married filing separately, $12,550
• Married filing jointly or Qualifying widow(er), $25,100
• Head of household, $18,800
• If you checked any box under Standard Deduction, see instructions.

For Disclosure, Privacy Act, and Paperwork Reduction Act Notice, see separate instructions. Cat. No. 11320B Form **1040** (2021)

KEY

1. What Form: 1040
2. Filing Status: Single
3. Who is filing: Personal Information
4. What deduction: Standard
5. Are you claiming or are you claimed as a dependent: No
6. How much did you make: Line 1
7. How much did you create: Line 7
8. Report your deduction: Line 12
9. Total Taxable Income: Line 15

4. STEP 4: E-FILE

If this is your first time filing or if you are under the age of 16, you will most likely have to mail in a physical copy of your tax return to the Internal Revenue Service, as the electronic filing will not be available.

For future filings or for repeat filers, you can choose to file and sign your tax documents electronically called an **E-FILE**. This is a more efficient and even safer way to file your taxes. To do so, you will need to create a **PIN (PERSONAL IDENTIFICATION NUMBER)** 5 number sequence as a password for your filing. Remember in Chapter 8 when you create a password, do not be predictable and make it random. It will be up to you to remember this PIN, so keep it in a safe place.

Next you will want to confirm filing and process at

SA.WWW4.IRS.GOV

From here you will go to your 'Your Online Account' and use your PIN to see the updates on the process.

5. STEP 5: CONNECT YOUR ACCOUNT.

Remember back in Chapter 4 when we set up your foundational Today & Tomorrow accounts?

Well, here is just one of the ways those will add value to you. During your filing process you will have the option of connecting your account to allow for a refund or to pay your liability, automatically.

- **TAX REFUND:** You overpaid taxes through the year and are owed money back from the government.
- **TAX LIABILITY:** You underpaid taxes through the year and owe money to the government.

 To connect your account, you will need the **BANK ACCOUNT NUMBER** and the **BANK ROUTING NUMBER** so the IRS will know where to send or request money.

Your routing number identifies which financial institution to connect with and your account number identifies which individual account to connect with. Automation is an advantage of the times and connecting your bank to E-File will allow for an efficient way to file.

Remember If you do not pay your taxes, there will be Interest and fines we discussed In Section 9.2.

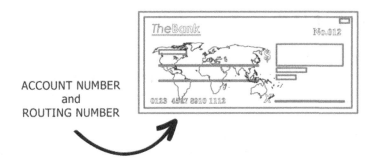

ACCOUNT NUMBER
and
ROUTING NUMBER

IS IT BETTER TO GET A REFUND OR TO PAY A LIABILITY AT THE END OF THE YEAR?

This is a confusing thought. Many Americans looks forward to and celebrate their 'tax refund' seeing it as 'extra' money. But as you come to understand the tax process, you realize the money paid to the government through the year is an estimate, an estimate of how much money you will owe at the end of the year. This means that if at the end of the year you are being returned money with a tax refund, you overpaid on the estimate throughout the year. While this is not necessarily a bad thing, it does mean the government was holding more of your money without paying you any interest!

Money Vehicle does not recommend stopping withholding taxes as that would set your Money Buckets up to fail come April when taxes are due. We are recommending you take another look at your W4 and review your elections. If too much money is being taken out through the year and you are getting a large tax refund, perhaps you can reduce how much is being withheld and have a little extra cash flow.

Owing taxes through a tax liability is also not a bad thing. We discussed in depth the amazing things that Society provides, having a tax liability just means your estimate from the year was off and you need to contribute a little more. This happens if you received some unexpected income or had too little withholding taken out through the year.

HOW CAN I PREPARE AND FILE MY TAXES?

Today there are really 3 options to file your taxes: You file on your own, a software files for you, a professional files on your behalf.

Taxes are a foreign language that you are beginning to understand, but do not feel like paying for software or professional help with your taxes is a waste of money. These are great resources, and they can find you more deductions or credits that will save you more money in the end. Few will want to take on the burden of trying to calculate and files taxes on their own, so Money Vehicle would guide you to research the tax software on the market today.

A **CERTIFIED PUBLIC ACCOUNTANT CPA** will become a necessary part of your team as your tax situation becomes more complex.

IS THERE ANY WAY TO FILE MY TAXES FOR FREE OR GET HELP FILING FOR FREE?

First a warning here, marketing today can be tricky. There are offerings that will sadly trick you into believing you are getting something for free, when in reality they are signing you up for something that costs money, just not today. Be on the lookout and before you sign up for anything free, confirm there are no strings attached.

 MONEY VEHICLE TIP:

If you get a FREE product, YOU are the product!!

There are ways to get help and file your taxes for free, there is even a **"FREE FILE ALLIANCE"** who provides their services for free. These are resources if you have a simple and straightforward return that will guide you through the filing process. Be on alert though if you do add complexity or need further help, that may come at a cost.

REQUIREMENTS TO GET FREE TAX HELP: [40]

01 Income under $72,000

02 No information complexities Ex. Single and No Dependents

03 No unique income or deductions Ex. Standard Deduction

Here are a few examples of the Free File Alliance offered by and governed through the IRS:

- 1040Now.com
- ezTaxReturn.com
- TaxAct.com
- TaxSlayer.com

Note: TurboTax has left the Free File Alliance, meaning they charge you money for all their services.

If you are looking for someone to talk to and ask questions, you can search this service out with **VITA (VOLUNTEER INCOME TAX ASSISTANCE).** VITA is run through the IRS and offers tax preparation services to those in need through partner organizations.

WHAT ROLLS UP INTO THE FORM 1040 OR THE TAX TABLE OF CONTENTS?

First off, we appreciate you using the Money Vehicle terminology ☺

Secondly, Money Vehicle does not need you to be a tax expert and will not test you on these forms, but we do want to introduce some other documents you will come across as you begin to file.

Tax Documents:
- **SCHEDULE A:** Report if you are taking the Itemized deduction
- **SCHEDULE B:** Report interest or dividends (9.3) that were paid to you
- **SCHEDULE C:** Report self-employment income and deductions Ex. You have an LLC
- **SCHEDULE D:** Report any Capital Gains or Losses (9.3)
- **SCHEDULE E:** Report income from rental properties, royalties, partnerships, S-corporations, trusts
- **SCHEDULE SE:** Report self-employment tax
- **SCHEDULE 1:** Report additional income from a business, rental property, or unemployment
- **SCHEDULE 2:** Report additional taxes paid
- **SCHEDULE 3:** Report additional tax credits

Understanding the documents and the terminologies when it comes to taxes is a major step. You do not need to become a CPA or tax professional to file your own taxes. However, as things get more complex, you will need the help of an accountant on your team.

Money Vehicle is NOT providing any type of financial or tax advice! We hope you have gained confidence in understanding the United States tax code and are more prepared to start filing your taxes.

KEEP IT SIMPLE, MOST STUDENTS WILL MAKE THESE TAXABLE ELECTIONS:

FILING STATUS	SINGLE
DEPENDENTS	NONE
DEDUCTION	STANDARD

SECTION 9.4
RECAP

1. W2 EMPLOYEES WORK FOR A COMPANY AND RECEIVE BENEFITS; 1099 CONTRACTORS WORK FOR THEMSELVES AND ARE RESPONSIBLE FOR MANAGING THEIR OWN TAXES.

2. YOU WILL NEED TO GATHER YOUR TAX DOCUMENTS BASED ON YOUR ACTIVITIES THROUGHOUT THE YEAR BUT REMEMBER YOU DO NOT KNOW YOUR FINAL SOCIETY CHOICE UNTIL YOU FILE FORM 1040.

3. USE THE E-FILE TO MAKE YOUR ELECTIONS AND SET-UP ACCOUNT AUTOMATION TO BE MORE EFFICIENT WITH YOUR FILINGS.

REVIEW

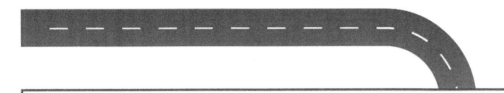

THE RULE: KNOW YOUR NET

When you take a good look at all that taxes do for us, you appreciate how valuable they are to our society. The Society Choices we encounter first are sales and income taxes. Understanding when sales tax occurs gives you a better perspective of how much of your money is really going into the Society Bucket as you buy goods or services. With a progressive income tax code, your next dollar earned will be taxed more than your first dollar earned, but you can also calculate your average tax rate too. Filing your taxes can feel overwhelming, but gathering all your documents and making simple elections should empower you to file your Society Choice!

ACTION

Plan for your Society Choice, understanding that 25% of your Gross Income will be contributed there.

- Calculate Marginal Tax Bracket and Effective Tax Bracket.
- Know when, where, and how to File a 1040
- Deduct $13,850 (2023) of taxable income through the Standard Deduction

OWNER'S MANUAL
FOR YOUR MONEY VEHICLE:

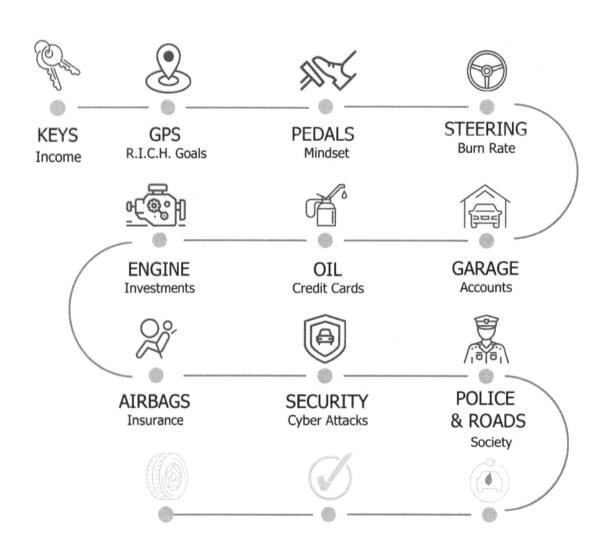

KEYS
Income

GPS
R.I.C.H. Goals

PEDALS
Mindset

STEERING
Burn Rate

ENGINE
Investments

OIL
Credit Cards

GARAGE
Accounts

AIRBAGS
Insurance

SECURITY
Cyber Attacks

POLICE & ROADS
Society

TAX ADVANTAGED ACCOUNTS

CHAPTER 10

WHAT IS MY BEST ADVANTAGE TODAY?

ACTION

Act like an Invest-OR, open a Roth account and grow your investments – tax free!

OVERVIEW

10.1: How to Prune Your Tax Tree

10.2: Types of Investment Accounts

10.3: Your Best Investment Vehicle: Roth Account

DRIVING YOUR MONEY VEHICLE

Once you finish reading your driver's manual, you start to think about what makes your car so great—its sunroof, its racing stripe, the dice that hang from its mirror...What's truly great about your car is that you have autonomy over it, not to mention the time to get where you want to go. But you are probably wondering if you can upgrade Your Money Vehicle to get even more mileage out of it, this leads us to the option of a Hybrid!

SECTION 10.1
HOW TO PRUNE YOUR TAX TREE

TERMS

SECURITIES INVESTOR PROTECTION CORPORATION (SIPC): the insurance provider for money in your brokerage account. Like the FDIC with banks, the SIPC will cover up to $500,000 ($250,000 in cash).

401(K): an employer sponsored 'defined contribution' personal pension account that is provided by a company you work for as a W2 employee, with a tax advantage for retirement savings.

DEFINED CONTRIBUTION: an account where contributions are made regularly by employer and employee, with a limit of how much you can contribute.

INDIVIDUAL RETIREMENT ACCOUNT (IRA): an individually owned defined contribution personal pension account that provides a tax advantage for retirement savings.

ROTH IRA: a type of IRA allowing after-tax savings up to a specified amount, where the contributions and earnings can be withdrawn tax-free after age 59.5.

ROLLOVER IRA: a type of IRA that allows you to move money from a former employer sponsored plan (401k) into an IRA.

TAX ADVANTAGE: an economic bonus to certain accounts or investments that can reduce your taxes, defer your taxes, or grow without taxes.

TAX DEFERRED: a type of tax advantage that allows you to delay paying taxes until later.

TAX FREE: a type of tax advantage that allows you to grow after-tax dollars tax-free

Think about how far you have come and all that you have learned. To connect the dots and take our final action Money Vehicle wants to introduce you to three types of investment accounts: Brokerage accounts, 401(k) or IRA accounts, and Roth accounts. We will want you to see the advantages and disadvantages of each type of account and to do that we are going to have to get a little dirty.

THE MONEY TREE EXPO: TAX ADVANTAGED INVESTMENT ACCOUNTS

The annual Expo for Money Trees is only a few weeks away, and you know you have three baby trees that could be in the running for 'Biggest Tree of the Year'!

You grab a shovel and head out to plant the young trees in the optimal place in your backyard. But just before you start digging, you think to yourself, "My goal is to grow the biggest tree I can, I wonder how each tree would grow if I treated each differently?"

1　　　**2**　　　**3**

You decide to conduct an experiment in which you trim each plant differently and even let them grow in different types of soil. The three different methods are:

 Tree One: This will be your base case and grown the traditional way you usually grow a tree. Before putting Tree One in the ground, you trim it into what you hope are the ideal growing dimensions. Then you plant it in normal soil and let it grow.

On the day of the Tree Expo, you will trim it again to give it the best vertical frame just before the judges come to measure it.

 Tree Two: This is where you begin to explore—how big would the plant get if you didn't trim it at all before you plant it in the ground? You take Tree Two and get it in the ground without trimming it into ideal growing dimensions, then sit back and let it grow.

On the day of the Tree Expo, you know that you will need to trim it quite a bit to give it the best vertical frame you can.

Tree Three: With two trees planted in the normal soil, you feel like you can try something new with Tree Three. This is where you will try out a secret soil called 'Roth Advantage' soil. The secret to the Roth Advantage soil is that once your tree is trimmed and placed in this special soil, you will never have to trim it again no matter how big it gets. Knowing this, you trim Tree Three today, pack some Roth Advantage soil around it, and let it grow.

On the day of the Tree Expo, you will NOT need to trim anything as your tree will already be in the best vertical frame you can.

ARE WE GOING TO TALK ABOUT INVESTMENT ACCOUNTS AND NOT TREES?

Fine! Let's move into how these three trees translate from a garden to your plan.

The three trees represent three different types of investment account with three different ways they are taxed. Let's discuss the types of accounts first.

BROKERAGE

We introduced brokerage accounts in chapter 6, but to refresh a brokerage account is a type of investment account that allows you to buy and sell (or broker) securities such as stocks, bonds, mutual funds, and index funds. Brokerage accounts can be opened by individuals or legal entities and are provided by a 'Brokerage Firm' which acts as an intermediary between the investor (you) and the investment (market).

Brokerage accounts can come with services such as research or analysis tools, some investment guidance, or other planning services such as a cash management tool. But be prepared as the more services available, the more fees will be available as well. There can be fees for trades, account maintenance, transfers, and even for the actual investment you are investing in.

These accounts will follow the rules set by the Financial Industry Regulatory Authority (FINRA) and are governed by the Securities and Exchange Commission (SEC). Where the FDIC insures money in your bank account, money in your brokerage account will be insured by **SECURITIES INVESTOR PROTECTION CORPORATION (SIPC).**

401(K)

The 401(K) account was introduced in 1978 and is named after the subsection 401(k) that the rule falls under in the U.S. Internal Revenue Code or tax laws. Put in Money Vehicle terms, the account got its name from the rule that made it. A 401(k) is an employer sponsored, **DEFINED CONTRIBUTION**, personal pension account. Put in Money Vehicle terms, this account will be connected to your job or employer. While it is your account, you have access to it because you are an employee of a specific company. There is a defined contribution or set maximum amount you can put into the account each year, in 2023 that maximum amount is $22,500.

$$\$22,500$$

401(K) MAXIMUM CONTRIBUTION FOR 2023

While your employer will be the 'Plan Sponsor' and owner of the account, typically they will hire a 'third-party administrator (TPA) to manage the accounts. These third parties will make sure all 401(k) rules are being followed and support each employee as they invest for their retirement. The fees for a 401(k) plan can be paid by your employer, by you, or by both. These third-party administrators will be governed by the Employee Benefits Security Administration within the US Department of Labor.

WHY ARE COMPANIES CLOSING PENSIONS AND OPENING 401(K) ACCOUNTS?

Why it is called a 'personal pension' is because back in Chapter 1 we discussed how the pension system was going away, well this is the new form of retirement planning that companies are moving toward. This also has to do with the lessons we learned in Chapter 6 around risk and diversification. With a pension plan, your company is responsible for every employee's retirement. Pensions are designed to be a fixed income for life, but what we learned in Chapter 6 is that investments are anything but fixed. Moving to the 401(k) account allows companies to offload the risk of your retirement from their responsibility onto your responsibility. You are driving Your Money Vehicle and this transition from pensions to 401(k) is a clear message that your company is not in the driver seat anymore.

CHAPTER 1 RULE:

YOU ARE DRIVING!

INDIVIDUAL RETIREMENT ACCOUNT (IRA):

The **INDIVIDUAL RETIREMENT ACCOUNT (IRA)** is intentionally named because it represents an individual's plan to retire. Unlike the 401(k) where you must be an employee of a company to participate, the IRA is available for anyone to open and use. It does act as a personal pension as the account holds investments targeted for an individual's eventual benefit in old age or retirement. Like the 401(k), the IRA is also a defined contribution or set maximum amount you can put into the account each year, in 2023 that maximum amount is $6,500.

There should not be many fees associated with opening this account, but some companies will charge a management or custodial fee. Since this account is not connected to your employer, there is only one real requirement, you must have an earned income. This allows for great flexibility in both what you invest in as well as this account staying with you no matter where you decide to work, many entrepreneurs begin their retirement planning with an IRA.

IRA MAXIMUM CONTRIBUTION FOR 2023

ROTH IRA

WHAT IS THE DIFFERENCE BETWEEN 401(K) AND IRA?

ROTH IRAs are still IRAs, so all the requirements and contribution limits stay the same. The real difference is in how these two accounts are taxed and that is what we will discover as we progress through the rest of this chapter.

401 (K)	You work at a company and even though it is my account and money, the 401(k) is setup through your employer. The employer will control what you can invest in and who is managing the account. If you are to leave that company you would most likely need to transfer your funs to an IRA, called a **ROLLOVER IRA**.
IRA	You work for yourself or want an account that is not connected to your company. In an IRA there is no one telling you what to invest in or helping you manage the account, that is all on the 'Individual'.

THE MONEY TREE EXPO: TAX ADVANTAGED INVESTMENT ACCOUNTS CONTINUED:

How you treat the three trees can also explain how the three types of investment accounts will be taxed. Instead of the judge coming to measure the trees, you are measuring how well you U.S.E. your money, and instead of trimming the trees, you are trimming your income or paying taxes on your money.

 **Tree One (Taxable Account: Brokerage):** The usual way to handle a tree and the first investment account format. With Tree 1, we trimmed the tree before we put it in the ground and then again before the judges measured it.

In a brokerage account, you will tax your earned income before you put it into the account and then down the road when you want to use the dollars, you will tax them again. First is income tax and later is capital gains tax.

 **Tree Two (Tax Deferred Account:** 401(k) or IRA): With Tree 2, you wanted to see how big the tree could grow before you trimmed it, so you did not trim it at first, putting it straight into the ground. Then, as the tree grew larger, you had to trim even more when the judge came to measure.

In a **TAX DEFERRED** account you get to place your earned income directly into the account before it is taxed. This is why it is a **TAX ADVANGTAGED** account; you do not pay income taxes before you deposit the money. Then as the account grows and you want to use the dollars later in life, you will have to pay income taxes then. The idea is that your income tax bracket in retirement will be much lower than your income tax bracket today.

 Tree Three (Tax Free Account: Roth): With Tree 3, you used the secret soil, trimming the tree and then putting it into this special Roth Soil. But then you did not have to trim the tree again when the judge came to measure.

In a **TAX FREE** account you contribute dollars after you pay income tax on them, but then as the account grows you will not be taxed on the growth of your dollars. This is why it is a tax advantaged account; you do not have to pay taxes on the growth of your money, no matter how big the account gets.

You quickly see that Tree One is not the biggest, because you are trimming it—or paying taxes on it—twice, and there is no advantage to that. You only had to trim Tree Two and Tree Three once, making them tax advantaged accounts. Which tree ends up being the biggest? We will find out in Section 10.2.

SECTION 10.1
RECAP

1. BROKERAGE ACCOUNTS ARE TAXABLE ACCOUNTS MEANING YOU ARE TAXED WHEN YOU PUT MONEY IN AND WHEN YOU TAKE MONEY OUT.

2. 401K/IRA ACCOUNTS ARE TAX DEFERRED ACCOUNTS MEANING YOU ARE NOT TAXED WHEN YOU PUT MONEY IN, INSTEAD YOU ARE TAXED LATER WHEN YOU TAKE MONEY OUT.

3. ROTH ACCOUNTS ARE TAX FREE ACCOUNTS MEANING YOU ARE TAXED WHEN YOU PUT MONEY IN BUT NEVER AGAIN.

SECTION 10.2
TYPES OF INVESTMENT ACCOUNTS

TERMS

AFTER TAX CONTRIBUTIONS: dollars that are placed into an account after they have been taxed.

PRE-TAX CONTRIBUTIONS: dollars that are placed into an account before they have been taxed.

MARGIN ACCOUNT: a type of brokerage account that allows you to purchase investments with borrowed money, after you meet a required deposit.

ACCREDITED INVESTOR: the SEC defines this investor as someone who EITHER has a gross income of $200,000 in each of last two years ($300,000 with spouse) OR has a Net Worth over $1,000,000.

EMPLOYER MATCH 'FREE MONEY': your employer can contribute more into your retirement plan account based on your contributions. Called a match because you contribute and then they will, called 'free' because this benefit does not cost you anything.

Looking at the money in your Tomorrow (savings) Account, you understand why you have used this vehicle, but may wonder if there is a more efficient account to place your money into to begin investing. In Chapter 6 we introduced a Brokerage Account that is deemed a 'taxable account' and now we are going to introduce you to two 'tax-advantaged' accounts.

Looking back at the trees for a moment, you see the three types of investment accounts:

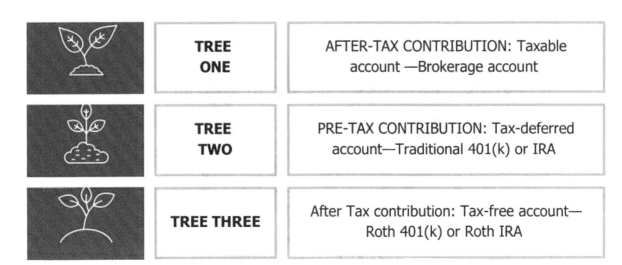

	TREE ONE	AFTER-TAX CONTRIBUTION: Taxable account —Brokerage account
	TREE TWO	PRE-TAX CONTRIBUTION: Tax-deferred account—Traditional 401(k) or IRA
	TREE THREE	After Tax contribution: Tax-free account— Roth 401(k) or Roth IRA

Each account will fill the Future Bucket and put you on course to achieve your R.I.C.H. goals. But now you are wondering which account is best or more advantageous to you today.

TREE 1: BROKERAGE (TAXABLE) ACCOUNT

To contribute to a brokerage account, you will need to pay your income tax first. With the after-tax dollars you can then deposit them into the brokerage account. As your investments grow and you want to use your dollars, you will need to pay Capital Gains tax on the growth of your investments.

 Advantage: Main advantages of brokerage accounts is the flexibility in use and the access to your money without penalty.

Disadvantage: In a brokerage account you will be taxed twice. You are taxed on the income you earn and then again on the growth of your investment.

 Example: You want to start investing in a brokerage account and just got your first paycheck of $1,000.

- **Step 1:** The $1,000 is gross income and we will need to take out income taxes of 25% (estimate), which equals $250.
- **Step 2:** You find a custodian you trust and decide to open your brokerage account there.
- **Step 3:** You have taken care of your other Money Buckets and want to invest the $750 you have after income taxes into your brokerage account.
- **Step 4:** You purchased an Index Fund tracking the S&P 500 and over the next few years your investment grows to $1,500.
- **Step 5:** You want to use the $1,500 to buy a car and pull the $1,500 out of your brokerage account. When you pull the money out, you will not be taxed on what you invested - the first $1,000, but you will be taxed on the growth $500 at capital gains rates.

WHAT DOES MARGIN MEAN?

When looking at to make purchases in your brokerage account, you will come across two types of ways to purchase the investment – cash or margin. In a cash transaction you will be required to purchase the investment in full in cash at the time of trade. In a margin transaction you will be able to borrow money to make trades.

Think about that for a moment, you are going to borrow money (risk) to invest money (risk). **MARGIN ACCOUNTS** get a lot of publicity, and you can hear many elaborate stories on how people got rich using other people's money but be very careful taking on the double risk of investing borrowed dollars. Money Vehicle does not recommend trading on margin for students or anyone who is not an **ACCREDITED INVESTOR** – having $200,000 of income or $1,000,000 of net worth.

TREE 2: TRADITIONAL 401(K)
OR IRA (TAX-DEFERRED) ACCOUNT

Before taxes are taken out, you can contribute earned income into a traditional 401(k) or IRA. This is why people call them 'pre-tax' dollars because they are before tax. As you look at your tax liability for the year, you will see these dollars are not included and you will save some money on taxes this year. This is truly practicing 'Pay Yourself First' because you are paying your Future Choice even before your Society Choice. As your investments grow and you want to use your dollars, you will need to pay income taxes on the growth of your investments.

 Advantage: Main advantage of a traditional 401(k) or IRA account is the tax savings today and the ability to defer your tax liability to later in life.

Disadvantage: In a traditional 401(k) or IRA you will not have full access to your money until full retirement age which is 59.5. This means if you withdraw your money before that age, you will receive a 10% penalty and then will be taxed on the money you pulled out. This restriction is intended to keep the tax advantage for the accounts purpose, retirement.

 Example: You want to start investing in the 401(k) account at work and just got your first paycheck of $1,000.

- **Step 1:** The $1,000 is gross income and you have taken care of your other Money Buckets, so these dollars are ready to be invested. The beauty of a 401(k) is that you can contribute money before it is taxed, so the entire $1,000 goes into the 401(k).
- **Step 2:** You purchased an Index Fund tracking the S&P 500 and over the next few years your investment grows to $1,500.
- **Step 3:** You want to use the $1,500 to buy a car but remember these dollars are meant for retirement and if you pull the money out before age 59.5 you will get a penalty.
- **Step 4:** At age 60 the original $1,000 you invested has become $10,000 and now you want to pull the $10,000 out of your 401(k). Now the $10,000 will be taxed at your ordinary income tax bracket.

WHAT IS THE BEST RETURN I CAN GET ON MY INVESTMENTS?

Second Advantage: **EMPLOYER MATCH** is 'Free' money from your employer in your 401(k).

FREE MONEY:

Take advantage of your employer match!

Money Vehicle continues to warn against any 'guarantee' when it comes to investing, but there is one way you can guarantee an investment return and that is through your company's 401(k) plan. Companies today want to retain their employees, but they also want to support their employees to achieve retirement. To accomplish both, companies will provide an employer match to your 401(k) contribution.

The employer match is an incentive for you to participate in your Future Bucket, and you will be rewarded with free money. Each company has its own way of determining how much the match is, but however much the match is for, there is a 100% guaranteed investment return for you.

 Example: Your company says it will 100% match your first 3% contribution and then 50% of your next 2% contribution. This means if you:

Contribute 0%	You put in 0% and are match 0%	**Total Contribution 0%**
Contribute 3%	You put in 3% and receive a 3% match	**Total Contribution 6%**
Contribute 4%	You put in 4% and receive a 3% match and then half (50%) of the other 1% for a total match of 3.5%	**Total Contribution 7.5%**
Contribute 6%	You put in 6% and receive a 3% match and then half (50%) of the other 2% for a total match of 4%	**Total Contribution 10%**

The percentages are based on your income, so if you make $50,000 and contribute 5% that will be $2,500 from you and with a 4% employer match that will add another $2,000 – for FREE!

TREE 3: ROTH IRA OR ROTH 401(K)
(TAX-FREE) ACCOUNT

A Roth account is unique, it was created in 1997 by the Taxpayer Relief Act and is named after William Roth, a politician from Delaware who wanted to lessen the impact of Traditional IRAs on the federal budget. In the short term he accomplished his goal, taxpayers must pay their taxes before contributing to a Roth IRA. But what we are starting to realize is that in the long-term, the federal budget is missing out on a lot of tax dollars. As you look at your tax liability this year, you will not get an advantage or deduction for contributing into a Roth. So why would you do it? Because as your investments grow through the decade lens of an 'Invest-OR', you will not have to pay anything to your Society Choice. Down the road, when you want to use these dollars, they will be tax-free!

 Advantage: Main advantage of a Roth account is that once you put money into this account, it will never be taxed again. Think about that for a moment, at twenty-three you could have sixty-plus years of tax-free growth!

Disadvantage: In a Roth account, you will be taxed today and will not have full access to your money. We will go into more specific details on this in Section 10.3.

 Example: You want to start investing in a Roth account and just got your first paycheck of $1,000.

- **Step 1:** The $1,000 is gross income and we will need to take out income taxes of 25% (estimate), which equals $250.
- **Step 2:** You find a custodian for a Roth IRA or your company for a Roth 401(k) that you trust and decide to open your Roth account there.
- **Step 3:** You have taken care of your other Money Buckets and want to invest the $750 you have after income taxes into your Roth account.
- **Step 4:** You purchased an Index Fund tracking the S&P 500 and at age 60 your investment is worth $10,000. You will be able to use the full $10,000 tax free.

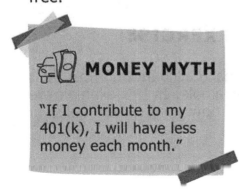

MONEY MYTH

"If I contribute to my 401(k), I will have less money each month."

Reality check: You are not losing the money you put into your 401(k) account, you are simply investing it into your Future Choice. Whatever amount you feel like you are losing, remember two things – first is that those dollars are going to work for you and second is that employer match is immediately creating more money. Now you know why the myth gets busted and in fact you have MORE money each month.

INVESTMENT ACCOUNT OVERVIEW TABLE:

	BROKERAGE	401(K)	IRA	ROTH IRA
OWNED	INDIVIDUAL	COMPANY	INDIVIDUAL	INDIVIDUAL
CONTRIBUTE	UNLIMITED	$22,500	$6,500	$6,500
ACCESS	YES	NOT BEFORE 59.5	NOT BEFORE 59.5	DEPENDS
TAX TIME	TWICE	LATER	LATER	NOW
TAX DEDUCTION	NO	YES	YES	NO
TAX TYPE	INCOME & CAPITAL GAIN	INCOME	INCOME	INCOME

WHICH ACCOUNT IS BEST EXERCISE:

There is no better way to show the uniqueness of each account and how their tax treatment will differ than to work through an example. In this example we will consider investing $10,000 today and compare how they will be taxed in the 3 different types of investment accounts.

BROKERAGE	401(K)	ROTH
1: $10,000 Taxed at 10% today before invested	1: $10,000 Not taxed today and put straight into investment for 40 years	1: $10,000 Taxed at 10% today before invested
2: How much goes into the account? ($10,000 * 0.9) = $9,000 in account	2: How much goes into theaccount? ($10,000 * 1.0) = $10,000 in account	2: How much goes into the account? ($10,000 * 0.9) = $9,000 in account
3: Invest the total from #2 for 40 years at 10%	3: Invest the total from #2 for 40 years at 10%	3: Invest the total from #2 for 40 years at 10%
4: How much do you have after investing #3 for 40 years? = $407,333.30	4: How much do you have after investing #3 for 40 years? = $452,592.56	4: How much do you have after investing #3 for 40 years? = $407,333,30
5: Tax the total from #4 by 15% Capital Gains (407,333.30 * .85) = After Tax in Box #6	5: Tax the total from #4 by 20% Ordinary Income (452,592.56 * .80) = After Tax in Box #6	5: Do you tax these dollars? NO! = After No Tax Box #6
6: How much Freedom do you have? = $346,233.30	6: How much Freedom do you have? = $362,073.60	6: How much Freedom do you have? = $407,333.30

Note: $10,000 is over the annual Roth IRA contribution limit, so let's assume it is a Roth 401(k).

SECTION 10.2
RECAP

1. 401K/IRA: RECEIVE A TAX DEDUCTION IN THE YEAR CONTRIBUTED, GROWS TAX FREE AND THEN PAY TAXES WHEN YOU TAKE MONEY OUT

2. 401(K)S ARE RUN THROUGH THE COMPANY YOU WORK FOR, AND IRAS ARE RUN THROUGH YOU AS AN INDIVIDUAL.

3. YOU CAN GET 'FREE' MONEY AND YOUR BEST INVESTMENT RETURN FROM YOUR COMPANY 401(K) EMPLOYER MATCH.

4. KNOW WHICH ACCOUNT REQUIRES AFTER-TAX (ROTH) OR PRE-TAX (401K/IRA) CONTRIBUTIONS.

SECTION 10.3

YOUR BEST VEHICLE: ROTH ACCOUNT

TERMS

CONTRIBUTIONS (SEEDS): are dollars you place into the Roth account.

EARNINGS (FRUIT): are dollars created while the money is invested in the Roth account.

FRACTIONAL SHARE INVESTING: the ability to buy less than a whole share of a company.

EXPENSE RATIO: the fee you pay to own the mutual fund or index fund.

WHICH ACCOUNT SHOULD I OPEN AS A STUDENT JUST STARTING OUT IN MY CAREER?

To answer this question, we will need to connect some of the Money Vehicle concepts we have learned.

Since you are just starting out in your career and are starting with a relatively low income compared to the income you will receive later in your career, you will fall into a lower tax bracket. Remember Chapter 9.3 ice-cream scoops, this would be taxing at the one scoop level and not the three-scoop level. Next, we want to look at the road ahead and remember Chapter 2.3 mindset of an 'Invest-Or' where we should not see just the next year of investing, but decades of time to invest. As a young adult just starting out in your career, your lower tax bracket today and long-term time horizon are two major advantages.

With a Roth account, 401(k) or IRA, you will benefit from your advantages. You will pay a lower tax bracket on your income today and allow your money to grow tax-free for the rest of your life! This is using the 8th wonder of the world to its fullest.

TWO REASONS TO CHOOSE A ROTH ACCOUNT:

YOU ARE IN A LOWER TAX BRACKET TODAY. **OR** YOU WANT YOUR MONEY TO GROW TAX-FREE FOR LIFE!

Second Advantage of a Roth 401(k): With a Roth 401(k) you will be able to contribute more dollars up the 401(k) limit of $22,500 in 2023, plus you could still get your employer match.

Second Advantage of a Roth IRA: With a Roth IRA there is a unique advantage to having 'after-tax' dollars, meaning you already paid income tax, in this account. That advantage is that your **CONTRIBUTIONS** can be withdrawn tax and penalty free. This is not the case for your account **EARNINGS.**

WHAT IS THE DIFFERENCE BETWEEN CONTRIBUTIONS AND EARNINGS IN A ROTH ACCOUNT?

Imagine you are a farmer planting seeds; the seeds would be your contribution. At any time, you can go and dig up a seed (contribution) for a quick snack. But, once those seeds develop into plants and start producing fruit (earnings), then the fruit must stay on the plant.

- Contributions (seeds): are dollars you place into the account.
- Earnings (fruit): are dollars created while the money is invested in the account.

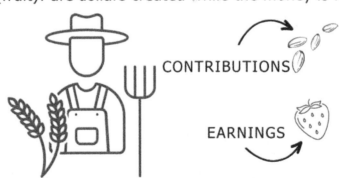

In a Roth IRA, the money you have earned, taxed, and contributed into the account is accessible to you at any time, for any reason.

In a Roth IRA, you can use the earnings as well, but to receive the penalty-free treatment on the earnings within the account, you must leave the money in the account until you reach the age of 59.5. There is an exception to this earnings rule under age 59.5, if you have had the account for five (5) years and are pulling the money out for a first-time home purchase or higher education.

Example: Let's say you contribute $5,000 into a Roth IRA, and a few years later, the account has grown to $7,000. If you want to use the $5,000 you contributed to buy a car, you can. The $2,000 of earnings, however, must stay in the account until age 59.5.

WHAT DO I NEED TO OPEN A ROTH IRA?

Requirement #1: Most important, you must have earned income.

Then you can contribute the lesser of either your earned income or $6,500 (as of 2023 and subject to future increases with inflation).

 Example: For example, if you made $3,000 this year, you could contribute up to $3,000; if you made $10,000 this year, you could contribute up to $6,500.

Requirement #2: Photo ID or Driver's License to confirm your identity.

Requirement #3: Social Security Number is a second form of identification and confirmation of United States citizen.

Requirement #4: Bank account and routing number to allow for contributions into the account.

Requirement #5: Employer or Income Information to confirm requirement #1, an earned income.

WHERE CAN I OPEN A ROTH IRA?

There are many custodians that offer Roth IRA accounts, it is up to you to find one that fits your situation. You can use resources such as NerdWallet.com or BankRate.com to compare different account offerings. Examples of where you can open:

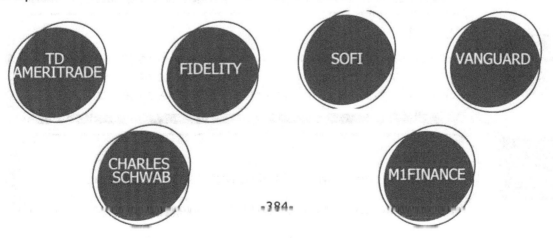

When you compare, you should look at the fees and account minimums, just like Chapter 4 Bank Accounts. The account fees are what they will charge you when you make trades or just to have the account open. The account minimums are how much you need to open the account. Some accounts will help you choose what to invest in and make the investments for you, this is often referred to as a 'Robo-Advisor'. Be aware that with these services there will be additional fees involved.

As a young investor, you should look for an account that have $0 fees and $0 minimums.

MONEY VEHICLE TIP:

Remove emotions from investing by setting up automatic contributions to your future.

HOW DO I TRANSFER MONEY INTO MY ROTH IRA?

01
Step 1:
You should have a Roth IRA open, if not go back to 'What do I need to setup a Roth IRA'.

02
Step 2:
Connect your bank account to your Roth IRA account, this is also a requirement from earlier.

03
Step 3:
Setup automatic transfers from your bank account to your Roth IRA and your Future Bucket.

04
Step 4:
Select how often (Monthly on the 1st) and how much (Up to your income or $6,500 in 2023) you want to be transferred in Step #3; then allow this transfer 3-5 business days to complete.

05
Step 5:
Confirm all the information is correct before submitting.

HOW DO I INVEST INSIDE MY ROTH IRA?

First you need to confirm that your transfer has settled, and the money is in the account. Then to choose your investment, follow these steps:

01

Step 1:
Go to your custodian and select 'Trade'

02

Step 2:
Select which account you want to trade in – 'Roth IRA'

03

Step 3:
Choose between investment, with Chapter 6 you should be confident in selecting stocks

04

Step 4:
Select which investment you want to make, remember Be Average = Index

05

Step 5:
Use **FRACTIONAL SHARE INVESTING** which means you can buy a piece of the stock's share and not the whole share

HOW DO I INVEST INSIDE MY ROTH IRA?

With a long-term time horizon, you can feel confident taking on the risks of investing. This means that you can take on the risk of being a part owner of companies or invest in stocks. This can be accomplished through investing in globally diversified mutual funds or ETFs (Exchange Traded Funds). For now, let's consider mutual funds and ETFs the same.

Whichever mutual fund or ETF you choose should have no trading fees and a low **EXPENSE RATIO**. The expense ratio is the fee you pay to own the mutual fund or index fund.

Money Vehicle recommends getting started with an index fund that has:

No trade fees: You shouldn't be trading much, but there's no reason to be charged when you do.

 Low or no management fees: With custodians fighting to get clients, there are accounts with very low management fees and sometimes can even be $0 management.

 Low or no expense ratio: Aim for under thirty basis points or 3/10 of 1 percent (0.003). With smaller initial deposits, you want low expenses.
Example: Thirty basis points (.003) on $1,000 is $3 ($1,000 * .003).

 Broad diversification: Domestic and foreign.

 Growth potential: This comes with risk, but you have the time horizon to withstand it.

Custodians are constantly updating their list of offerings, so it is important that you confirm these measurements for your investment. Money Vehicle does NOT give financial advice, but here are a few funds in no particular order that you can go review and get your investment portfolio started:

VOO	Vanguard S&P 500 ETF
FNILX	Fidelity ZERO Large Cap Index
SPY	SPDR S&P 500 ETF
IVV	iShares Core S&P 500 ETF
SWPPX	Schwab S&P 500 Index Fund
VTI	Vanguard Total Stock Market ETF

THIS IS NOT FINANCIAL ADVICE, FOR RESEARCH ONLY.

Ideally, at this point, you understand why Money Vehicle recommends opening a Roth IRA account to maximize the advantages of being a young invest-OR. If not, remember you are in a low tax bracket today and the money will be allowed to grow tax-free for thirty-plus years.

 Example: You put $10,000 into a Roth account by the age of thirty and invest at an average return of 10 percent until retirement at age sixty-five you will have $281,000 tax-free!

Now that you see the Roth advantage and know what to invest in, it's time to open a Roth IRA. If you are at a company that offers a Roth 401(k) then you should capitalize on it and contribute. If not, Money Vehicle would encourage you to go open a Roth IRA and contribute today.

> **MONEY VEHICLE MISSION IS TO EMPOWER STUDENTS TO OPEN ONE MILLION ROTH IRA ACCOUNTS!**

SECTION 10.3
RECAP

1. ADVANTAGE OF ROTH IRA FOR STUDENTS: YOU ARE IN A LOWER TAX BRACKET TODAY AND WILL PAY A LOWER TAX ON YOUR EARNED INCOME.

2. ADVANTAGE OF ROTH IRA FOR STUDENTS: YOU WILL RECEIVE DECADES OF TAX-FREE GROWTH ON YOUR INVESTMENTS.

3. ADVANTAGE OF ROTH IRA FOR STUDENTS: YOU WILL STILL HAVE ACCESS TO YOUR CONTRIBUTIONS (SEEDS) THAT YOU PLACE INTO THE ACCOUNT.

REVIEW

THE RULE: U.S.E. A ROTH!

Through empowering yourself to understand, strategize, and be efficient with your money, you will be on your way to achieving your R.I.C.H. goals. The best investment return you can guarantee will be the employer match within your 401(k) at work. However, when you look at the three types of investment accounts, each offer different advantages to build into your plan. As a young investor today, the tax-free growth and access to your contributions of a Roth IRA is likely the greatest advantage for you. Through this account, you immediately build in future returns by removing taxes. Synthesize all the lessons in Your Money Vehicle by opening and U.S.E.ing a Roth IRA.

ACTION

- Act like an Invest-OR, open a Roth account and grow your investments – tax Free!

OWNER'S MANUAL
FOR YOUR MONEY VEHICLE:

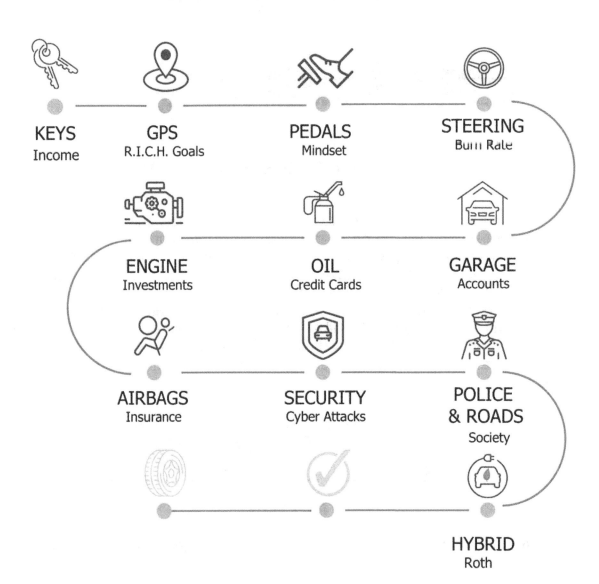

KEYS
Income

GPS
R.I.C.H. Goals

PEDALS
Mindset

STEERING
Burn Rate

ENGINE
Investments

OIL
Credit Cards

GARAGE
Accounts

AIRBAGS
Insurance

SECURITY
Cyber Attacks

**POLICE
& ROADS**
Society

HYBRID
Roth

DRIVING YOUR MONEY VEHICLE

OUTRO

WHY IS SO MUCH TAKEN OUT OF MY PAYCHECK?

OVERVIEW

11.1: How To Read a Paystub

11.2: Game of Inches Challenge

11.3: The Road to Freedom

ACTION

Find INCHES in your plan by learning to U.S.E. your paystub and benefits.

DRIVING YOUR MONEY VEHICLE

You are in Your Money Vehicle driving where you want to go and are more confident that you know how to U.S.E. money. But every vehicle breaks down, the oil runs out, the parts get rusty and the brakes fade. This is why you take your vehicle in to have a tune up and a chance to review what is happening and what needs to be improved.

SECTION 11.1
HOW TO READ A PAYSTUB

TERMS

PAYSTUB: a document outlining in detail how much was earned and then how much was taken out for taxes or deductions.

PAYCHECK: transfers the amount of money that was earned in a specific period.

PAYCHECK IDENTIFICATION NUMBER: the unique number on each paycheck so your employer can identify and track each earner.

PAY PERIOD: number of days that are accounted for in this paycheck.

NET PAY: the amount of money you TAKE home after taxes and deductions, Net Income.

YEAR TO DATE (YTD): summary of what has happened in a specific category since the beginning of the tax year (Jan 1).

EMPLOYEE BENEFITS: any compensation provided by your employer that is in addition to your wage or salary and intended to increase your overall satisfaction and productivity.

HEALTHCARE: the organization and offering of medical care to people.

TANGIBLE BENEFITS: employee benefits that can be measured in dollar amounts. Ex. healthcare benefits.

INTANGIBLE BENEFITS: employee benefits that cannot be measured but are still attributed to rewarding work experience. Ex. company culture.

FULL-TIME EMPLOYEE: employee working more than 35 hours a week and is required to have access to benefits offered through the company.

TERMS

PART-TIME EMPLOYEE: employee working less than 35 hours a week and their benefit package is at the discretion of the employer.

GROUP HEALTH: employer provided health insurance plan where employees can elect to be covered by the company policy.

HMO HEALTH MAINTENANCE ORGANIZATION: a type of group health policy where the company offers a list of network providers the insurance will cover.

PPO PREFERRED PROVIDER OPTION: a type of group health policy where the employee can choose from a larger group of providers or receive reimbursement for providers outside of the network.

FLEXIBLE SPENDING ACCOUNT (FSA): a tax advantaged account through your employer where you can contribute pre-tax dollars to be used for specific purposes such as medical costs, tax free.

HEALTH SAVINGS ACCOUNT (HSA): a tax advantaged account owned by the individual and connected to a high deductible health insurance plan, where you can contribute pre-tax dollars to be used for medical expenses.

HEALTH REIMBURSEMENT ACCOUNT (HRA): a type of employee benefit where a company will offer an account with a certain amount of dollars to reimburse the employee for healthcare-related costs.

PAID TIME OFF (PTO): negotiated time off from work that will still be paid salary.

EMPLOYEE STOCK OPTIONS (ESO): a type of benefit where a company will offer an employee the ability to purchase or earn ownership of the company.

CULTURE: company culture is how people within the company view what the companies' values are and how it operates.

BRAND: company brand is how people outside the company view the companies' values and how it operates.

WELLNESS PROGRAM: programs designed to improve and promote the health and fitness of an individual.

Now that you have begun to DRIVE YOUR MONEY VEHICLE and started to U.S.E. money, you should be ready to translate your paystub.

HOW IS A PAYSTUB DIFFERENT THAN A PAYCHECK?

We do need to callout the difference between these two. Your **PAYCHECK** is simple to read, it is the cash you have earned at your job that is available for you to deposit into your account. There are no calculations or definitions, a simple dollar amount on a check. A **PAYSTUB** will be a document with much more detail around how you arrive at the final dollar amount on your paycheck.

Paystubs summarize how much you have earned, how much you have been taxed, and how much either you or your company have deducted during this **PAY PERIOD**. How often you receive a paycheck may differ, for example some people may get a paycheck each week, every two weeks, or once a month. No matter how often you get your paycheck deposited, there will be a summary of what was taken out from your gross pay to your net pay on your paystub.

Wage
You will see your hourly rate and number of hours worked. If you earned any overtime, you would see this as well.

Salary
You will see the salary you earned during this pay period. If you earned any bonuses, you would see this as well.

WHY IS A PAYSTUB IMPORTANT?

Your income is essential in driving Your Money Vehicle, so understanding how your income is delivered should be important to you. Each pay period you will have the opportunity to take a pit stop and review how far you came in this section of your journey. These pit stops will serve as a good accountability check for both you and your employer. Each paystub is a chance for you to confirm that you are receiving the correct amount of earnings. It is on you to verify what is being taken out and confirm the correct amounts are being used.

We discussed all the way back in Chapter 1 that people break the Golden Rule because they confuse their Gross Income with their Net Income. This mistake can be avoided if you understand how to read your paystub and identify how much you will pay to your Society Choice. With this accurate estimation, you can build personalized Money Buckets and really set your plan up for success.

> **REMINDER: PAYSTUBS ARE JUST ESTIMATES. THESE ARE NOT OFFICIAL IRS CALCULATIONS OR DOCUMENTATIONS, THOSE FINAL CALCULATIONS COME IN APRIL WHEN YOU FILE YOUR TAXES, AFTER ALL YOUR INFORMATION IS KNOWN.**

WHEN WILL I NEED MY PAYSTUB?

If you are trying to set up your financial plan and establish your Money Buckets, you will U.S.E. your paystub to begin to calculate your Society and Future Choices. Net Pay will also provide clarity on how much you can spend.

If you are looking for a place to live, your landlord or even your mortgage broker will require some proof of income. This is where you can not only send them your paystub, but now be able to explain what everything on it means.

MONEY VEHICLE TIP:

When talking to your landlord, you should ask if your rent can be connected to your Credit score calculation.

If you apply for financial assistance from the government, a school, or a non-profit they may also want to confirm that you need resources. This will be accomplished through providing your paystub.

If you are filing your taxes, you can use your paystubs to confirm your W2 or 1099 statements. This double check will allow you to clear up any mistakes before you file your taxes. This clarity will also allow you to hold your employer accountable as you will have proof of any issues.

WHY DID COMPANIES BEGIN TO TAKE THINGS OUT OF MY PAYCHECK?

The government began requiring companies to deduct taxes from a paycheck because people were not preparing for their tax liability. April would come and individuals would be hit with a tax liability that they were unprepared for and had no cash to cover.

By automatically removing taxes and deductions from W2 paychecks, your company is helping you manage your Society Choice.

If you feel your company should not withhold as much of your paycheck, you can change your elections to reduce your withholdings. This reduction will increase your short-term cash flow, but you should understand that your tax liability will be due in April regardless of the withholding.

HOW DOES A PAYSTUB DIFFER FROM W2 TO 1099 WORKERS?

Paystubs for W2 and 1099 workers are completely different!

When you are a W2 employee, your company will withhold money for taxes and contributions to retirement accounts. However, as a 1099 independent contractor, the company you contract with is not responsible for your financial health or future.

A 1099 contractor will receive their gross pay from the company they worked for and are responsible for withholding taxes on their own. That's right, as a 1099 contractor you now need to truly manage and own your Money Buckets on your own. With each paycheck you will need to place a percentage into a separate savings account or somewhere that you can safely hold the dollars that you will owe in your tax liability.

A 1099 contractor will also not receive any support in their retirement or Future Choice planning. No contributions will be directed to a 401(k) and there will be no employer match because you are your own employer. Each 1099 contractor is responsible for contributing a part of their paycheck to their Future Choice on their own.

AS A 1099 CONTRACTOR YOU ARE RESPONSIBLE FOR SOCIETY AND FUTURE CHOICES.

HOW CAN I FIND MY PAYSTUB?

As a W2 employee, you will need to access your company payroll system using a login you received when you started with the company. If you cannot gain access, then you should reach out to someone in your HR department.

As a 1099 contractor, you will receive a 1099 Form from each company you contracted with. This 1099 Form represents your paystub but remember this is your Gross Pay and not your Net Pay.

HOW DO I READ MY PAYSTUB?
MAIN POINTS OF A W2 PAYSTUB

1. Paycheck Identification Number
- The unique number on each paycheck so your employer can identify and track each earner.

2. Pay Period
- Number of days that are accounted for in this paycheck.
  - Wage: you will see your hours
  - Salary: you will see your days

3. Pay Date
- The day your payment was issued.

4. Personal Information
- Address: Where you live and the state you will file your taxes in.
- Social Security Number: A 9-digit number used to identify and track individuals for taxes.
- Filing Status: As a W2, this is the tax election you have made on W4. As a 1099, this election will impact your taxes but not be seen on your paystub.

5. Gross Pay
- The amount of money you MAKE before taxes or deductions.
  - Overtime Pay: For wage employees, they will receive at least 1.5X their regular pay for hours worked above 40 hours in a week.
  - Bonus Pay: For salary employees this is extra compensation above regular earnings.

6. Withholdings

- Federal Income Tax: This is a mandated amount by the IRS that is withheld from each paycheck by your company for the Federal progressive Income Tax code. This is automatically sent to the IRS to reduce your tax liability when you file in April.
  - Can be seen as FED, FIT, FITW but they all mean Federal Income Tax Withheld.
- FICA – Social Security: Your contribution to the Social Security system, which is an income payment in your retirement years. You will pay 6.2% and your employer will also pay 6.2% into this system.
  - Self Employed (1099) must pay both Employee and Employer: 12.4% of Gross Income.
  - Can be seen on your paystub as OASDI, FICA, SS.

- FICA – Medicare: Your contribution to the Medicare system, which is the health insurance in your retirement years. You will pay 1.45% and your employer will also pay 1.45% for this system.
  - Self Employed (1099) must pay both Employee and Employer: 2.9% of Gross Income.
  - Can be seen on your paystub as MED.
- State Income Tax: Amount withheld by your company for your State Income Tax. Not all states have a state income tax so this could be as little as 0%.
  - Can be seen as State, SIT, SITW but they all mean State Income Tax Withheld.
- Municipality or City Taxes: Amount withheld by your company for your City or Municipality Income Tax. Not all areas have these income taxes so this could be as little as 0%.
- Unemployment = These contributions will go to support unemployment benefits.
  - Can be seen as FUTA.

7. Pre-Tax Deductions
- Dollars contributed for specific purposes that are taken out before taxed.
- Health Insurance Premiums: If you elected the employer provided health insurance policy, you will see your premium payment deducted from your paycheck.
  - Can be seen on your paystub as HS or HI.
- Dental Insurance Premiums: If you elected the employer provided dental insurance policy, you will see your premium payment deducted from your paycheck.
- Life insurance: If you elected the employer provided life insurance policy, you will see your premium payment deducted from your paycheck.
- Flexible Spending Account (FSA): If you elected the employer provided flexible spending account for healthcare or childcare, you will see your contribution deducted from your paycheck.
- Health Savings Account (HSA): If you elected the employer provided high deductible health insurance policy, you will see your premium payment deducted from your paycheck.
- 401(k) EE Contribution: You will see the contributions you elect to put into this account.
- 401(k) ER Contribution: You will see the contributions your employer matches into this account. This is considered 'free' money but calculated as compensation by your employer.
- IRA Contribution: This will NOT be seen on your paystub.

8. After Tax Contributions
- Roth Contribution: If you elect to contribute to a Roth 401(k) you will see your contribution deducted from your paycheck but will not receive a tax deduction.
- Disability Insurance = If you elected the employer provided disability insurance policy, you will see your premium payment deducted from your paycheck.

9. Employer Paid Fringe Benefits
- These are the benefits the employer has paid on your behalf and will be treated as a type of compensation unless the tax code allows exemption.

10. Net Pay
- The amount of money you TAKE home after taxes and deductions.

11. Year to Date (YTD)
- Summary of categories since the beginning of the tax year (Jan 1)

COMPOUND INTEREST EXAMPLE:
$100 AT 5% OVER 10 YEARS:

YEAR	STARTING BALANCE	INTEREST EARNED	ENDING BALANCE
1	$100	$5	$105
2	$105	$5.25	$110.25
3	$110.25	$5.51	$115.76
4	$115.76	$5.79	$121.55
5	$121.55	$6.08	$127.63
6	$127.63	$6.38	$134.01
7	$134.01	$6.70	$140.71
8	$140.71	$7.04	$147.75
9	$147.75	$7.39	$155.14
10	$155.14	$7.76	$162.90

> **COMPOUND INTEREST CREATES EMPLOYEES (MONEY) AND THEN THOSE EMPLOYEES (MONEY) CREATE EVEN MORE EMPLOYEES (MONEY)!**

THE TIME VALUE OF MONEY

You are beginning to understand why there is value in not only earning money, but also creating money through compound interest, and it is time to put a name to this value. The value of money over time is conveniently called: the **TIME VALUE OF MONEY (TVM).**

Time Value of Money (TVM): states that money is worth more today than in the future because if you put the money to work, it can create more money!

TVM states that $1 today is worth more than $1 a year from now, due to its earning potential. When you U.S.E. money to create more money, it becomes your employee, and the TVM calculation reflects how hard your money is working.

When you understand the time value of money you see that $.01 is worth a lot when you can make it go to work. Money will be more valuable today than in the future because of your opportunity to make it your employee. Begin to base your decisions on the time value of money and realize that your money will never be more valuable than today.

WHAT IS THE MOST IMPORTANT PART OF THE TIME VALUE OF MONEY?

This is why Money Vehicle is so excited that you are here, because the most important factor is also your second greatest asset – TIME. Time is what makes the exponential difference in the formula and time is why the $.01 ends up being more valuable than the $5 million.

The best part of this is that time is also the part of the formula that you control the most. No matter the amount of dollars you have today (PV), the longer you allow them to work for you, they will get exponentially bigger in the future (FV).

PLUGGING INTO A COMPOUND INTEREST CALCULATOR, YOU WILL NEED TO KNOW:

- **PRINCIPAL:** what you start with
- **ADDITIONS:** will you make any more additions
- **TIME:** how long you will put the money to work
- **INTEREST:** the rate you intend to receive
- **COMPOUNDING:** how often you think the money will compound (annually or 1 is typical)

COMPOUND INTEREST TABLE

QUARTERLY	4 TIMES A YEAR
WEEKLY	52 TIMES A YEAR
SEMIANNUALLY	2 TIMES A YEAR
MONTHLY	12 TIMES A YEAR
DAILY	365 TIMES A YEAR
ANNUALLY	1 TIME A YEAR

CAN WE GET BACK TO SUZY AND RICKY. WHO CAME OUT AHEAD?

It is hard to believe, but by now I am sure you have started to guess that it was Suzy! Using a 7 percent return and a long-time horizon, here are the results:

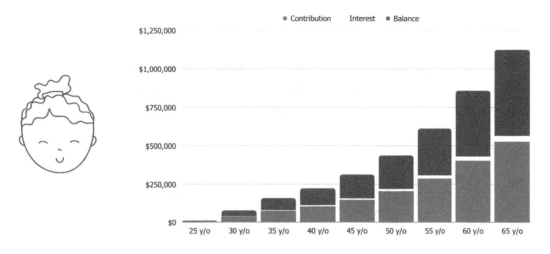

Suzy:
Saves $5,000 a year <u>until</u> age thirty-five , then stops= $562,682

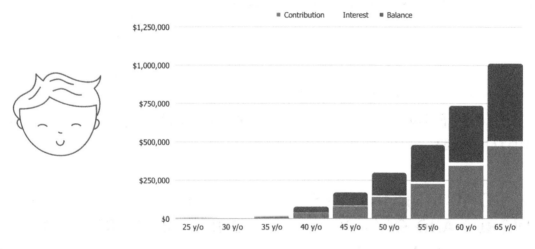

Ricky:
Saves $5,000 a year <u>starting</u> at age thirty-five = $505,354

Even though Suzy only saves $50,000, versus Ricky's $150,000, she comes out $57,000 ahead at her freedom date!

How is that possible? Suzy understood how to make money go to work for her like an employee. Using time and letting her investment compound, she was using the secret of the wealthy —compound interest!

Putting compound interest and the Time Value of Money concepts into action changes your relationship with money. No longer are you just working for money, now money is working for you too!

SECTION 2.2
RECAP

 MONEY VEHICLE TIP:

Stop just working for money, Start making money work for you!

1. SIMPLE INTEREST IS MONEY CREATED OFF OF THE PRINCIPAL.

2. COMPOUND INTEREST IS THE 8TH WONDER OF THE WORLD AND OCCURS WHEN MONEY GETS CREATED OFF THE PRINCIPAL AND PRIOR INTEREST.

3. MOST IMPORTANT FACTOR IN THE TIME VALUE OF MONEY FORMULA IS TIME!

SECTION 2.3
TREAT YOUR MONEY LIKE AN EMPLOYEE

TERMS

SPEND-OR: sees money on a day-to-day basis and money goes out as it comes in.

SAV-OR: sees money on a month to money basis and protects money for a specific purpose.

INVEST-OR: sees money on a decade-to-decade basis and puts money to work for their financial future.

What kind of 'OR are you? Spend-OR, Sav-OR, or Invest-OR? (We know not grammatically correct 😊)

You can find out what type of OR you are by answering two simple questions:

When you **earn** money, do you spend or save?

When you **create** money, do you spend or invest?

Spendra, Salvador, and Investina all want to see the new blockbuster movie coming out this summer, The Capitalist Games. They are each so motivated to see it that they go out and get summer jobs to help pay for tickets.

After two weeks, their first paychecks arrive, and each of them is faced with the decision: spend or save?

SPENDRA

Spendra can't wait. After taxes, rent, and life's expenses are taken out, she has just enough left to head to the half-off matinee showing of the new film. She doesn't have any extra cash to get snacks at the movie or even to go out again before her next check comes in. This is Spendra's decision; she has earned her money and it is her decision to spend it.

 Spendra is a Spend-OR— she sees money on a day-to-day basis and money goes out as it comes in.

SALVADOR

Salvador doesn't just want to go see the movie, he wants to make a night out of it —going out to dinner beforehand and getting some of the best movie treats ever, REESE'S Pieces. He saves a little money from each paycheck until he gets his third one.

As the money adds up, he has a decision to make about his savings: spend it or put it to work?

Once he has saved enough for this specific purpose, Salvador goes out and enjoys his night—dinner, movie, and candy.

 Salvador is a Sav-OR—he sees money on a month to money basis and has his money protected for a specific purpose.

What Spendra and Salvador both failed to ask was if there was a way to see the movie and keep some of their hard-earned money.

INVESTINA

Investina has a system that allows her to see the movie for "free." Investina knows she will only need 50 percent of her paycheck to live on and wants to have as much of her paycheck working for her as she can. Instead of all Investina's paycheck staying in her checking account, she automatically sends 50 percent to her investment account. With this system she knows she can cover her Burn Rate while also making money work for her.

Investina avoids listening to Spendra when she discusses the movie's plot twists but enjoys hearing the non-movie details of Salvador's night out. With each check that comes in, Investina feels good knowing she is one step closer to seeing the movie with money she created, not money she earned.

When she got a job, Investina began earning money—every hour she clocked was money that went into her pocket. Then she decided to save her money rather than spend it all. Once she was comfortable with her savings, she looked into investing and putting her money to work. When money started to work for her without her time, she began to create a new stream of income.

EARNED INCOME **MONEY YOU WORK FOR**

CREATED INCOME **MONEY THAT WORKS FOR YOU**

With the money Investina created, she had another choice: does she spend it or invest it?

This is where Salvador made the decision to take his savings and go out for the night, but Investina decided to put all her money—earned and created—to work for her! This newly created income is her employee, and she tells it to go back to work to create new employees. Now the money she is creating begins to create even more money, and that is the power of compound interest.

- **Spend-OR:** sees money on a day to daytime frame
- **Sav-OR:** sees money on a month to month or year to year time frame.
- **Invest-OR:** sees money on a decade-to-decade time frame.

This process doesn't happen overnight, but with this strategy, Investina will be able to see the movie, get dinner, and even grab some REESE'S Pieces, all while the money she earned from her job is still working for her.

 Investina is an Invest-OR—she sees money in a long-term time horizon and treats money like an employee, making it go to work for her financial freedom.

Investina decided not to spend her earned income right away, or protect it in a Savings Account to spend on a specific activity. Instead, she decided to U.S.E. money to create new money. By following this mindset, Investina will break free from making decisions paycheck to paycheck or splurge to splurge and start to see each paycheck as her employee.

As you begin earning money, it isn't easy putting off what you want now for your R.I.C.H. goals. But, with every paycheck that you prioritize what you want MOST, R.I.C.H. goals, over what you want now, you will create a new employee!

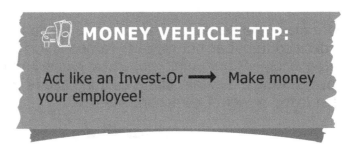

MONEY VEHICLE TIP:

Act like an Invest-Or ⟶ Make money your employee!

SECTION 2.3
RECAP

1. WHO ARE YOU: SPEND-OR (DAY-TO-DAY) -VS- SAV-OR (YEAR-TO-YEAR) -VS- INVEST-OR (DECADE-TO-DECADE).

2. YOU EARN MONEY WHEN YOU WORK FOR IT; YOU CREATE MONEY WHEN IT WORKS FOR YOU.

3. ACT LIKE AN INVEST-OR AND MAKE MONEY WORK FOR YOU.

SECTION 2.4
HOW A LOAN WORKS

TERMS

DEBT: when money is owed.

CONSUMER DEBT: when money is owed for purchases used by an individual or family.

BUSINESS DEBT: when money is owed for purchases used by a company.

INSTALLMENT LOAN: an agreement where the borrower will pay back the principal amount and the interest being charged in regularly scheduled payments. Where each payment is called an installment and upon completion of the installments, the borrower will no longer be in debt but own the asset outright.

AMORTIZE (AMORTIZATION SCHEDULE): to gradually write off or payback the cost of an asset over time. The Amortization Schedule will show you exactly how much is being paid in each installment and how much of that installment is going towards principal or interest.

TRUTH IN LENDING ACT: protects you against inaccurate and unfair credit billing or credit card practices, requiring lenders to provide clear information on costs.

FIXED INTEREST RATE: the interest rate is locked in the life of the loan.

VARIABLE INTEREST RATE: the interest rate can go up or down during the life of the loan.

PREPAYMENT PENALTY: a fee vendors charge if you pay off all or part of your loan early.

HOW DOES THE LOAN ACTUALLY WORK?

As a consumer when you are forced to purchase anything that you do not have the cash to pay for with other people's money (OPM). This can be called many things – debt, credit, loans, etc. but it is the same relationship we discussed in Section 2.1 where there is a lender and a borrower. The introduction to debt occurs in many of our lives when we decide to buy those new shoes, go to college, buy a car, or settle into our dream house!

Many will hear the word 'DEBT' and get a cold chill up their spine. But Money Vehicle wants to show you that debt is not a good or bad thing, debt is a tool, and its impact depends on how you U.S.E. it. You wouldn't say a hammer is a bad thing, would you?

When you U.S.E. debt wisely, it can be a good tool for Your Money Vehicle. However, when you do not use debt wisely, it can destroy Your Money Vehicle.

> ## WHEN YOU U.S.E. DEBT WISELY, IT CAN BE A GOOD TOOL FOR YOUR MONEY VEHICLE

OK, SO WITH DEBT I MUST PAY MORE THAN I BORROWED, THAT MAKES SENSE. BUT HOW DO I UNDERSTAND THE BREAKDOWN OF PAYMENTS?

Loan payments are broken down into two pieces – the Principal and the Interest.

The PRINCIPAL in a loan is how much you borrowed, the original amount of the loan, and the amount the seller sees as the value of the asset you are purchasing. When looking at your loan payments, the principal will go towards paying back the amount you borrowed and slowly be reduced as you take ownership of the asset.

If you could make purchases with your own money in cash, the total amount would be the same as the amount you are purchasing today.

The **INTEREST** in a loan is how much it will cost you to borrow the principal. You see that the asset is valued at a price beyond what you have in cash and will need to take out debt to purchase it. In this case, the total price will then be the original amount AND the interest you paid.

If you are not using your own money, you will be charged interest on the debt you take out, and the total amount would then be the principal plus the interest you paid.

When we are discussing debt here, it must be stated that we are talking about **CONSUMER DEBT**. This form of debt is what the typical person, you, or me, takes on when we want to buy things for ourselves as opposed to **BUSINESS DEBT,** that is debt meant to invest in or buy an appreciating asset. Consumer debt is often tied to something that is consumable or will decrease in value over time. Yes, this includes your car and house!

When you take out consumer debt such as Auto loans, Home Mortgages, or even Student Loans, you enter into an agreement called an '**INSTALLMENT LOAN**'. Credit cards (Chapter 5) are not amortized because there is not a regular payment schedule. Credit cards are revolving debt which means they continually open and close as opposed to amortized debt that has a completion date.

The installment loan is an agreement that the borrower will pay back the principal amount borrowed, and the interest being charged in regularly scheduled payments overtime. Each payment is an installment and upon completion of the installments, the borrower will no longer be in debt. If there is a car or house involved, you would then own this property outright.

Anytime you enter this type of 'installment' relationship, you will want to confirm exactly how the loan will work and how the loan will **AMORTIZE** over time. Amortize literally means to gradually write off the cost of an asset over time. When you amortize a loan, you will see exactly how much is being paid in each installment and how much of that installment is going towards paying back the principal through the amortization schedule.

The '**AMORTIZATION SCHEDULE**' is a table showing how exactly you will reduce your debt gradually over time. Almost every installment loan contract you sign will have a big table on it that explains exactly how your payments will work overtime or how the loan will 'amortize'.

This schedule will show you how many installments you will make, when installments are due, what the breakdown of each installment will be (principal and interest) and perhaps most importantly when your loan matures, or when the payments will be completed to make you the new owner.

However, using an amortization schedule will not be as simple as exchanging $1 for $1. The lender wants assurance that they will get the most out of the deal. What the lender has the authority to do is direct how much of each installment goes toward the amount you borrowed (principal) and how much goes toward the cost of borrowing (interest).

The **TRUTH IN LENDING ACT** is meant to protect you from inaccurate or unfair lending practices. The law requires lenders to provide you with the details of your loan costs and how they will be calculated so that you are able to compare this offering verse other lenders. But, this only is valuable if you understand how the costs work and how to compare.

LET'S BREAK DOWN WHAT DETAILS YOU NEED TO SEE HOW THE INSTALLMENTS WILL BEGIN TO AMORTIZE OVER TIME.

- How long is the loan for: Number of installments
- How much is being loaned: Principal amount
- How much is each installment: Total payment due
- How much is being paid to interest: Percent of total payment paying interest
- How much is being paid to principal: Percent of total payment paying principal
- How much is left after this installment: Current balance of the loan
- How installment is being divided: How much of installment goes toward paying off interest and how much to paying down principal

EXAMPLE: $21,000 LOAN PAID BACK OVER 11 INSTALLMENTS AT 7% INTEREST.

AMORTIZATION SCHEDULE EXAMPLE						
LOAN AMOUNT	PAYMENT	INTEREST	PRINCIPAL	BALANCE	% TO INTEREST	% TO PRINCIPAL
$21,000	$2,800	$1,470	$1,330	$19,670	52.5%	47.5%
$19,670	$2,800	$1,377	$1,424	$18,246	49.2%	50.8%
$18,246	$2,800	$1,277	$1,523	$16,723	45.6%	54.4%
$16,723	$2,800	$1,171	$1,630	$15,093	41.8%	58.2%
$15,093	$2,800	$1,056	$1,744	$13,349	37.7%	62.3%
$13,349	$2,800	$934	$1,866	$11,483	33.4%	66.6%
$11,483	$2,800	$804	$1,997	$9,486	28.7%	71.3%
$9,486	$2,800	$664	$2,136	$7,349	23.7%	76.3%
$7,349	$2,800	$514	$2,286	$5,063	18.4%	81.6%
$5,063	$2,800	$354	$2,446	$2,617	12.7%	87.3%
$2,617	$2,800	$183	$2,617	0	6.5%	93.5%

HOW TO READ AN AMORTIZATION TABLE AND BREAKDOWN AN INSTALLMENT LOAN:

- **Installment Number:** Which installment this is.
  - **Example:** Installment #3 begins with $18,246
- **Principal Amount:** Start with the original loan amount and then decrease as the principal payments are paid.
  - **Example:** Original Loan is $21,000 but after installment #3, the loan amount will be $16,723 for installment #4
- **Total Payment:** The total amount you pay each period installment, the formula for calculating this payment is beyond the scope of this course.
  - **Example:** Each installment will be a payment of $2,800
- **Interest Paid:** Each installment will pay the Interest on the loan. Find out how much by multiplying the current balance of the loan by the interest rate.
  - **Example:** Installment #3 = $18,246 * .07 = $1,277.22 of interest paid this installment
- **Principal Paid:** Each installment will also pay down the principal remaining. Find out how much by subtracting the interest from the total payment.
  - **Example:** Installment #3 = $2,800 - $1,277 = $1,523 of principal being paid off this installment.
- **Current Balance:** After your installment pays down a portion of the remaining principal, you will have a new loan amount that will be charged interest. Subtract the principal being paid this installment from this installment's loan amount.
  - **Example:** Installment #3 = $18,246 - $1,523 = $16,723 balance to begin installment #4.
- **Installment Breakdown:** As the current balance decreases, the amount of interest you pay will decrease with it. However, your total payment will not change, then the excess payment will go to pay down the principal.
  - **Example:** Installment #3 sees 54% of the payment go to principal and then installment #4 sees 58% go toward principal.

 3 TAKEAWAYS FROM BREAKING DOWN A LOAN:

1. The lender will be paid their interest first.
2. The borrower must confirm the payment fits in their cash management system.
3. The total cost of a loan will be the purchase price plus interest.

WHY WILL MORE OF THE PAYMENT GO TOWARDS INTEREST AT THE BEGINNING OF THE INSTALLMENTS?

If you did not amortize and split your payments into these categories, then you would simply be paying the interest off. Upon your last payment you would still owe the entire principal and you would own nothing.

Amortizing is meant to benefit both parties in this borrower and lender relationship. Paying the debt back with consistent installments where each is divided into what you borrowed (principal) and what it cost (interest) provides a clear understanding for both parties of how the agreement will proceed.

> **For the borrower,**
>
> each payment will be stated as a monthly responsibility and continue to establish them as the new owner of the asset.

> **For the lender,**
>
> each payment will provide a monthly income and reduce the risk of not receiving their principal loan amount back.

At the beginning of the loan a higher percentage goes toward paying the interest to ensure the lender will receive their reward for lending their money. Then as the installments continue, you can see that more and more of the payment goes towards the principal, because the loan amount continues to decrease and therefore the interest charged on that installment decreases. Even though the interest being paid goes down, your installment remains the same and the excess payment will then go to paying off the principal.

WILL I KEEP PAYING 7% INTEREST EVERY INSTALLMENT?

That depends on the type of interest rate you agreed upon when you took out the original loan. Was it a fixed or variable interest rate?

FIXED INTEREST RATE **THE INTEREST RATE IS LOCKED IN THE LIFE OF THE LOAN.**

VARIABLE INTEREST RATE **THE INTEREST RATE CAN GO UP OR DOWN DURING THE LIFE OF THE LOAN.**

These two types of interest rates are clear in their definition but get a little more complex when you begin to wonder which is going to be better for you.

With a fixed rate, you have the security of consistent payments. Knowing the interest rate will not change allows you to build your cash management system around this loan payment.

With a variable rate, you will usually be enticed with a lower starting rate. For example, a fixed rate at 4% but a variable rate starting at 3%. Then you must identify how much can the rate fluctuate and what would cause the interest rates to go up. There is always the chance that the rate will go down, but that is never an event that you should depend on. If that happens U.S.E. the extra cash wisely.

Remember the FED decided the Federal Funds rate, so if it rises, so will the rate on your loan, but there are many other factors that can impact interest rates.

If the payment on variable debt is pushing your cash management to the limit and an increase in payments would cause you to break the Golden Rule, then you should look at the security of a fixed loan.

If the payment on any debt is pushing your cash management limits, you should question if this debt is the right decision for your plan. Debt is not inherently bad, but how people use it can be.

WILL THIS SCHEDULE INCLUDE THE FEES ASSOCIATED WITH TAKING OUT THE LOAN?

Yes, there are additional fees that can come with taking out a loan. There can be taxes that are unknown to you, insurance policies that you did not know you needed, penalties for paying the loan back early, and extended vehicle warranties. These additions can be automatically included in your loan cost!

It is not guaranteed that your lender will include transaction fees in this amortization schedule breakdown. Make sure to ask your lender if there are fees or additions included in the Amortization Schedule. If your numbers seem off from the conversation you have been having and the calculations you have been making, that is probably because there have been additional fees included.

The Truth in Lending Act allows you to inquire about what they are and see which can be lowered, or even removed.

WAIT A MINUTE! I CAN GET A PENALTY IF I PAY BACK MY LOAN TOO SOON!?

When a lender allows you to use their money, they are doing so with the amortization table in mind, expecting that over the next number of months they should expect your payment as income. When you begin to alter this schedule, they are not so thrilled because you are altering their income.

This is a **PREPAYMENT PENALTY** from a lender. When you start the loan, the lender expects to get paid interest for the term of the contract. If you decide to reduce the term by paying the loan back early, the lender will lose interest. To prevent the notion of losing money, lenders can put a 'Prepayment Penalty' in your loan contract. This penalty states that if you are to pay off the loan or a significant amount of the loan before the term of the contract is up, you will be charged a penalty. This fee is to recover the interest that the lender will miss out on.

 MONEY VEHICLE TIP:

Make sure to ask your lender if there are any prepayment penalties or fees.

SECTION 2.4
RECAP

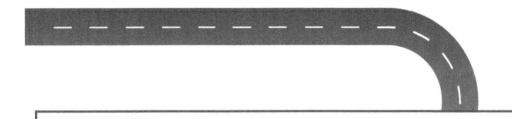

1. DEBT IS A TOOL THAT YOU CAN U.S.E. WITHIN YOUR PLAN.

2. THE AMORTIZATION TABLE BREAKS DOWN YOUR LOAN INTO INSTALLMENTS THAT YOU PAY REGULARLY.

3. THE TOTAL COST OF SOMETHING YOU BOUGHT WITH A LOAN WILL BE THE PRICE PLUS THE INTEREST YOU PAID.

REVIEW

THE RULE: EMPLOY YOUR MONEY

What does it take to borrow money? More money called interest! Every lender–borrower relationship begins with someone looking to make more money. Knowing the value of money is the first step in understanding how the wealthy create money using the "eighth wonder of the world," compound interest. Identifying how long you see money and which type of 'OR you are —spend-OR, sav-OR, or investor-OR—will show you if you are U.S.E.ing compound interest. Debt is a tool and understanding how it works will allow you to identify when or if you can U.S.E. debt in your plan. Acting like an Invest-OR means you are putting money to work for you and U.S.E.ing the most important factor in the TVM formula – time!

ACTION

Start thinking and acting like an invest-OR, by employing a percentage of your paycheck to start working for future you!

- Identify where you are a borrower and understand the amortization of the loan.
- Classify an amount of money you want to begin creating money with – Pay Yourself First.
- Act like an Invest-OR = Stop just working for money, Start making money work for you!

OWNER'S MANUAL
FOR YOUR MONEY VEHICLE:

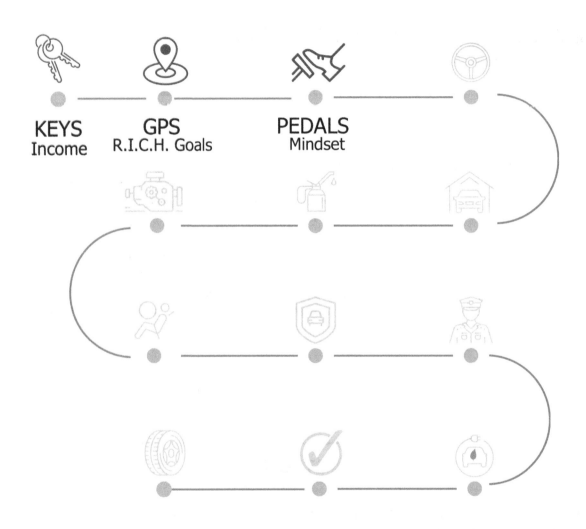

KEYS
Income

GPS
R.I.C.H. Goals

PEDALS
Mindset

CHAPTER 3

WHAT CAN I DO TO CONTROL MY MONEY?

OVERVIEW

3.1: The Costs of Not Choosing

3.2: Create Habits, Achieve Success

3.3: Money Buckets: 5 Choices with your Paycheck

ACTION

Establish and set up your Money Bucket cash management system.

DRIVING YOUR MONEY VEHICLE

Knowing how to slow down and stop is vital, but now you see where you want to go on your GPS and wonder how you're going to get there. This is where the steering wheel comes into play in directing the journey. Turning the steering wheel right and left is just like making choices with your money. Making choices that steer you toward your R.I.CH. goal help develop the foundation of your financial plan.

SECTION 3.1
THE COSTS OF NOT CHOOSING

TERMS

OPPORTUNITY COST: the positive alternatives you gave up with your decision.

MARGINAL COST: the additional cost of producing, buying, or consuming one more unit.

MARGINAL BENEFIT: the additional benefit of producing, buying, consuming one more unit.

CONSUMER FINANCIAL PROTECTION BUREAU: agency of the U.S. government responsible for consumer protection in the financial sector.

"What major are you going to choose?" Every senior in high school is asked the same question and immediately feels the implications of this life-altering decision. Let's say it's you, and you're beginning to measure the following options:

OPPORTUNITY A

History: You have always loved learning about civilizations and how humans have evolved over time. Writing papers in school has been easy for you, and the reading assignments feel more like rewards than homework.

Pre-Med: This will be a challenging major, but you have always liked helping people. Not to mention that your mother is a doctor and having you follow in her footsteps would make her proud.

OPPORTUNITY B

OPPORTUNITY C

Management Information Systems: Information systems and computers will be a big part of whatever the future holds. While this is not your favorite subject, you see the positive impact it could have on your career.

This internal debate is a perfect example of not just weighing the opportunities before you, but also the costs associated with each decision. This thought experiment is an introduction to **OPPORTUNITY COST**. Opportunity Cost calculates the loss of whatever positives the opportunities you did not choose could have brought you.

In other words, ask yourself the reason why you would choose something, and that reason is the opportunity cost if you do not choose it. Here are some examples:

When you choose a salad over a burger, the opportunity cost of that choice is the deliciousness of the burger.

When you choose to go out instead of studying, the opportunity cost of that choice is getting a better grade on the test.

When you choose to lease (rent) a car instead of buy it, the opportunity cost of that choice is ownership of the vehicle.

Back to choosing a college major, choosing one major inherently means you do not choose the other two. The positives that could come from the two that you do not choose are the opportunity costs.

History: Pursue an interest of yours and place what you want as the priority.

To be a historian you give up following in your mother's footsteps and a future career in technology.

Pre-Med: Pursue a passion for helping others and make your mother proud when you become an MD.

To be a doctor you give up what you are passionate about and a future career in technology.

Management Information Systems: Pursue employment with the understanding that it will be essential in future careers.

To be in technology you give up what you are passionate about and following in your mother's footsteps.

How do you weigh the impact the choice has on your present, as well as your future? Take comfort in knowing there is no right or wrong answer. There is only a measurement of your choice and the cost associated with it. No one can tell you which is the correct path for you to walk. You must lay out the opportunities along with their costs and choose your own way.

The next time you have a choice to make, ask yourself: What is the cost of not choosing that opportunity?

LET'S LOOK AT HOW ADRIAN IS WEIGHING THE OPPORTUNITIES HE HAS AS A STUDENT:

GETTING A PART TIME JOB

If Adrian chooses to take on a part-time job while still in school, he will have the opportunity to build his resume and earn some cash. The opportunity cost of working is the lost opportunity to devote that time and energy to academics, sports, band, debate, or just hanging with friends.

GOING OUT WITH FRIENDS

If Adrian chooses to spend Thursday night out with friends, he has the opportunity to enjoy quality time and not miss out when crazy Larry does something crazy. The opportunity cost of socializing is the lost opportunity to study for the Friday exam or be rested for the Friday performance.

MAJORING IN FILM

If Adrian chooses to study film next year while at college, he has the opportunity to enjoy pursuing a passion. Perhaps even achieve his dream of making his own film one day. The opportunity cost of this major though is that there is not as high paying of a financial opportunity. Adrian would be choosing his passion for Film over a more potentially more profitable major.

WHAT IF THE QUESTION IS NOT EITHER OR BUT MORE OF A SHOULD I GET MORE?

This takes us into an economic term of 'Margin', which is the measurement of what producing one more unit will provide you or what one more unit will cost you. When you begin to make decisions and weigh your opportunity costs, you will want to understand what the marginal cost or marginal benefit of one more is.

- **MARGINAL COST:** the additional cost of producing, buying, or consuming one more unit.
- **MARGINAL BENEFIT:** the additional benefit of producing, buying, consuming one more unit.

When you make a decision you must make a choice between two things, you will weigh the opportunity cost, but when choosing between one or more of something, you will weigh the marginal impact of the next unit.

Economic Example: A chair factory is deciding between making 10 or 15 of their new models. To set up and produce 10 chairs, it costs the factory $1,000 or $100 per chair and they can sell the chairs for $250. To produce one more chair the marginal cost would be $100 and the opportunity cost if they decide not to produce it would be the possible $250 sale.

Life Example: Adrian's friends are going to play soccer at the park, but he knows he has a big Algebra exam tomorrow as well. Adrian has put in an hour of studying and is debating the benefit of another hour. He believes if he studies another hour, he could increase his grade from a C+ to a B-. The Marginal Benefit of an hour of studying would be changing that C to a B, but the opportunity cost of this decision is playing soccer at the park.

Tax Example: Preview Chapter 9 '**MARGINAL TAX BRACKET**' is the tax bracket your next dollar would fall into, or if you made $1 more what it would be taxed at.

This measurement of margins will be used as you encounter marketing tools daily. Weighing the costs and benefits of your purchases. Every time you decide to 'upgrade' or see a '50% off' sign, you know you are weighing the marginal cost or benefit of that decision as well.

Consumer Example: Buy a medium drink for $5.00 or a large drink for $7.00. The marginal cost is $2.00, and you must choose if the marginal benefit of the extra drink is worth it.

Business Example: When a company offers you a 'Buy 1 get 1 Free' deal, you may believe you are getting the better end of the deal. But what if the marginal cost of making one more unit was $1, and the profit the company makes if you buy one unit is $2. In this scenario, the company is better off 'giving' you the second unit at no charge if it entices you to purchase the first unit then they will still make money ($2 profit - $1 marginal cost).

WHO HELPS PROTECT ME IN THESE DECISIONS AND HELPS WEIGH THE OPPORTUNITY COSTS?

The **CONSUMER FINANCIAL PROTECTION BUREAU (CFPB)** is a part of the Federal Reserve. While it is not directly connected to the United States government, it does act as an agent of the government and is responsible for overseeing consumer protection in the financial sector.

SECTION 3.1
RECAP

The CFPB is responsible for overseeing banks, credit unions, securities firms, payday lenders, mortgage services, foreclosure relief, debt collectors, and other financial companies. One of their missions is to better understand how companies use social media to target and market to influence its customers.

Opportunity Cost is the value of the things you did not choose. It is the understanding that when you make a choice, something else is given up. Opportunity Costs occur in daily life decisions, at school, at work, at a store, at a friend's house, or even at a larger economic level. Be conscious of your choices and the costs that come with them.

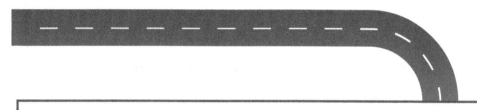

1. THERE IS A MARGINAL COST OR MARGINAL BENEFIT TO EVERY DECISION YOU MAKE.

2. OPPORTUNITY COSTS ARE THE POSITIVE ALTERNATIVES THAT YOU GAVE UP WITH YOUR DECISION.

3. BE CONSCIOUS OF THE CHOICES YOU MAKE AND WEIGH THE OPPORTUNITIES THAT YOU GIVE UP.

SECTION 3.2
CREATE HABITS, ACHIEVE SUCCESS

TERMS

CUE: the trigger— the thing that tells your body and mind to start.

ROUTINE: the action— the process that your body will begin to automatically do.

REWARD: the payoff— the reason you are building a habit.

U.S.E. MONEY: Money Vehicle wants you to - Understand your money, Strategize your money, & be Efficient with your money - U.S.E. Money!

What do you do when someone waves to you?

What do you do when you hear The Pledge of Allegiance?

What do you do when it's time to get ready for school or work?

When you are just simply responding, you have developed a habit. A habit is something you do so regularly that you don't even think about it. Even though they can be unconscious, habits can begin to define who we are.

 Watch your thoughts, for they become words. Watch your words, for they become actions. Watch your actions, for they become habits. Watch your habits, for they become your character. Watch your character, for it becomes your destiny! What we think, we become.
—Margaret Thatcher

Habits were initially formed out of a need for survival, when human brains began to fight for two things: energy conservation and safety.

Energy conservation: When you brush your teeth, you don't have to make the effort to tell your brain exactly how to brush; you already know how to do it.

Safety: When there is danger, your brain does not think but rather responds with the habit of fight or flight. Is this a natural reaction? Sure, one that has been created through the cue-routine-reward cycle of survival.

To Money Vehicle, forming a habit is learning a better way to do something by repeating what works. There is an expression 'success leaves breadcrumbs'. What it means is that people who have continued to find success can show you the way to get there by repeating what they did. But success is not a one-time event, it is a series of repetitive events. Building habits creates those events and it is as if you are sending a message to your future self about how to find success.

Cue
The trigger
The thing that tells your body and mind to start.

Routine
The action
The process that your body will begin to automatically.

Reward
The payoff
The reason you are building a habit.

 MONEY VEHICLE TIP:

Financial success is about being consistent more than clever, the best way to be consistent with your money actions is to build habits.

LET'S LOOK AT SOME COMMON HABITS YOU HAVE THAT YOU MAY NOT EVEN BE AWARE OF:

Brushing your teeth:
1. **Cue:** The trigger—Time for bed.
2. **Routine:** The action—Brushing your teeth.
3. **Reward:** The payoff—Tingling clean feeling in your mouth, and your dentist backing off.

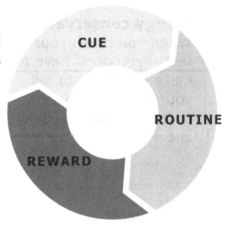

Oncoming danger:
1. **Cue:** The trigger—Feeling of danger.
2. **Routine:** The action—Run faster than you ever have.
3. **Reward:** The payoff—You're safe.

Received a paycheck:
1. **Cue:** The trigger— You just got paid.
2. **Routine:** The action—How do I spend these dollars.
3. **Reward:** The payoff— You got something new.

With a better understanding of why habits were created and how they work, we can begin to use this to create good money habits.

HOW DO I CREATE A NEW MONEY HABIT?

1. First, recognize a cue you have, or identify a new reward that you want.

Let's look at the teeth brushing example for a minute. When toothpaste companies wanted to sell more of their product, they began research on habits. Identifying that if people got a reward in the habit, they would do the routine (brush their teeth), more. Do people brush their teeth because the dentist said so? No! They do it for the rewarding feeling after they are done.

Review your Money Values and R.I.C.H. Goals, these will be your rewards you build habits to achieve.
Review your Money Values and R.I.C.H. Goals, these will be your rewards you build habits to achieve.

HOW CAN I U.S.E. THIS?

2.

Next, ask yourself, "Where is the cue that begins the spending habit?"

If you identify the cues—when you receive a paycheck, when you are at the mall, or when you are just bored online—then you can begin to create new habits. Becoming more conscious of what is starting your habit will allow you to begin to control it. If you are conscious of that store or when that time of day is when you do things you want to change, then you can begin to avoid that trigger.

All the time, people say, "I don't know where all my money goes!"

But they are missing the cue: the moment they receive a paycheck or money. This cue kicks off a money habit that you may or may not be conscious of yet but is the place we will begin to create your first money habit.

The next time you receive money, instead of asking, "How can I spend this?" notice your cue and create a new routine, saying "**How can I U.S.E. this?**" instead. Not a big change, but you will have a new answer to that question, and soon, a new reward.

HOW DO I CHANGE A BAD MONEY HABIT?

It's hard to get rid of old habits, but you can change them. Now that you know the three components of your bad money habit (cue, routine, reward), you can change your habits by following these laws of behavior change.

The four laws of changing a behavior according to James Clear's "Atomic Habits" are: [13]

1. Easy: Start small and remove as many steps as possible.
   a. I went to the gym for just 15 minutes a day to start.
   b. I automatically send $20 every paycheck to my Savings Account.
2. **Obvious:** Make it easier to remember.
   a. Want to brush my teeth before the gym, so I put my car keys near my toothbrush.
   b. On the 8th of each month, I review my subscriptions.
3. **Attractive:** Add in fun things with your habits.
   a. At the gym I listen to a podcast.
   b. Each time I review my Burn Rate I put on music.
4. **Satisfying**: Reward yourself after you finish or have a punishment for a bad habit.
   a. Every time I go to the gym, I get to watch an episode of my favorite show.
   b. Every month I fill my Money Buckets, I get to 'Treat Yo-self' for one purchase.

> What is immediately rewarded is repeated, what is immediately punished is avoided
>
> -James Clear

Using these laws, you can begin to see how you can change the cue, routine, or reward to change your habit and behavior.

EXAMPLE: YOU WANT TO STOP BUYING A COFFEE AFTER CLASS WITH YOUR FRIENDS.

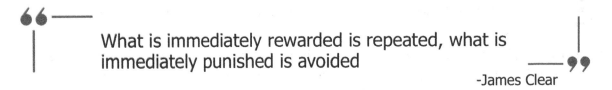

Cue ⇒ school is done and you want to keep hanging out

Routine ⇒ going into a coffee shop and getting a latte

Reward ⇒ hanging out with friends

NOW, HOW CAN YOU CHANGE THE ROUTINE TO MAKE IT MORE VALUABLE?

Your goal is to stop spending money at the coffee shop as you save up for a vacation. Instead of going to a coffee shop, you could go for a walk or hang out at the park or community space. You would maintain the same cue and reward, but you would have changed the routine in your habit by making it more valuable not to go and spend money.

WANT TO INCREASE YOUR CHANCES OF KEEPING A NEW HABIT?

Start by finding support. Whenever people make a change in a group or community, they are more likely to stick with that change. This is why we asked you to find an accountability partner at the beginning of the program. Have you ever heard the saying "Together Everyone Achieves More"? This is an acronym for TEAM and is the reason some average people can accomplish GREAT things. Because they had support to consistently keep doing the things they knew would bring success.

Another way to increase your chances of keeping a new habit is adopting the mindset James Clear shares in Atomic Habits of 'Don't Miss Twice'. This is an athletic mindset that means if you have a bad play, move on, and do not let one bad play turn into two bad plays.

As you try to change your behaviors you will realize it is a daily measurement of opportunity and daily choice. You will not win every day, but do not beat yourself up. Identify and callout the behavior you want to change and simply do not let it happen the next time, 'don't miss twice'.

TOGETHER
EVERYONE
ACHIEVES
MORE

The next time you are facing a decision and beginning to weigh the opportunity costs around your money, take the following four steps.

01

Identify

what is your habit—cue, routine, reward?

02

Change

replace your routine question of spend with "How can I U.S.E. each option?"

03

Measure

the opportunity costs of your decision, which align with your values and goals?

04

Evaluate

Take a day and decide if you want to spend the money now, or put it toward your RICH goal?

REPLACE "HOW CAN I SPEND MONEY?" WITH "HOW CAN I U.S.E. MONEY?"

SECTION 3.2
RECAP

1. A HABIT BROKEN DOWN: CUE + ROUTINE + REWARD.

2. THE ONLY WAY TO REPEATEDLY FIND SUCCESS AND ACHIEVE YOUR R.I.C.H. GOALS IS THROUGH BUILDING HABITS.

3. MAKE YOUR HABITS: EASY, OBVIOUS, ATTRACTIVE, AND SATISFYING.

SECTION 3.3
MONEY BUCKETS: 5 CHOICES WITH YOUR PAYCHECK

TERMS

BUDGET: an estimate of income and expenses for a specific period of time. This term has had a limiting mindset attached to it and that is why Money Vehicle does not use it.

CASH MANAGEMENT: a management of income and expenses before money even arrives. This term is more empowering to a growth mindset.

FIXED MINDSET: with a Fixed mindset, you believe that your talents and abilities cannot change, and you focus on what you already know you can do.

GROWTH MINDSET: with a Growth mindset you believe that with effort and perseverance, you can develop new abilities to take on new challenges.

SAVE: protecting your money from risk.

INVEST: putting your money at risk.

BURN RATE: your monthly lifestyle needs, combining your past and present choices.

Every month, it happens: you get to the thirtieth and are out of money. You didn't meet your savings goal this month and are confused as to where all the money went!

Sure, you took the first steps in writing down your goal and have begun asking, "How do I U.S.E. this?" but now we must develop a plan. The plan begins with understanding how you are choosing to spend your money and placing each choice into a bucket.

Identifying which bucket you want to fill up will allow you to U.S.E. your money throughout the month and not just spend blindly until it runs out.

Before we dive into the Money Bucket system, let's talk about why Money Vehicle does NOT use the 'B' word (BUDGET) and instead frame this process as **CASH MANAGEMENT.**

Carol Dweck is a well-known researcher on mindsets and has concluded that there are really two types of mindsets: fixed and growth. With a **FIXED MINDSET**, you believe that your talents and abilities cannot change, and you focus on what you already know you can do. With a **GROWTH MINDSET** you believe that with effort and perseverance, you can develop new abilities to take on new challenges.

The 'B' word often places you into a fixed mindset where you feel confined to what you know about budgets and that this thing will be in control of you. When we change this concept and practice to cash management it produces a mindset shift into the growth side. Now you see this new world of income and expenses as something you can continue to develop and eventually be in control of, as opposed to it controlling you.

With this mindset shift, let's introduce the Money Vehicle cash management system – Money Buckets. These buckets represent the 5 choices you will make with every paycheck you receive. But by developing this system, you will have weighed the opportunity costs of your decisions and begun to build habits of putting your money to work before it even hits your account.

The Five Money Buckets will decide—where every dollar you make goes.

1. SOCIETY CHOICE
2. PAST CHOICE
3. PRESENT CHOICE
4. FUTURE CHOICE
5. COMPASSION CHOICE

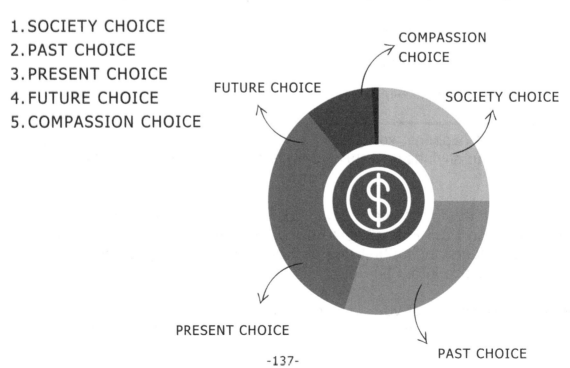

 **SOCIETY CHOICE** Dollars investing into the society we choose to belong to, known as Taxes. These dollars support everything not owned by individuals. Ex. Schools, hospitals, military, and roads.

The first reality that hits when you begin getting paid is that taxes are real. Taxes are the cost of protecting and caring for everything between what you own and what everyone else owns.

You may be asking if this is a choice or a law. Well, yes, it is a law, but you choose to belong to this society and the choices you make in your plan decide how much you will pay.

For a Chapter 9 preview, which deduction you choose will impact your Society Choice.

Money Vehicle is changing the naming of taxes to 'Society' to try and change the negativity people have towards taxes. Taxes may not be a fun choice but think about all the things that taxes provide—emergency response from fire and police departments; repair of the roads that you drive on; funding of public schools; health coverage; retirement income for the elderly; and military protection for all of us. Or how about the public pool you and your friends use or the national park you want to visit?

This mindset shift from what taxes take to what they provide in our society will allow you to make this choice in your system and challenge the notion of taxes being 'worth it'.

EXAMPLES OF SOCIETY CHOICES:
- Sales Tax
- Income Tax

 **PAST CHOICE** Dollars that have already been spent before the month even begins. Example: debts, bills, and rent.

Anything due before the month even begins, you know there are payments that you already owe such as rent, bills, and debt, these payments can be referred to as a 'Fixed Expense'.

But as you categorize these choices into your Money Buckets begin to see them as decisions you have made in the past and place them in your Past Choices bucket. Regardless of what you do throughout the month, these Past Choices will remain constant

EXAMPLES OF PAST CHOICES OR FIXED EXPENSES:

- Where you live—No matter if you rent or buy, the cost associated with where you chose to live will be due this month.
- Bills—The signed contracts for services like electricity, phone, or insurance that have a monthly payment associated to them.
- Debt – The signed contracts for loans you have taken out and have a monthly interest payment associated with them. Credit Card payments would land here because you take a loan out to use them – Preview Chapter 5.

 **PRESENT CHOICE** Dollars being spent today on your wants and needs. Examples would be buying gas, groceries, or games.

Every day, you are faced with hundreds of choices, many of them revolving around how you are going to use your money today.

These choices that you make and can change throughout the month are called 'Variable Expenses' but as you categorize them into your Money Buckets place them into the Present Choice bucket.

These Present Choices will rise and fall depending on what you do throughout the month. For now, the goal is to simply recognize when you are making these choices and start to consider if this choice is a want or a need.

- **Need:** something you feel you cannot make it through the day without – food or clothes
- **Want:** something you feel will improve the quality of your day – smoothie or jewelry

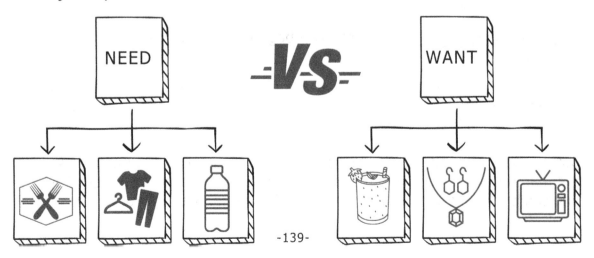

As your financial literacy grows, so will your attention to the impact of these decisions, but for the moment we just want you to begin practicing Mindful Money. This is where you begin to have a mental log to track what you are spending your money on. Being mindful does not mean you are always thinking about money or that you know your list down to the dime. Mindful just means that you are aware of the decisions you are making.

Developing this list will give you more clarity as to what is a want or a need for your life. Our decisions are personal and what is a need for you may not be for your neighbor or your friend. For now, start to see the decisions you are making and be mindful of which list the choice would fall under – want or need, perhaps begin with:

- Do you bring your lunch, or go out?
- Do you go to the movies on the weekend, or stream one at home?
- Do you buy new jeans or wear your old ones?

EXAMPLES OF PRESENT CHOICES:

- The breakfast you ate.
- The gas in your car or the bus ticket to get downtown.
- The movie or band you went to see.
- The book or new pair of jeans you bought.

HOW DO WE FIND OUR LIFESTYLE SPEND OF 'BURN RATE' USING THE MONEY BUCKET SYSTEM?

Utilizing the Money Bucket system will show you what the amount of money you need to live each month. This measurement is your monthly Burn Rate. Your Burn Rate will be your Past and Present choices added together.

BURN RATE=YOUR MONTHLY LIFESTYLE CALCULATED BY ADDING UP YOUR PAST AND PRESENT CHOICES

We only count the Past and Present buckets for your monthly burn because they are requirements for you to get through the month. If something were to happen, you could stop the payments into the other buckets for a short period of time. Your burn rate represents the wood being thrown onto the fire in the Golden Rule analogy.

For example, if you lose your job then you will not continue to pay Society Choice on Income, you could pause your Future Choice, and you could delay your Compassion Choice.

 **FUTURE #4 CHOICE** Dollars going towards the future you are creating. Examples: saving and investing.

Far too often, we get to the end of the month and then suddenly try to hit our goal of saving or investing. We end up looking at the choices we made throughout the month and wish we could get some back. What if you could hit your goal first! Start out each month knowing you will put money away first and then go make your monthly decisions. This would be when you stop playing checkers with your money and start playing chess!

Why we began with R.I.C.H. Goals is because that is the future you want to become. Those destinations you set on your journey are meant to make money personal to you. Yes, you need to celebrate when you reach a landmark and take pride in setting the next destination.

Remember the Future – if you do not care about future you, who does?

When you look at starting in your Future Choice there are two ways to begin filling the bucket:

SAVING: PROTECTING MONEY FROM RISK OR ### INVESTING: PUTTING MONEY AT RISK

 MONEY VEHICLE TIP:
Measure the opportunity cost (3.1) of which bucket you are choosing to fill; your choices depend on this measurement.

WHERE SHOULD I START MY FUTURE CHOICE?

You must begin your Future Choice Bucket with a cushion of savings before you can invest. This cushion becomes the 'Spare Tire' on your Money Vehicle and is going to protect your plan from those unexpected potholes in the road. We will discuss more in Chapter 4. For now, see the difference in saving and investing and understand that your plan needs protection from risk before it can take on more risk.

EXAMPLES OF FUTURE CHOICES:

- The $20 you saved so you can go get the $100 shoes.
- The $100 you invested to go to work for you.

COMPASSION CHOICE

Dollars going to people, place, or purpose outside of yourself. Example: giving back to charity, church, or family.

Recently, science has made incredible discoveries regarding the emotional connection to helping others.

When you spend money on yourself, you no doubt receive enjoyment for a moment, but research is showing that when you spend money on others, you create social connections that will lead to feeling greater happiness throughout your life.

This is why the Compassion Choice is also known as the Happy Bucket.

Today, you may not have the means to fill this bucket with your treasure (money), instead, you can fill your Compassion Choice by giving your time or talent. Just find something you are passionate about and get involved.

START WITH A SIMPLE THOUGHT EXPERIMENT:

- Who has helped you get where you are today?
- What place have you gone to for support?
- Where do you see a cause bigger than yourself you would want to impact?

Answering these questions will lead you to identifying your Compassion Choice. Do not worry, we are not going to ask you to give all of your time or treasure, but we do ask for your to start the habit of practicing compassion. That way when you do have the resources, the habit will already be there.

EXAMPLES OF COMPASSION CHOICES:

- The birthday present for your sister.
- The Saturday you went to serve at the local food bank.
- The $100 donation to those in need.

MONEY VEHICLE TIP:

Measure the opportunity cost of which bucket you are choosing to fill. Make sure they reflect you values and prioritize the R.I.C.H. Goals you set for yourself.

HIGH-LEVEL MONEY BUCKET STRATEGY

25%	SOCIETY
30%	PAST
34%	PRESENT
10%	FUTURE
1%	COMPASSION

EXAMPLE: $50,000 INCOME

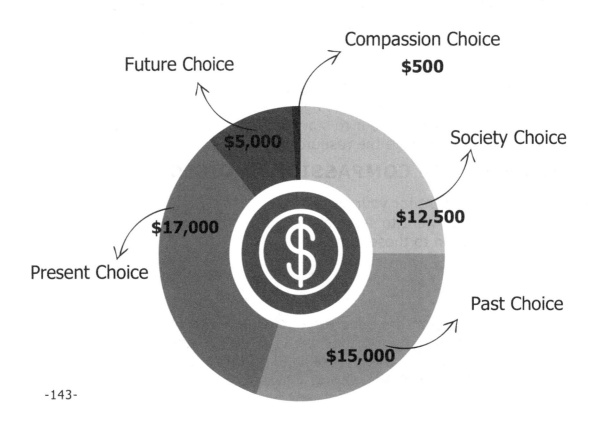

Compassion Choice $500

Future Choice $5,000

Society Choice $12,500

Present Choice $17,000

Past Choice $15,000

EXAMPLE: $2,000 PAYCHECK

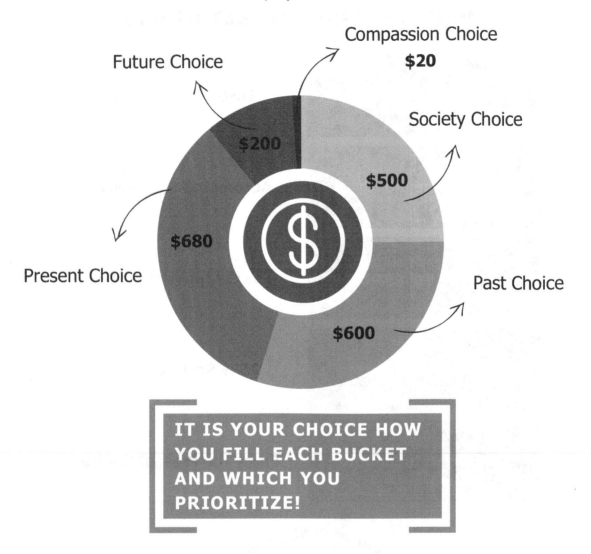

Compassion Choice
$20

Future Choice

Society Choice

$200

$500

Present Choice

$680

Past Choice

$600

IT IS YOUR CHOICE HOW YOU FILL EACH BUCKET AND WHICH YOU PRIORITIZE!

HOW DO I U.S.E. THE MONEY BUCKET SYSTEM?

Now that you can categorize how your money is going into these Money Buckets, you can begin to be proactive about how you will handle your paychecks by building habits. Let's identify 5 monthly habits that align to the 5 Money Buckets.

MONTHLY MONEY BUCKET HABITS

1st of the month	10% Future Choice
8th of the month	Automate Past Choices
14th of the month	1% Compassion Choice
25th of the month	25% Society Choice
Last day of the month	Enjoy the Present Choice

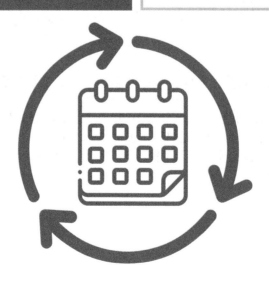

SECTION 3.3
RECAP

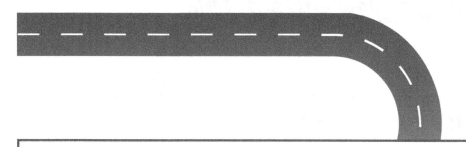

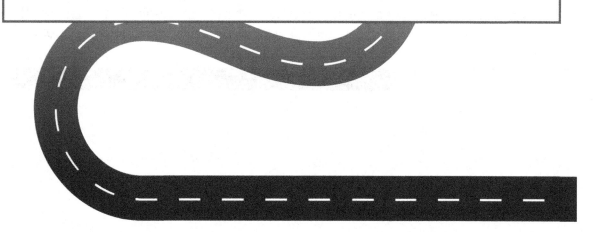

1. YOUR MONEY BUCKET CHOICES:
SOCIETY (TAXES), PAST (DEBTS/BILLS), PRESENT
(WANTS/NEEDS), FUTURE (SAVING/INVESTING),
COMPASSION (FAMILY/IMPACT).

2. BURN RATE IS YOUR PAST & PRESENT CHOICE
COMBINED EACH MONTH TO LIVE ON.

3. PRIORITIZE: FUTURE WITH PAY YOURSELF FIRST
AND COMPASSION WITH YOUR HAPPY BUCKET.

REVIEW

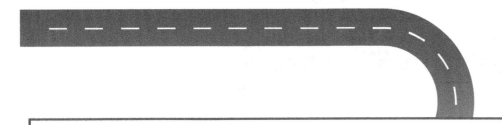

THE RULE: MONEY IS A HABIT

Seeing money as a verb, not a noun, will give you the perspective that money is a vehicle—a vehicle that will get you to your destination and stop being your destination. Seeing money as a verb allows you to focus on the opportunity cost of each choice you make. These practices will become your habits—measure the cost and ask, "How can I U.S.E.?" Developing good money habits will allow you to prioritize which bucket you will be filling first and how you fill each one. No longer will you come to the end of the month with questions; now, you will have a plan that leads to your freedom!

ACTION

Set up your Money Bucket cash management system, beginning each month by paying yourself first and calculating your Burn Rate throughout the month.

OWNER'S MANUAL
FOR YOUR MONEY VEHICLE:

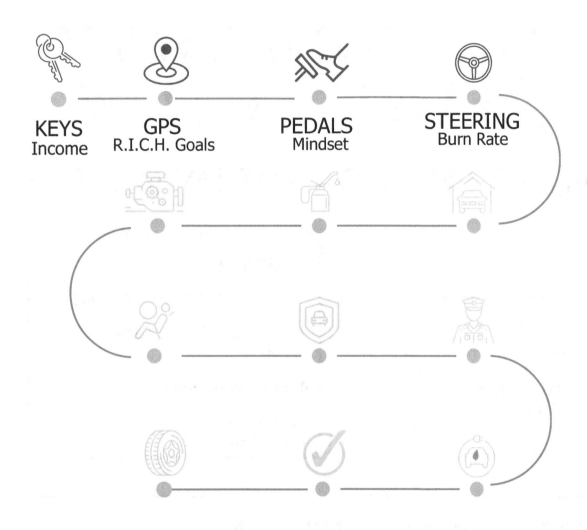

KEYS
Income

GPS
R.I.C.H. Goals

PEDALS
Mindset

STEERING
Burn Rate

CHAPTER 4

WHERE SHOULD I PUT MY MONEY?

ACTION

Setup the foundational accounts for your Money Bucket system, automate your Past Choices and establish a Corona Cushion.

OVERVIEW

4.1: The Business of Banking

4.2: "Today" and "Tomorrow" Accounts

4.3: Banking Rules

4.4: Balancing and Reading Your Statements

DRIVING YOUR MONEY VEHICLE

Where is the safest place to park your car? In the garage. The garage will provide safety, easy access, and even some rewards, like not having to scrape off snow or ice. The safest place to park your Money Vehicle is in a bank; it can provide many of the same benefits.

SECTION 4.1
THE BUSINESS OF BANKING

FEDERAL DEPOSIT INSURANCE CORPORATION (FDIC): created by the Banking Act of 1933, this is a United States government corporation providing insurance on deposits to American commercial banks.

NATIONAL CREDIT UNION ADMINISTRATION (NCUA): the counterpart of the FDIC for credit unions, it is an independent agency of the Federal Government to regulate and insure credit unions deposits.

LIQUIDITY: the ability to access your money in cash either in person or electronically whenever needed.

LENDER: a person who receives interest for giving someone else the privilege of using their money.

RESERVE RATIO: the minimum amount the central bank requires that each commercial bank keeps in liquid assets, or cash.

FRACTIONAL RESERVE BANKING: the practice that allows the bank to U.S.E. any remaining dollars above the reserve ratio requirement at their own discretion.

FOR-PROFIT: business organization whose goal is to produce a profit.

NOT-FOR-PROFIT: business organization whose goal is to benefit a social need.

BANK: a for-profit financial institution that will accept deposits from the public.

SHAREHOLDER: an owner of shares in a company, for example a bank.

CREDIT UNION: a not-for-profit financial institution that will accept deposits from the public.

WHERE SHOULD I PUT MY MONEY?

This is the first question everyone asks once they begin to have more than enough money for a weekend's worth of fun. When you really start to understand that you need a cash management system, you quickly discover the need for foundational tools to direct those choices.

Getting started, you really have two choices: under the mattress or in a bank. We can all agree that the days of stashing money under mattresses or in a hole in the backyard are over.

WHERE SHOULD I PUT MY MONEY?

1. With a financial institution, there is no longer a concern surrounding the location and tracking of each of your dollars. The financial institution has the capability of showing you exactly where every dollar goes and even providing some tools to control your spending.

2. The financial institution will provide your money with a layer of security that cannot be found under your mattress. In fact, the **FEDERAL DEPOSIT INSURANCE CORPORATION (FDIC)** will insure up to $250,000 per person in each of your bank accounts if they qualify. With credit unions, which we will discuss in a moment, the **NATIONAL CREDIT UNION ADMINSTRATION** will insure up to $250,000 per person, per credit union. Accounts such as Checking, Savings, Certificate of Deposits, and Money Market Accounts will be insured, while any account that has investment risk will not be insured, it is always best to ask.

What isn't covered by the FDIC is anything with an investment component. The insurance on your money means that if something were to happen to it— let's say the bank was hacked and your money was stolen—up to $250,000 of your account total would be covered by the FDIC. If, however, your money is in an account where you have put it at risk—such as placing the funds into bonds or stocks—the FDIC will not cover it. It should also be pointed out that online third-party platforms such as Venmo or PayPal do not receive this protection.

3. You would think that handing your money over to someone at a bank would make it less accessible, but part of a bank's value is that the money you deposited is readily accessible. This easy access is called **LIQUIDITY.**

> **LIQUIDITY IS THE ABILITY TO ACCESS YOUR MONEY IN PERSON OR ELECTRONICALLY WHENEVER NEEDED; THIS CAN BE DONE AT YOUR LOCAL BANK OR AT AN ATM.**

4. If you are not yet sold on opening an account, the next advantage may just convince you—the financial institution ends up paying you money! Remember, the **LENDER** (Ch.2) receives interest for giving someone the privilege of using their money. When you give your money to a financial institution, you become a lender, and the bank becomes a borrower of your money. This relationship means that the financial institution must pay you interest for the privilege of holding your money at their branch. While it may not be a lot of money, the more money you place in a savings account, the more the bank will end up paying you on your savings. To create more money, you will need to take on more risk, and we will discuss that in Chapter 6.

WHY WOULD THE FINANCIAL INSTITUTION PAY YOU TO HOLD YOUR MONEY?

When a financial institution offers you a small, guaranteed interest rate to take possession of your money, it is because they are acting like invest-OR's and believe they can find a higher return on your dollars elsewhere. More specifically, it means the bank is willing to take on more risk to get a higher return. In this case, you take on low risk when you deposit your money, and you get a low return from the bank (more on this when we discuss the fundamentals of investing).

For example, in your bank account, you might receive a guaranteed 1% interest rate. This interest rate says the bank believes it can go out into the financial market and find someone or something to pay an interest rate higher than that 1%. So, when you go to the bank and deposit your money, the bank pays you 1% and then goes to lend it or invest it in something else to earn a higher percentage than they paid you.

WAIT A MINUTE! THE FINANCIAL INSTITUTION CAN'T GIVE MY MONEY TO SOMEONE ELSE, CAN THEY?

Technically, financial institutions are only required to keep a certain amount of your money or physical cash on hand at their location, which is called the **RESERVE RATIO**. This reserve ratio is set by the FED to protect against customers making withdrawals and the institution running out of cash to give out.

This was more of a necessity when we used physical money, but let's use an example where the reserve ratio is 10%. If a bank has $1,000,000 in total deposits, it is only required to have reserve cash on hand of $100,000 for daily withdrawals.

Knowing the financial institution is only required to keep a certain percentage of the cash in 'reserve' you are introduced to the term **FRACTIONAL RESERVE BANKING.** This system allows financial institutions to U.S.E. the deposits beyond the reserve ration as they see fit.

> **INFLATION FACT:**
> Another resource the FED has to control inflation is found in Regulation D where it can raise and lower the reserve ration. When the ratio is higher, less money can be loaned out and it will reduce inflation. Opposite of that is making the ratio low, lending out more money and increasing inflation.

WHAT HAPPENS WHEN I DEPOSIT MY MONEY AT A FINANCIAL INSTITUTION?

A deposit cycle at a bank refers to the process of depositing funds into a bank account. The cycle typically involves several stages, including:

1.	Deposit	The customer deposits money into their account, either in person or through an electronic transfer.
2.	Processing	The institution receives the deposit and processes it, checking for accuracy and authenticity.
3.	Verification	The institution verifies the deposit by confirming that the funds are available and that the account number and other information is correct.
4.	Posting	The deposit is posted to the customer's account, increasing the customer's available balance.
5.	Hold	Depending on the institution's policies, a hold may be placed on some or all the deposit amount to ensure that the funds are available and to protect against fraudulent activity.

6.	Reserve	The institution is required to keep a percentage of this deposit in cash reserves. Then with the amount of the deposit over the reserve the institution is free to U.S.E. the money as they would like.
7.	Interest	If the account earns interest, the institution will calculate and post any accrued interest to the account on a regular basis.
8.	Withdrawal	The customer can withdraw funds from their account up to the available amount, either in person or through an electronic transfer.
9.	Statements	The institution will provide regular statements to the customer detailing all account activity, fees and interest earned.
10.	Reconciliation	The customer should reconcile their account regularly, comparing their records to the institution's records to ensure that there are no discrepancies or errors.

Overall, the deposit cycle at an institution ensures the safe and secure transfer of funds into an account while allowing the institution to U.S.E. the deposits as an Invest-OR. This balance is meant to maintain the accuracy and integrity of the financial system.

DO FINANCIAL INSTITUTIONS MAKE MONEY OFF MY MONEY?

Well, we are going to discuss banking fees in 4.2, but they will make money through fees. Yes, a financial institution is allowed to U.S.E. your money above the reserve ratio however it sees fit. In our example above, that would be the other $900,000 being used in loans or invested into different assets.

What each financial institution does to run its business ultimately comes down to whether it is a FOR PROFIT or NOT FOR PROFIT institution.

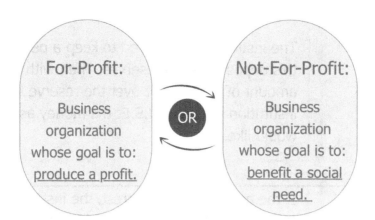

The two types of financial institutions for-profit and not-for-profit we need to introduce here are Banks and Credit Unions. The biggest difference between these two institutions will be found in their purpose as a for-profit or not-for-profit business.

A **BANK** is a for-profit business, where a credit union is a not-for-profit business. This means that banks and credit unions have different purposes for existing and with that purpose will provide different values to you as a customer.

A bank's purpose is to produce a profit for its owners which are its **SHAREHOLDERS**. The shareholders are people who invested in shares of that specific bank. With this purpose, everything in a bank is designed to be efficient and effective in producing more profit.

Advantages banks will have come from the variety of products or services they can provide. The more a bank can offer, the more you can purchase, and the more profit. Banks will also have an edge in physical locations, while this may not be as much of an advantage today with money changing to more virtual offerings, it is still a benefit to have access to a physical bank location in your city or in your travels.

WHY DO WE HEAR MORE ABOUT BANKS THAN CREDIT UNIONS?

You are probably wondering why you have heard of so many more banks than credit unions, that is because banks have a much larger marketing budget. With excess profits, banks have an opportunity to invest dollars into marketing, product development, and technology. It is hard for credit unions to compete with much larger technology budgets because the credit union is not trying to create a profit and you will see this in their online and mobile banking platforms.

WHY WOULD WE CHOOSE A CREDIT UNION?

With **CREDIT UNIONS** being not-for-profit, their mission is aimed at a social benefit to its community over making money for shareholders. A credit union is also designed to benefit its owners, but here the owners are the members of the credit union. That's right, the members of the credit union own the credit union, as opposed to shareholders owning a bank. The members are not paid a profit at the end of the year but instead receive benefits such as lower fees and better interest rates.

 A bank may offer you an auto loan at 5% and make 1% of that as profit. A credit union does not need that profit, so they can offer you the same loan at 4%.

To join a credit union, you typically must have some qualifier or connection such as having the same employer, living in the same area, or being a part of a school or union.

 For example, members of the military have specific credit unions like Navy Federal Credit Union. Nowadays, some credit unions are trying to grow and provide their service to more people, so you may not even need to meet that qualifier to join.

The mission of the credit union is to serve their community and this mission is felt in its operations. While things like customer service depend on who is providing it, credit unions take pride in the neighborhood atmosphere of their locations and providing the best resources for the members within that.

- More products and services.
- More branches and wider footprint.
- More investment in marketing and technology.

- Lower account fees or requirements.
- Focused on community and being local.
- Better rates on savings and loans.

WAIT A MINUTE, ARE YOU SURE I SHOULD U.S.E. A FINANCIAL INSTITUTION?

Yes, both banks and credit unions will offer your plan:

	System	Cash Management tools
	Security	FDIC or NCUA
	Liquidity	Easy Access
	Interest	Guaranteed created money

HOW TO DEPOSIT FUNDS INTO A BANK ACCOUNT

1. Prepare the funds: Gather the funds you wish to deposit, such as cash or a check made out to you.

2. Endorse the check: If you are depositing a check made out to you, endorse the back of the check by signing your name.

3. Fill out a deposit slip: If depositing cash or a check, fill out a deposit slip with the amount of the deposit and the account you want to deposit it into. Some banks offer electronic deposit options, which may not require a deposit slip.

4. Approach the teller, use an ATM, or electronic option: If you prefer to make the deposit in person, approach the teller and provide them with your deposit slip and the funds. Alternatively, you can use an ATM to deposit the funds, which will require you to follow the on-screen instructions. Nowadays, there are many electronic deposit options that allow you to take a picture of a check and treat it as a deposit slip.

5. Verify the deposit: After the deposit is made, you will receive a receipt and be shown how much of your deposit is 'available' to you. Verify that the amount of the deposit and the account information is correct.

6. Wait for the deposit to clear: Depending on the type of deposit and the bank's policies, there may be a hold period before the funds are 'available' for use. This hold period can range from one to several business days.

SECTION 4.1

RECAP

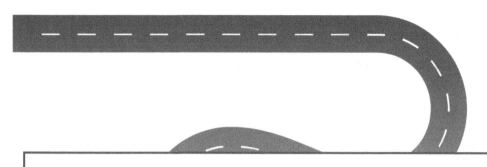

1. BEYOND THE RESERVE REQUIREMENT, FINANCIAL INSTITUTIONS ARE ALLOWED TO U.S.E. YOUR MONEY.

2. THE FIRST TEAMMATE YOU WILL NEED ON YOUR MONEY VEHICLE JOURNEY IS A BANKER.

3. FINANCIAL INSTITUTIONS OFFER SECURITY, LIQUIDITY, INTEREST AND A SYSTEM.

SECTION 4.2

TERMS

ACCESSIBILITY: ability to withdraw money from a specific account.

REQUIRED MINIMUM BALANCE: minimum amount of cash you must have in a specific account or face a fee.

FEES: a payment made to an institution for a service.

ALERTS: a resource provided by financial institutions to tell you important messages about your account.

CHECKING ACCOUNTS (also known as TODAY ACCOUNTS): intended for use on purchases and activities that you do today. With a checking account, you can pay for lunch, buy those shoes, or just take out cash to have.

SAVINGS ACCOUNTS (also known as TOMORROW ACCOUNTS): intended to be used for a specific purchase on a day in the future. Tomorrow may not be the next day, but tomorrow represents a day in the future where you would want to buy something bigger like a car, vacation, college, or new phone.

CONSUMER FINANCIAL PROTECTION BUREAU (CFPB): an agency of the United States government responsible for consumer protection in the financial sector.

FED REGULATION D: created from the Securities Act of 1933 this imposes a reserve requirement on certain deposits and specifies how the institution classifies different deposits.

THE FEDERAL FUNDS RATE: the interest rate at which financial institutions lend their reserve balances held at the Federal Reserve to one another.

ANNUAL PERCENTAGE YIELD (APY): the total amount of interest paid on an account based on the interest rate and frequency of compounding over a 365-day period.

MONEY MARKET ACCOUNTS (MMA) or MONEY MARKET DEPOSIT ACCOUNT (MMDA): a type of account that can provides a higher interest rate like a savings account while providing accessibility like a checking account.

CERTIFICATE OF DEPOSIT (CD) or SHARE CERTIFICATES: a type of savings account at a financial institution that can be used to protect money and earn a higher interest rate than a traditional savings account, but your cash will not be liquid.

MATURITY DATE: the date at which the final payment on a loan is due and the principal is due to be returned.

Imagine walking into a bank with the $1,000 you saved from working over the summer. You now know the advantages of a bank account and want to make sure you are using the right account for what you need.

You already know that about half of your money is being spent on the Present Choice Bucket and half is being spent on your Future Bucket. Now you are wondering what type of account is best for each Money Bucket.

Financial Institutions offer many different types of accounts—checking, savings, money market accounts, certificates of deposit, and many more. Each one has its own specific use and potential reward. So, you will need a good way to compare the different types of accounts being offered.

KEY FEATURES IN BANK COMPARING ACCOUNTS:

	**Accessibility**	Are there any restrictions on withdrawing money from this account?
	**Intended Use**	Does this account interact with accounts within the bank or outside the bank?
	**Required Minimum Balance**	Is there a certain amount required to open or always be held in this account?
	**Fees (account & transaction)**	Are there fees associated with opening or using this account?
	**Alert/Perks**	What features or benefits can you assign to this type of account? What are the mobile banking capabilities, how is the customer service? When does the account provide rewards?
	**Interest**	How much will my money create while in this account?

For now, we are going to focus on the two main types of accounts that will set the foundation for your plan:

CHECKING AND SAVINGS ACCOUNTS

CHECKING ACCOUNTS can be called **TODAY ACCOUNTS** because they are intended for use on purchases and activities that you do today. With a checking account, you can pay for lunch, buy those shoes, or just take out cash to have.

 Example: Going to the movies tonight, you would take $20 out of your checking account to be spent TODAY.

SAVINGS ACCOUNTS can be called **TOMORROW ACCOUNTS** because they are intended to be used for a specific purchase on a day in the future. Tomorrow may not be the next day, but tomorrow represents a day in the future where you would want to buy something bigger like a car, vacation, college, or new phone.

 Example: You work all summer to earn that $1,000 but you do not want to spend it today, instead you want to save it for when you go off to college next year.

HOW DO TODAY (CHECKING) ACCOUNTS COMPARE TO TOMORROW (SAVINGS) ACCOUNTS?

As you begin to compare these two account types, remember that the accounts do not change, the purpose you are using them changes. Identify which account you will need for the specific dollars you have targeted in your Money Buckets.

Let's walk through the Key Features in comparing each account:

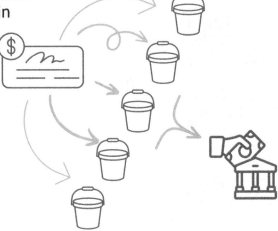

TODAY (CHECKING) ACCOUNTS

	Age	You must be 18 years old to open or have an adult co-sign the account with you.
	**Accessibility**	These accounts are to remain very liquid, which you understand now means being able to access cash daily. Through using checks, cards, or communications with your bank, you should be able to access your money at any time. The only accessibility requirement hurdle you will find is if your account balance drops to $0 and you have no more cash in the account.
	Intended Use	These accounts are intended to be used outside of your bank. They can connect to shops and stores and anywhere you will need to access your money.
	Required Minimum Balance	There is typically not a required minimum to open or have in your checking account, however you should be aware that if you go below $0 there will be penalties.
	**Fees (account and transaction)**	According to the **CONSUMER FINANCIAL PROTECTION BUREAU (CFPB)** checking account holders average $9.97 in fees a month or $118 over the year. Banks being businesses will have more fees for these accounts than credit unions. Some fees are unavoidable and some are worth the value the account features provide, we will review reducing fees in Section 4.3.
	**Alert/Perks**	These accounts will help you manage and track your expenses by providing you with a constant transaction list of where your money is going. With these transactions, you can receive alerts for when money leaves, comes in, or you are close to $0. These checking accounts receive FDIC insurance at a bank or NCUA insurance at a credit union up to $250,000 per owner per account. Another feature of checking accounts is that you can set your 'Auto-8' payments up in them.
	Interest	These accounts are meant to be transactional, and your institution will not pay you for money they cannot U.S.E. elsewhere. You can receive a small interest rate 0.1% - 1% but nothing that is going to help you outpace inflation.

TOMORROW (SAVING) ACCOUNTS

Age

You must be 18 years old to open or have an adult co-sign the account with you.

Accessibility

These accounts used to have restrictions on how many times you can pull money out of them each month, this was issued by the FED IN REGULATION D. The idea was twofold, first it would allow banks to measure their reserve ratio better and second it would keep your Tomorrow (Savings) account funded for future events and big purchases, not pull money out every week when you want something. Confirm with your bank how often you can pull from this Savings account and if it is accessible via ATM or to pay monthly bills. (Update: Through the Covid-19 Pandemic, this Regulation D has been suspended and you can now pull from your Savings account an unlimited number of times. You should confirm that your individual bank is not enforcing Regulation D.)

Intended Use

These accounts are intended to be used within your bank and mostly just with your Checking account. You will transfer money from your checking into your savings or pull money from your savings into your checking account. You can set up some automatic payments for large Past Choices such as rent or bills, but these accounts are truly meant to protect the money you target for your R.I.C.H. goals and Corona Cushion. Having these dollars in a separate account than your checking account will limit the temptation to spend them.

Required Minimum Balance

These accounts will typically have a required amount to open the account as well as a required amount to be kept in the account. You can see requirements from $50 to $500 with banks and requirements all the way down to $1 with credit unions. While not every account has a requirement anymore, the ones who will pay you more interest will maintain a requirement. This requirement is because they want to loan the dollars you save out to the market and need to know what they must work with. Confirm with your institution when opening your Tomorrow (Savings) account what the minimum balance to open is and if there are any requirements to have a checking account or automatic deposit set up.

Fees (account and transaction)

In these accounts, you should not incur many fees if you meet the required minimum balance. There are not typically fees in a savings account because the institution is going to U.S.E. your money to create more money and that is how they make money in Savings accounts.

TOMORROW (SAVING) ACCOUNTS

| Alert/Perks | These accounts allow you to keep your savings in a liquid and accessible fashion while building toward your R.I.C.H. goals. A neat feature is the ability to see the progress you are making to achieve these goals. These checking accounts receive FDIC insurance at a bank or NCUA insurance at a credit union up to $250,000 per owner per account. |

| Interest | The rate an institution will pay you for your savings account will depend on what the FEDERAL FUNDS RATE is at the time and how much money you want to put into the account. These types of accounts can receive different levels of interest payments over the year measured in ANNUAL PERCENTAGE YIELD (APY), but you can seek out interest in the 2-4% range that will help you keep pace with inflation. |

HOW DO TODAY ACCOUNTS COMPARE TO TOMORROW ACCOUNTS?

	CHECKING	SAVINGS
Accessibility	Liquid	Confirm Liquidity
Use	Outside Accounts	Checking Account
Required Balance	No	Possible
Fees	Yes	Rare
Alerts	Overdraft	Goals Achieved
Interest	0-0.1%	1-4% (online)

Walking into the bank, you will want to be prepared with some questions to ask about the services and products provided by the institution. The list below is not comprehensive, but it should help you get more clarity in the conversations around your accounts.

QUESTIONS FOR YOUR BANKER:

- What is the minimum balance required for this account?
- What fees will the bank charge me for this account?
- What interest will the bank pay me on money held in this account?
- How many monthly withdrawals am I allowed to make from this account?
- What is the minimum balance required for this account?
- Does this account have any special alerts, rewards, or advantages?

MONEY MARKET ACCOUNTS (MMA) or **MONEY MARKET DEPOSIT ACCOUNT (MMDA)** are a type of account at a financial institution that can be seen as a hybrid checking/ savings account and a possible addition to your foundational accounts. These types of accounts will provide a higher interest rate than typical savings accounts and, if you ask, can offer check writing or ATM capabilities like a checking account. To receive these benefits, the MMA will usually require a larger minimum balance to open or maintain the account.

You should approach these accounts with the same questions as above and inquire as to the liquidity of the account. It must be noted that Money Market Mutual Funds (MMMF) are not the same as Money Market Accounts (MMA). A Money Market Mutual Fund is an investment account and not insured by the FDIC.

Example: You want to get a better interest rate on your short-term savings but also may need access to the money.

CERTIFICATE OF DEPOSIT (CD) or **SHARE CERTIFICATES** is a type of savings account at a financial institution that can be used to protect money and earn a higher interest rate than a traditional savings account. The CD account will pay you a fixed interest rate in exchange for the U.S.E. of your money over a fixed period of time. This means to earn the higher interest, you will not be able to use the money deposited until the fixed period is over, occurring on the MATURITY DATE. The length of time ranges from 3 months up to 5 years and usually will see the longer the time period, the higher the interest rate. But the longer the time period, the longer you will not be able to access those dollars.

You will also not be able to make more contributions into this account, you can contribute into a new CD, but once you make the initial deposit you will not be able to add more during the fixed period. Upon 'maturity' you will have your deposit returned plus the interest earned and often will have an option from your bank to renew your deposit into a new CD. You should confirm that the CD does not automatically renew upon maturity.

There should not be many (or any) fees in a CD account because the institution will have the ability to U.S.E. the money elsewhere over the time period. The biggest fee will come if you need to access the money before the maturity date through an **EARLY WITHDRAWAL PENALTY.** These accounts are seen as very secure and still insured by the FDIC.

 Example: You want to purchase a car next year and want your dollars to be protected while creating some interest, you could open a 12-month CD to achieve this R.I.C.H. goal.

TODAY (CHECKING) ACCOUNT IS INTENDED TO PULL MONEY OUT.

TOMORROW (SAVINGS) ACCOUNT IS INTENDED TO PUT MONEY IN.

WHO HELPS MONITOR FINANCIAL INSTITUTIONS?

While we know the FED helps set the Federal Funds Rate and can control features of financial institutions, it is not necessarily their job to monitor or police these institutions. That is where the Consumer Financial Protection Bureau (CFPB) comes in.

The CFPB states on their website that it is 'a United States government agency that is dedicated to making sure you are treated fairly by banks, lenders, and other financial institutions.' The CFPB also provides financial relief and support to those in need.

If you are interacting with a bank or credit union and feel that you have been misled or something is inaccurate, you have the right to file a complaint. You can file a complaint on actions involving a checking or savings account, credit card or credit report, student loan, auto loan, mortgage, debt collection, or any type of money transfer.

STEPS TO FILE A COMPLAINT:

01
Go to CFPB website
ConsumerFinance.gov/complaint

02
Provide information
Build your report on the key details of what happened and what actions you have taken so far to resolve.

03
Gather documents
Any documents that are relevant to the issue should be in the report filed.

04
Define success
Write out what you think a fair resolution would be for this issue.

There are other organizations that regulate financial institutions based on their makeup, but for now we wanted to focus on the CFPB.

CHOOSING AN INSTITUTION (TEAMMATE)

Establishing your foundational accounts can and should feel like you are choosing a teammate. No different than building the mindset within yourself, when you select a teammate, you will want to make sure that they know how to Be A Pro.

This means your teammate will need to be confident they know how to do what you are asking; you trust that they will do what you are asking, and when they do what you ask that it adds value to your overall financial plan.

This is an important decision and Money Vehicle wants to help you guide the interview process with these tips:

1. Begin with the End in Mind. Think about what you need from this institution, what accounts or types of offerings you are looking for, then confirm that they have all the products you will need.

2. Comparative Fee Analysis. Review the institutions you are considering for their fees. Do they charge higher or lower fees, do they charge fees for different activities, and if they are not charging fees, how are they making money?

3. Interest Rate Comparison. You will review both what the institution decides to pay you in accounts like Savings Accounts, but also how much the institution will charge you in loans like an auto loan.

4. Compare how you will interact with this teammate. Are you going to need physical locations to walk into, ATM machines around town, or will you primarily be an online customer. If strictly online, then work through their mobile and virtual experience. No matter if it is online or in a location, you should also compare the other resources this institution will have for your plan. Confirm that however you choose to engage with this institution you will be able to easily do so.

5. Read Customer Service Reviews. This will take two forms, cybersecurity and problem solving. The first should be a priority and one we will discuss in depth in Chapter 8. You need to confirm this institution has the correct security measures in place to protect your information, your account, and your transactions from cyber-attacks. Secondly, look at the reviews of customer service, you will no doubt find yourself in a situation where you need help fixing a banking error and you will want someone who is there to help. You can find these reviews at sources such as Consumer Reports, Better Business Bureau, or Yelp.

SECTION 4.3
RECAP

1. BUILD A 'CORONA CUSHION' BY PROTECTING A FEW MONTHS OF YOUR BURN RATE.

2. SET UP AUTOMATIC BILL PAYMENTS AND ALERTS WITHIN YOUR ACCOUNTS.

3. NEVER LET YOUR ACCOUNT GO BELOW $0!

SECTION 4.4

BALANCING AND READING YOUR STATEMENTS

TERMS

BALANCING A CHECKBOOK: a traditional way to review how much money was in your account by looking at the deposits and withdrawals you tracked in your checkbook. With virtual banking, this has become less of a practice but still a good concept to understand.

ACCOUNT STATEMENTS: monthly reports of what occurred in your account and can be delivered physically or virtually.

Ok, stay with me here as we go back in time, to a world where there was NO INTERNET!!!

Can you even imagine? Honestly it is hard to envision a place where we did not have access to this endless stream of information. But back in this time, banks were only accessed by going to a building and waiting in line. You would walk up to the bank teller and either get some money out of your account or deposit money into your account. Upon completion of the transaction, they would give you a 'balance' of how much money was in your account after this money landed.

The only other way to really know how much money was in your account was to 'balance' your checkbook and tally the money that went in and out that month. Sure, your bank would send you monthly statements showing the transactions that they were able to track, but with interest, bills, pending charges, returns, and delays, it was common for these two balances to differ. It was up to you to verify these transactions based on your 'balancing act'.

Now, come back to today, where we can access all the information we need in a matter of moments. Today, we have a resource called 'online banking' that can provide information on your account balance and a clear report of all the transactions you have made up to a few minutes ago. With this process, **'BALANCING A CHECKBOOK'** is not as vital as it once was, but it is still beneficial to understand the principles that this process is based on

STEPS TO BALANCE YOUR CHECKBOOK:

1. **Establish** your beginning account balance.
2. **Record** the date and amount of each deposit including cash and interest.
3. **Record** the date and amount of each withdrawal including cash and interest.
4. **Compare** with the statement that your bank has provided you, being aware of the transactions that do not match.
5. **Reconcile** the differences. Identify why or how the disagreement between your checkbook and bank statement occurred and make the necessary adjustments.
6. **Calculate** your ending balance. After all transactions have been confirmed or reconciled, find the ending balance for your account by adding the deposits and subtracting the withdrawals.
7. **Start** the next month with your ending balance as Step #1 and work through the process again.

LET'S LOOK AT ADRIAN'S TRANSACTIONS TO HELP HIM TRACK AND BALANCE HIS CHECKBOOK.

At the beginning of March Adrian has $350 in his Checking account then has the following transactions:

DATE	MEMO	AMOUNT
3/1	PAYDAY	(+) $200
3/5	GROCERY SHOPPING	(-) $75
3/8	CELL PHONE BILL	(-) $50
3/15	PAYDAY	(+) $100
3/19	GROCERY SHOPPING	(-) $75
3/20	SUBSCRIPTIONS (NETFLIX, HULU, AMAZON)	(-) $40
3/22	SHOE SHOPPING	(-) $100 CREDIT
3/29	MOVIE NIGHT	(-) $20

USING THE 'STEPS TO BALANCE A CHECKBOOK' ABOVE, WE WILL:

1. Establish your beginning account balance: **$350**
2. Record the date and amount of each deposit:

3/1 PAYDAY:	+$200
3/15 PAYDAY:	+$100

3. Record the date and amount of each withdrawal including cash and interest: -$75

Note: Notice the Credit Card is NOT listed as it is not connected to Checking account

3/5 GROCERY SHOPPING:	-$50
3/8 CELL PHONE BILL:	-$75
3/19 GROCERY SHOPPING:	-$40
3/20 SUBSCRIPTIONS:	-$20
3/29 MOVIE NIGHT:	-$260
TOTAL WITHDRAWALS.	

4. Compare with the statement that your bank has provided you, being aware of the transactions that do not match.

- Adrian's calculation = **$650** available-**$260** withdrawal = **$390** ending balance
- Account Statement from Adrian's bank: ending balance: **$340**

ADRIAN'S BANK STATEMENT			
DATE	**MEMO**	**AMOUNT**	**BALANCE**
	STARTING BALANCE		**$350.00**
3/1/2023	INCOME	(+) $200.00	**$550.00**
3/5/2023	GROCERY	(-) $75.00	**$475.00**
3/08/2023	CELL PHONE BILL	(-) $50.00	**$425.00**
3/15/2023	INCOME	(+) $100.00	**$525.00**
3/19/2023	GROCERY	(-) $75.00	**$450.00**
3/20/2023	SUBSCRIPTIONS	(-) $40.00	**$410.00**
3/29/2023	GAS STATION	(-) $50.00	**$360.00**
3/29	MOVIE	(-) $20.00	**$340.00**
	ENDING BALANCE -179-		$340

5. Reconcile the differences. The ending balance between these two calculations is different. When Adrian goes back to compare his transactions, he finds that there was a withdrawal on March 29 at a gas station for $50.00 that he does not remember doing. Reaching out to his bank they find the error and correct this transaction, removing the withdrawal from his account.

6. Calculate your ending balance. The ending balance for the month of March and starting balance for April will be $390.00. Then you can start back at step #1.

Balancing your checkbook is just confirming how much money is in your account. With transactions sometimes taking a day or two to 'post', it is important to keep track of how much is currently available and how much is being withdrawn. While you will have a great resource with online banking these days, it is always good to know how to work through this process manually. When you need to verify your account balance, use the 'Steps to Balance'.

IF I DO NOT NEED TO BALANCE MY CHECKBOOK, WHAT WILL WE USE FROM THE BANK TO HELP WITH OUR PLAN TODAY?

A document that will be extremely helpful for you as you build your financial plan will be your ACCOUNT STATEMENTS. These are monthly reports of what occurred in your account and can be delivered physically or virtually. Be aware that some institutions will charge you a fee for physical copies as it costs them money to print and mail.

This document will list out your account information:

- Statement Period: the amount of time that this statement will cover, found in the top right corner of statement and usually covering a month.
- Account Information: the details of your account such as account number and type.
- Transactions: a list of all transaction details, the date, and the description, during the statement period that have been posted to that specific account. If you have multiple accounts, you will have multiple transaction lists.
- Account fees: any fees you paid during the time period. Review these for accuracy and use the examples from Section 4.2 and 4.3.
- Interest paid: any interest that you have been paid during the time period for each account.

(1) **ABC BANK**
PO BOX 12345
ANYSVILLE. US. 12345

(2) March 01, 2023 through May 30,2023
Account Number: **000000593037148**

CUSTOMER SERVICE INFORMATION	
Web site:	**ABCBANK.COM**
Service Center:	**1-800-222-2222**
Hearing Impaired:	**1-800-333-3333**
Para Espanol:	**1-800-444-4444**
International Calls:	**1-800-555-5555**

(3) JOHN DOE
123 MAIN STREET
ANYSVILLE AA, 12345

CHECKING SUMMARY
Business Select Checking

	INSTANCES	AMOUNT	
Beginning Balance		**$15,050.80**	**(4)**
Deposits and Additions	2	130.00	
Electronic Withdrawals	2	-356.04	
(7) Checks	0	0.00	
Ending Balance	4	**$14,824.76**	**(9)**

(8) Your monthly service fee was waived because you maintained an average checking balance of $7,500.00 or a minimum checking balance of $5,000.00 or more during the statement period.

DEPOSIT AND ADDITIONS

DATE	DESCRIPTION	AMOUNT	
09/15	ATM Check Deposit	$125.00	**(10)**
09/15	ATM Cash Deposit	5.00	
Total Deposits and Additions		**$130.00**	**(5)**

ELECTRONIC WITHDRAWALS

DATE	DESCRIPTION	AMOUNT	
09/30	Qwest 8002441111 Telephone 2063864199818 CCID ID : 9Qc0273801	$249.96	**(11)**
09/30	Qwest 8002441111 Telephone 2063654528111 CCID ID : 9Qc0273801	106.08	
Total Electronic Withdrawals		**$356.04**	**(6)**

DAILY ENDING BALANCE

DATE	AMOUNT
09/15	$15,180.80
09/30	14,824.76

KEY

1. Institution
2. Statement Period & Account #
3. Account Holder Information
4. Beginning balance
5. Total Deposit
6. Total Withdrawals
7. Checks Written
8. Account Fees
9. Ending Balance
10. Summary of Deposits
11. Summary of Withdrawals

-181-

SECTION 4.4
RECAP

Knowing how to balance your checkbook and keep track of how much money you have in each account will provide you with a clear picture of your spending habits and give you an opportunity to correct any problems that arise. The sooner you correct problems the better and the better you track, the sooner you will see the problem.

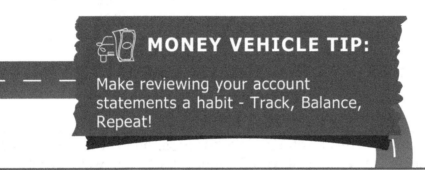

MONEY VEHICLE TIP:

Make reviewing your account statements a habit - Track, Balance, Repeat!

1. ONLINE BANKING HAS CHANGED HOW YOU 'BALANCE' YOUR CHECKBOOK OR ACCOUNT, BUT IT IS IMPORTANT TO KNOW THE FUNDAMENTALS OF THIS PROCESS.

2. CONFIRM THAT THE ENDING ACCOUNT BALANCES IN YOUR ACCOUNTS ARE CORRECT FOR ALL TRANSACTIONS IN THAT TIME PERIOD AND RECONCILE ANY DIFFERENCES.

3. MAKE BALANCING YOUR ACCOUNT A HABIT - TRACK, BALANCE, REPEAT.

REVIEW

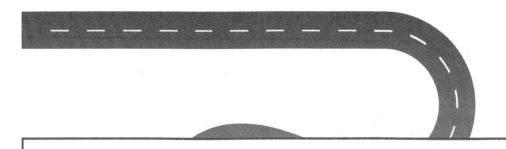

THE RULE: ESTABLISH YOUR FOUNDATIONAL ACCOUNTS

The first member of your financial team is a financial institution, a bank or credit union. Remember, this institution is a business, and it will find ways to U.S.E. your money, so you must U.S.E. your money as well. What this teammate can offer is a system, security, liquidity, and interest. You must choose the most efficient account for your plan and how you intend to U.S.E. your money. The Today (checking) account is intended for your daily activities, and the Tomorrow (savings) account is intended for your future activities. Start building your Corona Cushion in your savings account. Use the questions we have discussed to verify the features your teammate is offering, and make sure they will be a good fit for your plan. Keep track of your transactions and make sure your ending balance is always heading toward your R.I.C.H. goals!

ACTION

Open your foundational Checking and Savings accounts.
- Find a Checking and Savings account that will meet the needs of your plan.
- Setup automations within your foundational accounts to pay your Past Choices.
- Begin to build your Corona Cushion, 3-6 months of your Burn Rate.

OWNER'S MANUAL
FOR YOUR MONEY VEHICLE:

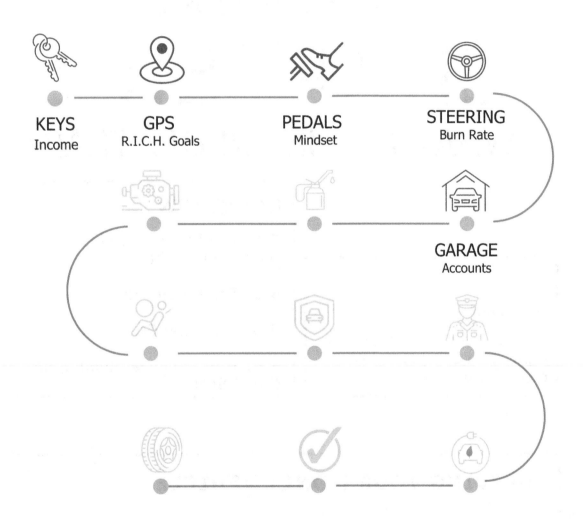

KEYS
Income

GPS
R.I.C.H. Goals

PEDALS
Mindset

STEERING
Burn Rate

GARAGE
Accounts

CREDIT SCORE

CHAPTER 5
WHAT IS THE CREDIT TRAP?

OVERVIEW

5.1: The Difference Between Debit and Credit

5.2: The Credit Trap

5.3: Avoid the Credit Trap

5.4: Your Financial Reputation, Credit Score

ACTION

Start building your financial reputation by opening a credit card.

DRIVING YOUR MONEY VEHICLE

The first big mistake people make with their car is not checking the oil. This damage to your engine is avoidable, but if not corrected it is devastating. What is the first big mistake people make with their Money Vehicle? People forget to check their financial oil, known as 'Credit'. You can avoid this damage by learning how to build your credit and financial reputation.

SECTION 5.1
THE DIFFERENCE BETWEEN DEBIT AND CREDIT

TERMS

DEBIT CARD: a payment card that can be used to pull cash from your account.

CREDIT CARD: a payment card that borrows credit from a third party.

SECURED LOAN: a type of loan with an underlying asset to secure the payment.

UNSECURED LOAN: a type of loan that has no underlying asset to secure the payment.

When you're out for lunch with friends, buying concert tickets, or getting a new pair of shoes, you are faced with the same question: should I use my debit or credit card?

You think of a commercial that made your credit card look like a wise financial decision—I mean, credit is everywhere, what could go wrong? The commercial talked about building up your credit score and even went so far as to entice you with the possibility of receiving "amazing rewards!" However, to make the right decision, you must understand the difference between the two payment options and why that company is so eager to get you to use their credit card.

- **DEBIT CARD:** a payment card that can be used to pull cash from your account.
- **CREDIT CARD:** a payment card that borrows credit from a third party.

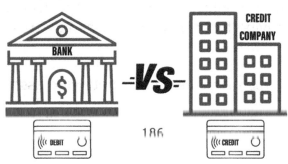

The differences between a debit card and a credit card can be summarized by these three questions:

01 Where does the money come from?

02 What is being transferred?

03 Will I be charged interest?

Let's look at an example. You get out of your car to pump some gas, then swipe your card to pay for it. Who is being contacted? What are they sending? What does it cost? Some would say it doesn't matter, as long as the transaction goes through, but there is a significant difference in how you choose to fill up your gas tank.

WHERE DOES THE MONEY COME FROM?

When you swipe a debit card, a signal is sent directly to your bank, alerting them that some of the funds you have in your account are being used to complete your purchase.

When you swipe a credit card, a signal is sent to a third party—not you or your bank, but a credit company. This third party is being alerted that funds are necessary to complete your purchase.

WHAT IS BEING TRANSFERRED?

With a debit card, your bank will be sending over cash from your bank account. So, if you have $100 in your bank account and use $20, you will now have $80 in your bank account.

With a credit card, the credit company will be sending credit to the gas station and a loan balance to your account. The credit being sent is not cash, it is a promise that you will pay cash later. Credit is based on trust and allows you to buy something without paying for it. I say it is based on trust because the loan is unsecured.

- **SECURED LOAN:** a type of loan with an underlying asset to secure the payment.
- **UNSECURED LOAN:** a type of loan that has no underlying asset to secure the payment.

Unlike with a secured loan for a home or a car, in the case of an unsecured loan, there is nothing the company can take away if you decide not to pay. They must trust that you will pay your loan back in the future. So, if you have $100 in your bank account and charge $20 on your credit card, you will still have $100 in your bank account.

WILL I BE CHARGED INTEREST?

Debit cards don't charge you money to make the transaction, because you are using your money and the transaction is done. Remember, from Section 4.1, Business of Banking, the bank is paying you a small amount of interest for the privilege of using your money.

Credit cards charge you interest, because when cash is sent to the gas station, a loan or credit is made to you, and there are always strings attached when you use other people's money. Regarding credit cards, the string is called an Annual Percentage Rate (APR). The APR is the percentage of interest that will be charged over an entire year.

Circling back on the idea of an unsecured loan because there is nothing guaranteeing the loan, there is a higher risk of you not paying the loan back. For example, if you do not pay your car loan, the lender will take your car, but if you do not pay your credit card loan, there is nothing for the lender to take. Due to the higher risk, the credit company will charge a higher interest rate.

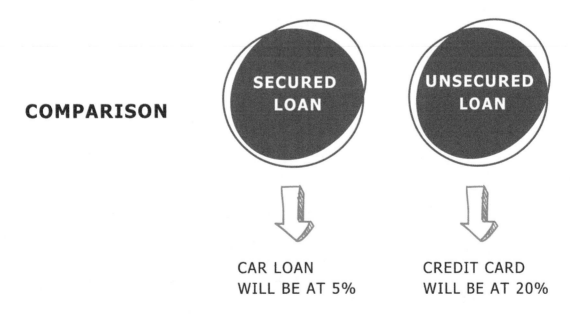

COMPARISON

SECURED LOAN

UNSECURED LOAN

CAR LOAN
WILL BE AT 5%

CREDIT CARD
WILL BE AT 20%

This should shock you a little. The understanding that credit is a loan but moreso that it will charge a VERY high interest rate. In our next section we will look at what happens if you do not U.S.E. your credit cards wisely.

Anytime you swipe your credit card, answer the following questions:

01 Where will the card payment be coming from?

02 What will the company be sending?

03 Will I be charged interest if I do not take another action?

SECTION 5.1
RECAP

1. DEBIT CARD: YOUR BANK SENDS CASH AT NO CHARGE TO YOU TO COMPLETE A TRANSACTION.

2. CREDIT CARD: YOUR CREDIT COMPANY SENDS CREDIT, WHICH WILL COST MONEY IF UNPAID, MAKING YOU A BORROWER.

3. SECURED LOANS HAVE AN ASSET TO MAKE THE DEBT LESS RISKY AND UNSECURED LOANS (EX. CREDIT CARDS) DO NOT HAVE AN ASSET AND ARE RISKIER WHICH MAKES THEM MORE EXPENSIVE.

SECTION 5.2
THE CREDIT TRAP

TERMS

CREDIT TRAP: when something you purchase ends up costing more than the original price due to interest paid on credit card.

ELECTRONIC FUNDS TRANSFER ACT: debit card allows only 2 days to report fraudulent activity, before you are liable for up to $500.

FAIR CREDIT BILLING ACT: protects information gathered by credit bureaus and removes liability for fraudulent transactions.

"Hey Steve, did you see my new seventy-two-inch Smart TV? It was only $2,000," Billy bragged.

"Awesome! Can't wait to watch the big game on it," Steve replied enthusiastically. Then he asked, "By the way, how did you afford a new Smart TV?"

"It was easy. I used my credit card, and my credit company says I only have to pay forty dollars a month," Billy stated with a false sense of security.

Billy doesn't fully understand how the credit system works and is in jeopardy of falling victim to...the credit trap!

HOW DOES THE CREDIT TRAP HAPPEN?

The **CREDIT TRAP** occurs when something you purchased ends up costing more than the original price. The trap is set when you use other people's money with your credit card. The card is going to charge interest on your balance.

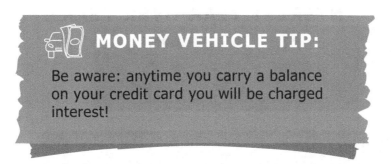
Let's look at our friend Billy with his new TV. He went out and bought a $2,000 TV with his credit card, making the balance he borrowed and the amount he still owes $2,000. The interest rate on his credit card is at an annual rate of 15 percent. This means he will be charged $25.00 every month, or $300 for the year, if he doesn't pay off the $2,000 balance. So that sweet new TV Billy bought doesn't end up costing $2,000, after one year of the credit trap, the TV costs $2,300! The scary part is that each month you do not pay off the amount, the credit trap deepens.

> **THE CREDIT TRAP IS WHEN SOMETHING YOU BOUGHT ENDS UP COSTING MORE THAN THE PURCHASE PRICE.**

The credit trap occurs when your purchase (new TV) ends up costing more than what was on the price tag. This means that compound interest (Chapter 2) is working against you to make a TV that was probably already out of your price range cost even more. The brutal reality is that the trap makes compound interest not a friend but an enemy, the 8th wonder of the world is now making YOU an employee.

Let's say Billy doesn't pay off his balance, and after a year he owes $2,300, due to the interest the credit card company has charged him. Now, his 15 percent interest will be charged on the entire balance of $2,300, making the trap get bigger, rising from $300 in year one to $345 in year two and widening the trap even bigger.

INTEREST YEAR OVER YEAR

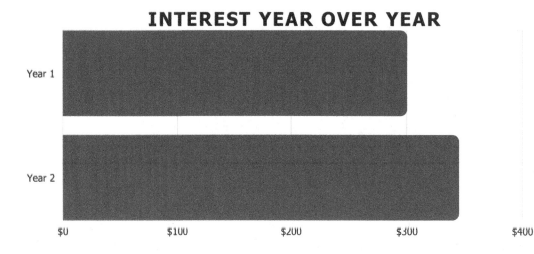

IF THE CREDIT CARD COMPANY IS LAYING A TRAP, CAN'T I JUST AVOID IT BY NOT USING ONE?

Yes and no. You can avoid using a credit card altogether, but you will be penalizing yourself by not building a good credit score. Your credit score will become a factor when you want to get a car loan, acquire a home mortgage, rent an apartment, attain insurance policies, set up your utilities, or even apply for a job! We will discuss the details of what makes up your credit score in future chapters, so for now, just understand that credit is something you will have to U.S.E. to your advantage.

Now that you know you need credit and see the trap that has been laid, how do you strategize a way around it? The first step to breaking away from the credit trap is understanding how it occurs. The next step is avoiding the trap altogether.

- **ELECTRONIC FUNDS TRANSFER ACT:** Debit card allows only 2 days to report fraudulent activity, before you are liable for up to $500.
- **FAIR CREDIT BILLING ACT:** Protects information gathered by credit bureaus and removes liability for fraudulent transactions.

Remember the quote from Albert Einstein in Chapter 2 'Those who understand it get paid it and those who do not, pay it'. This concept touches on the second part of that Einstein quote about how those who don't understand compound interest end up paying it. Albert never used a credit card, but he saw the importance of the concept and how it could—and would—be exploited.

Standing at the register and thinking about which card to insert into the payment device, understand when you swipe your credit card that the credit trap has been laid.

SECTION 5.2

RECAP

1. IF YOU HAVE A BALANCE ON YOUR CREDIT CARD, YOU WILL BE CHARGED INTEREST.

2. CREDIT TRAP: ANY TIME YOUR PURCHASE ENDS UP COSTING MORE THAN YOU ORIGINALLY PAID.

3. U.S.E. CREDIT CARDS TO GET ADVANTAGES LIKE:
   - 1) REWARDS YOU CAN EARN
   - 2) ACCEPTED MORE PLACES
   - 3) PROVIDES INSURANCE
   - 4) LOWERS PERSONAL RISK
   - 5) BUILDS CREDIT SCORE.

SECTION 5.3
AVOID THE CREDIT TRAP

TERMS

GRACE PERIOD: the time between the end of a billing cycle and when your bill is due, you are given this time to pay off your balance before interest begins to accrue.

ANNUAL PERCENTAGE RATE (APR): the interest rate the credit company will charge you on a yearly (annual) basis, 365 days.

DAILY RATE: the interest rate the credit company will charge you on a daily basis, 1 day or the APR divided by 365.

MINIMUM AMOUNT DUE (MAD): the lowest amount the credit company will allow each month for you to pay off from your balance. The MAD is instead of paying your balance off in full, you would only pay off 2-3% of the balance and this is how most people fall victim to the credit trap.

ANNUAL FEE: a yearly cost a credit company will charge you to have a specific credit card.

CASH ADVANCE: allows you to withdraw cash from your credit limit and the moment you pull the cash out, interest begins to accrue on your balance with no grace period.

CHARGED OFF: if you have missed payments for six (6) months, the credit company will write off your debt as uncollectable and negatively impacts your credit score. You are still liable for this debt; it will just transfer to a debt collector or bankruptcy.

SECURED CREDIT CARD: a credit card that has an asset (cash) deposited into an account to secure the loan. Good introductory step to build your credit.

AUTHORIZED USER: for minors wanting to use credit, this is a way to connect your name onto someone else's account and begin to build your credit.

Now you see the risk of the credit trap but also the idea that you need to start your credit history to begin establishing your credit score. We will dive into credit reports and scores in the next section, for now we want to answer the question rolling around in your head.

HOW DO I AVOID THE CREDIT TRAP?

We learned that the credit company can only charge you interest when you carry a balance. So, if there is no balance, then there will be no interest charged. Simple enough strategy stating if you pay off your balance on time every month, your credit card will start feeling more like a debit card—no fees, no interest—AND you will benefit from those rewards that the credit company is selling.

RULES TO USING YOUR CREDIT CARD:

1. Do not break the Golden Rule:

Understand that your credit card will allow you to buy more than you have in your bank account – spend more than you make. To avoid breaking the Golden Rule you must know how much you have in the bank, and not let a line of credit change the amount you spend on Present Choices.

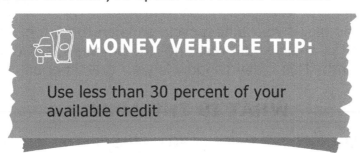

MONEY VEHICLE TIP:

Use less than 30 percent of your available credit

2. Do not forget your payment:

Pay your credit card bill on the same day every month. Making sure you do not miss a payment is making sure you will not lose money due to penalties. If possible, automate your payment. Sure, it is a better practice to log in every month and not only review your purchases but also verify that you made all the transactions, however, if you don't trust yourself to do that monthly, automate!

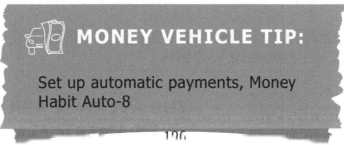

MONEY VEHICLE TIP:

Set up automatic payments, Money Habit Auto-8

3. Do not carry a balance:

Pay off your credit card in full every month, treating it just like a debit card. No balance means no interest, and those reward points you are accruing really will be a reward.

WHAT IS A GRACE PERIOD?

Notice in the last section we said 'if you pay off your balance on time every month.' There is a purpose for the callout, and it is the introduction to your GRACE PERIOD.

A grace period is the amount of time you are given to pay off your balance before interest begins to accrue. This period is the time between the end of a billing cycle and when your bill is due.

 For example, if your billing cycle ends on the 5th of the month, you will not be charged interest until the payment is due on the 9th of the month. This 4-day window is your grace period.

WHAT IS THE APR?

The **ANNUAL PERCENTAGE RATE (APR)** is the interest rate the credit company will charge you on your balance on a yearly (annual) basis, over 365 days.

 For example, if your APR is 17 percent, and you had a $100 balance for an entire year, you would be charged 17 percent times $100 which equals seventeen dollars (17% X $100 = $17).

APR does not mean you will be charged the full APR every day that you carry a balance, because the annual rate is broken down to a daily rate. To see what your **DAILY RATE** is, you would divide the APR by 365, representing 365 days in a year.

 For example, 17 percent APR = 17 percent/365 = 0.046 percent per day. So, the daily rate is .046%.

 **THE AVERAGE APR IN AMERICA**   16

WHAT IF I AM PAYING THE MINIMUM AMOUNT DUE?

You are falling straight into the credit trap! The **M.A.D. or MINIMUM AMOUNT DUE** is the lowest amount the credit company will allow each month for you to payoff. This is instead of paying your balance off in full, you only pay off 2-3% of the balance. Paying only the minimum amount due is how most people fall victim to the credit trap.

The credit card company wants you to believe that you are making a smart financial decision by paying the M.A.D., making a smaller payment, and having more cash to do other things with. But now that you understand your credit card is a loan you begin to ask yourself: who benefits from paying the M.A.D. - you or them?

When you only pay the M.A.D., you will fall into the credit trap and be paying the credit company interest for years. Trying to pay off your credit by using the minimum amount due is like trying to bail out a sinking ship with a spoon.

 Imagine being out on a boat and realizing there is a leak. Your boat is filling up quickly and you must make a choice about how you are going to get the water out. Looking around, you see a spoon, a bucket, and a water pump.

It seems obvious that no one would grab the spoon in a moment like that, but the spoon represents the minimum amount due—trying to solve a big problem with a tiny solution—and water keeps pouring into your boat. Grabbing a bucket and getting to work is the right tactic, but still the wrong tool. You will never solve the problem if more water keeps coming in than you can bucket out. The bucket symbolizes paying down chunks of your credit card balance but still letting water pour in. The best method is to first close the leak, then use the water pump to get the rest of the water out quickly. The water pump signifies paying off your credit card balance completely, and then paying it again every month.

The best method is to first close the leak, then use the water pump to get the rest of the water out quickly. The water pump signifies paying off your credit card balance completely, and then paying it again every month.

FOR A MATHEMATICAL EXAMPLE:

Let's say you have a $3,000 balance with a 20% APR. The credit company says your M.A.D. is only 2% of the balance or in this case $60 a month. You pay the $60 and you think your new balance is $2,940. With a 20% APR, you would owe $49 in interest for that month alone!

That is if all $60 went to paying down the balance, which we will show in this video of the M.A.D. calculation that it does not.

M.A.D. SHOULD MAKE YOU MAD!

Put simply, if you are paying off the minimum amount due (M.A.D.), you are going to lose a lot of money and that should make you MAD! Paying large chunks of your balance is better, but you're still falling into the credit trap. Your #1 priority in a financial plan should be to get out of credit card debt as fast as you can because there is almost nothing that can overcome a 20% APR!

WHAT IF I AM INVESTING THE MONEY OR GETTING REWARDS?

In the boat scenario, this would be like saying, "I understand the water is pouring in, but I feel my time is best served by trying to catch fish." It doesn't matter how many fish you catch if your boat sinks!

Plus, ask any financial professional what they can expect on a yearly basis to 'create' off investments and they will tell you 15 to 18 percent (the average APR in America) is a hard number to consistently match—let alone beat—with any investment.

As for the rewards, who do you think is benefiting from those, the person receiving them or the person giving them out? You pay for those rewards when you fall victim to the credit trap and pay the credit company interest. Credit companies are businesses, and if the cards didn't make them money, they wouldn't offer them. If you treat your credit like a debit and pay off your balance in full, then those rewards will truly be rewards.

IS VISA OR MASTERCARD MY CREDIT CARD COMPANY?

Oddly enough, the answer is neither. Those companies are payment networks that allow credit cards to transact in their network. They are the connector of your credit company to the store.

The credit card company will be a third party, which is also listed on your card, such as Bank of America, Capital One, Chase, Wells Fargo. Be aware that most credit cards are also traditional banks as well.

HOW SHOULD I GET MY FIRST CREDIT CARD?

You must be at least eighteen years old, and if you are under twenty-one, you will need to show income from a job. So, start out by getting a job—have money coming in before it is going out.

If you have been working with a bank, try applying with this already established relationship. If you are at college, look for a student credit card. If you aren't having luck, look to a retail store that you use often; they typically have favorable approval odds.

Utilize sites such as BankRate.com, NerdWallet.com, or CreditKarma.com to review your approval odds for specific cards, targeting those that do not require a high credit score or long credit history. Then compare the rates and fees of the card. Don't forget to read the reviews!

When you are ready to apply, you will need to give your full name, date of birth, Social Security number, address, employment information, and income.

WHAT DO I NEED TO AVOID WITH MY FIRST CREDIT CARD?

For your first card, you should avoid any type of **ANNUAL FEE**, a yearly cost to just have this specific card. You should not be using this card enough to cover that type of fee. Also be on the lookout for gimmicks, as some cards waive the fee upon signing up, but will begin to charge it after a few months.

Avoid at all costs a **CASH ADVANCE.** A cash advance allows you to withdraw cash from your credit limit. When you do this, you accrue interest immediately, without a grace period, and the interest rate will be even higher than your APR!

Never get **CHARGED OFF,** which refers to missing payments for six months and your credit company writing your debt off as uncollectable. This offense will negatively impact your credit score and you will still be liable for this debt, only now it will transfer to a debt collector or bankruptcy.

Regardless of your credit limit, you should try to use a maximum of only 30 percent. Meaning that if you have a credit limit of $1,000, you should only use $300.

ARE THERE ANY TOOLS THAT CAN HELP ME MANAGE MY CREDIT CARD MORE LIKE A DEBIT CARD?

Yes, there are! Remember your new teammate from chapter 4, the banker? Well, you can set up an automatic payment from your Today (checking) account to be sent every month to your credit card account. There are also applications that can help you perform these tasks. Just Google "Apps to pay off my credit card" and find a free one!

WHAT IF I WANT TO BE INTRODUCED TO CREDIT, BUT NOT GET AN UNSECURED LOAN?

Understandably getting a credit card has risks and that can make people nervous. There are ways to step into this credit world, without taking on a traditional unsecured credit card.

First you can look into a **SECURED CREDIT CARD.** Secured credit cards are where you make a deposit of money—say $500—and that serves as your security and credit limit. If you fail to make the payment, you will lose some of the money you used to secure the card. A secured credit card can be a great introduction to credit and will even work to build your credit score.

Another option for those who are minors and want to begin developing credit is to become an **AUTHORIZED USER** on another account. If there is someone you trust, family or mentor, who has a credit card and they feel confident in your ability to handle the responsibility of credit, they can add your name to the account as an authorized user. This will allow you to begin building credit from a younger age.

Be warned, this ties your credit to that person. Meaning if they make a mistake, it impacts you and if you make a mistake, it impacts them.

WHY, HOW, WHAT AND WHEN—THE STEPS TO PAY OFF CREDIT CARDS

WHY — REVIEW WHY YOU FELL INTO THE CREDIT TRAP.

HOW — WHAT IS THE APR ON EACH CARD AND WHAT IS THE BALANCE?

WHAT — SET UP YOUR PLAN OF ATTACK, CHOOSING EITHER THE SMALLEST BALANCE OR HIGHEST APR FIRST!

WHEN — AUTOMATE YOUR CREDIT CARD PAYMENT.

SECTION 5.3
RECAP

1. M.A.D. MAKES YOU MAD! DO NOT FALL INTO THIS CREDIT TRAP.

2. TREAT CREDIT LIKE DEBIT, DON'T SPEND WHAT YOU DON'T HAVE AND AUTOMATE YOUR PAYMENT.

3. AVOID ANNUAL FEES OR TAKING A CASH ADVANCE AND TRY TO ONLY U.S.E. 30% OF YOUR CREDIT LIMIT.

SECTION 5.4
YOUR FINANCIAL REPUTATION, CREDIT SCORE

TERMS

FAIR CREDIT & REPORTING ACT: Federal legislation to promote the accuracy, fairness, and privacy of consumer information captured by consumer reporting agencies.

FICO: Fair Isaac Corporation is perhaps the best-known company that calculates personal credit scores.

FANNIE MAE & FREDDIE MAC: mortgage companies created and backed by the United States Government to purchase mortgages in a secondary market, neither institution issues their own mortgages.

FINANCIAL REPUTATION: how lenders will measure how much they can trust you and a key indicator is your Credit Score.

CREDIT REPORT: a list of every credit-related action you have taken in a period of time.

CREDIT SCORE: a single number derived from the transactions in your Credit Report that will provide a comparative benchmark between lenders.

FEDERAL TRADE COMMISSION (FTC): established in 1914 to administer and protect fair competition in the marketplace.

HARD INQUIRY: when your credit report is pulled in connection with requesting more credit or debt. Ex. Applying for credit card or auto loan.

SOFT INQUIRY: when your credit report is pulled but there is no request for more credit or debt. Ex. Insurance companies or property managers.

CREDIT BUREAU: a company that collects information relating to your credit and makes the information available to financial institutions.

EXPERIAN: member of the 'big three' credit reporting agencies.

THE CREDIT CLASS

Adrian walks into Mrs. Musk's Algebra classroom with a plan to try an improve his grade. He saw his grade yesterday, a C+, and was really hoping to have gotten a B. Approaching Mrs. Musk with a smile, Adrian says "Hey, Mrs. Musk how is your day going?"

A seasoned teacher, Mrs. Musk welcomes the approach, but is not fooled into why Adrian is here."

"Wonderful, Adrian, just going through some of the extra credit and second-attempts students have turned."

"You know Mrs. Musk; I was just coming in to talk to you about that." Adrian says. "Students these days just do not appreciate the in-person conversation. I am thinking about my grade yesterday and wanted to come and talk to you directly about how I can improve that grade?"

Mrs. Musk is pleased that that Adrian's charade wrapped up quickly, and responds: "Adrian, when you start to look at being late to class, missing an assignment, forgoing the extra study groups, and an all in all lack of focus on the syllabus guide, then there is not a whole lot you can do about changing the final grade,"

Adrian looks confused, so Mrs. Musk goes on.

"The final grade is important, but it is more a reflection of everything you have been doing in class. Your grade is made up of your class attendance, your homework assignments, your quizzes, and your final exam.

There are a few ways to impact your final grade, but it is more important to go look through the entire semester and see where you took some missteps. If you can look at where you lost points and try to fix those assignments or turn in some extra work, then you should be able to move that grade up."

That is exactly what I am going to do, Mrs. Musk!" Adrian says excitedly. "I know I made a mistake on assignment three and missed a quiz. If I fix those mistakes, will it be enough to get to a B?"

"You can give assignment three a second attempt, but you can't retake a missed quiz," responds Mrs. Musk. "That is a mistake you must learn from, and just try not to repeat."

Adrian stands to leave with his hope being strengthened and already thinking through that assignment. But before he can get out of the classroom Mrs. Musk calls out: "Adrian, don't forget to check for any mistakes I may have made as well. I am human after all."

HOW DID WE GET TO A "CREDIT SCORE"?

Before we can break down what a credit score is, we should establish where it came from and why it will be so important in your life. This topic will play a part in deciding where you live, where you work, and even where you go to the doctor.

Debt has been around for 5,000 years but tracking and reporting it have only been around for 200 years. How people used to verify people to loan to was by asking a neighbor or someone in town to vouch for them. But as population grew, you could see how this system begins to break down.

In 1841, Lewis Tappan founded the "Mercantile Agency," and set out to create the first attempt for the United States to have a system to measure if you should lend money to other businesses, known as commercial credit. The agency would attempt to validate both the character and the actual assets of businessmen generating massive ledgers in New York City.

This was the beginning of the credit score, an idea that scholar Josh Lauer has called your "financial identity." This identity summarizes your financial history and threatens to plummet should you make certain financial choices.

But each advancement established the pillars needed for commercial credit reporting in the modern era, those pillars being:

Private sector surveillance of people's transactions

Sharing of information between bureaus and the agencies collecting the data

A ratings system that made everything measurable.

It wasn't until the late 19th century when people began to work less and make more that department stores wanted to find new ways to get more money into their stores. This new consumer credit would allow individuals to buy things they perhaps could not afford right away with the trust it would be paid back.

In the 1960s, data was being collected from over 2,000 credit bureaus across the country, by paper! This was before the daily use of computers. But then everything changed in 1970 with the passing of the "**FAIR CREDIT REPORTING ACT,**" and an attempt to remove bias or prejudice from the closed doors of credit bureaus. The Fair Credit and Reporting Act required bureaus to begin sharing their information with the public, expunged data on race, gender, or disability, and issued that negative information be deleted after a period of time.

Over time, the credit bureaus were bought up and consolidated into three major credit bureaus that compute millions of people's financial identities each day: Experian, TransUnion, and Equifax. However, even with the consolidation into these three bureaus, they were still unsuccessful in succeeding to produce a national credit report. There was still an inability to compare the three different reports produced by the three different bureaus.

With computers in full swing now, they began working with a technology company to develop an algorithm that could score these credit reports. The technology company was called "Fair, Isaac and Company," but you may know it better as **FICO**.

In 1989, FICO worked with the national credit bureaus to create an algorithm that would provide a scoring model that could be used to compare the different credit reports. This algorithm that is amazingly like the one used today has become known as your credit score.

By the mid-1990s, **FANNIE MAE** and **FREDDIE MAC**, two companies that purchase mortgages from lenders to stabilize the money supply in the market, began requiring mortgage applicants to submit their credit score as part of the decision-making process to lend money for homes.

TODAY, FICO CLAIMS THEIR CREDIT SCORE IS USED BY 90% OF TOP LENDERS IN THE COUNTRY.

The system is no doubt imperfect, whether you want to point to too much power being in the hands of the few or too much surveillance invading your privacy or to the idea that there are still social hierarchies and prejudices in the system, the credit score is not without flaw. But the idea of the alternative, a world where there is no centralized measurement to know who you can financially trust would be an even more chaotic system.

Why is this topic so important today, as there are over 26 million Americans who are considered credit "invisible." If these people needed a loan to buy a car or home, they would sadly be declined.

The Credit Game is not perfect, but it is how people will know not only if you can pay your debts, but if your will. That is why we here at Money Vehicle refer to your credit score as your **"FINANCIAL REPUTATION"**. It is how people will begin to know if they can trust you financially before they even meet you.

> Your credit score is your financial reputation in the world and determines how much people will or will not trust you.

Trust is very important when you think about handing a stranger some of your money and the world needs a benchmark of financial trust. A way of being able to compare one person they could lend money with another; this benchmark is your credit score.

If you want to know what people think about you financially or if they would trust you with a loan, look no further that your "financial reputation," it will typically reflect their answer.

GOOD HISTORY LESSON BUT WHY IS THIS SO IMPORTANT TO ME NOW?

The importance of credit scores will be seen throughout your financial plan and anytime someone wants to have a measurement of your past financial decisions. This person could be selling you a car or a home, hiring you for a job, providing insurance coverage, or simply selling you a phone. Every one of them will use your financial reputation as a measurement of if they should do business with you AND what type of business, they should offer you.

1. APPLYING FOR A JOB

Why would your future employer be concerned with your credit score? According to a survey by Salary Finance   half (50%) of workers suffer from financial stress, and these workers are more likely to lose sleep, be depressed, not finish daily tasks, turn in lower quality work, and have poorer relationships with their colleagues.   [18]

One study by Benefits Pro   estimates that financial stress costs companies in the USA around $4.7 BILLION PER WEEK! That is why your credit score is included when you apply for a job, because it will cost your company money if you feel too stressed about your finances.

Every day, hiring committees question if they should bring on a new teammate who is already showing signs of this issue. When these committees begin to look at a stack of resumes, many of which are worthy candidates for the job, a credit score can be a differentiator. Wouldn't it be easier to hire the person who is more trusted with their paycheck?

Having a poor financial reputation can make you seem like someone who cannot handle their personal finances or possibly someone who should not be trusted in a business setting.

2. BUYING A CAR

You're about to graduate from high school, and one of your dreams is to drive up to graduation in a new car! You know that the car will cost more than you have, but you are confident you can get a loan and make the payments. As you go to the dealership, they show you around and once you select your wheels, they begin to ask for some information. This information will begin with your financial reputation.

The dealership is only concerned with one thing, will you make your payments on this new car loan? If your reputation is low or if it is just too short of a period of time, they will either decline to lend you the money or offer it at an interest rate you should decline.

3. APPLYING FOR AN APARTMENT, PHONE, ETC.

Your credit score can even come into play when signing a contract for something like a new cell phone or an apartment.

We will learn an investing principle is "Risk equals Return," which states that there must be risk to provide return, but also that if the risk increases so should the return. When applying for a new phone, apartment, or anything else, your contract may be at a higher price, and you may be required to put down a larger deposit due to your risk being higher.

The risk of you not fulfilling your obligations is higher because that is what your financial reputation is and that means the company will want more in return.

4. CREDIT CARDS

Of course, your credit score will come into consideration when taking out a credit card. The irony of course is how do you start to build credit without using a credit card? But again, you will receive a higher interest rate or not even have access to certain reward cards until your reputation is built.

THE $100,000 EXAMPLE!

Let's look at two friends who are trying to buy a house and need to borrow $300,000.

Harper has not handled her credit very well and has a low credit score of 560, where Darrel has been building his credit score since he was a senior in high school and has a high credit score of 760 (do not get too lost in the actual score as we will dive into that shortly, for now, just understand that one is higher than the other and that both are looking for a $300,000 mortgage).

Darrel will receive a 30-year fixed rate mortgage at 3.8% with a monthly payment of $1,398.

Harper will receive a 30-year fixed rate mortgage at 5.39% with a monthly payment of $1,683.

THAT IS A $285 DIFFERENCE EACH MONTH, AND OVER THE LIFE OF THE MORTGAGE, WILL COME TO OVER $102,000!

Is that enough to see why your financial reputation is so important?

None of this is to say that people with bad credit are bad people because that could not be further from the truth or this conversation. We are not talking about the type of person here; we are talking about their financial health.

How have they handled debt in the past and should they be trusted to handle more in the future. Those are the only questions future lenders are concerned with. How much of their decision will be made begins and ends with your financial reputation – credit score!

CLASS VS. GRADE = REPORT VS. SCORE

We began this section with an identification of what the difference between a **CREDIT REPORT** (Class) and a **CREDIT SCORE** (Grade) is. Lots of attention will be given to your credit score as it becomes your financial reputation and a number that often introduces you to strangers, but the truth is you have more control over what is going into that report than the calculation of the score.

Your credit report will be a collection of all your financial transactions (much like your classwork) that will document all your lender relationships and how you have been managing your payments. These reports are meant to keep track of how you handle money in your life.

Can enough time pass to dull the impact of a mistake? Absolutely. But there is a reason it is called Credit History: because your decisions will be reported to credit bureaus whose job is to keep track of how you have been managing your finances, both recently and in your past.

The government understands how important these reports are and they want you to have free access to them once a year. The Fair Credit Reporting Act ensures that you can access all your information by going to AnnualCreditReport.com

WARNING!

Call them scammers, schemers, or successful but there are many attempts to trick you into PAID credit monitoring services using a connection to the Fair Credit Reporting Act. You have access to a FREE report once a year.

Use AnnualCreditReport.com as a resource to look up your credit report and confirm that there are no errors. These credit bureaus are run by humans and sometimes have human errors in them.

ONE IN FOUR CONSUMERS IDENTIFIED ERRORS ON THEIR CREDIT REPORTS THAT MIGHT AFFECT THEIR CREDIT SCORES.

Your credit score will be a three-digit number that reflects the category of trust a lender will provide you with. Much like your final grade, these scores reflect what you have been doing with your money. Your credit score becomes your financial reputation, it is what people will know about you before they ever actually meet you. This score will show how you have been handling the current debt relationships you are in and answer the question of how easily you should be given the opportunity to U.S.E. more.

Financial institutions saw how vital knowing your credit score is, and many have begun offering credit score tools in their service offering. These resources can show you your score and even why it has gone up or down in the past weeks.

The federal statutes and regulations are not to mislead you in believing credit reports are perfect. In fact, the **FEDERAL TRADE COMMISSION (FTC)** has reported there are over 40 million mistakes on credit reports, going so far as to say "one-in-five" contain "material" errors that could be dinging your credit score.

Make sure you review your credit report and look for common credit report errors such as:

- Incorrect personal information such as your name being misspelled or someone with a similar name having accounts show up on your account.
- Incorrect accounts opened from identity theft. The FTC reports over 167,000 fraudulent credit cards being opened in a year.
- Incorrect account owner. Having someone else's name by the main owner instead of your own.
- Accounts you have closed that are still showing as open.
- Duplicate accounts with different names or owners.
- Inaccurate payment history or outdated information.

SHOULD I CHECK MY CREDIT SCORE OFTEN?

It is not necessary to constantly check your credit score, because much like your actual reputation, it takes a long time to build. Your score should not drastically go up or down and if it does, you should be able to pinpoint exactly why. Keeping tabs on your credit score a few times per year will be enough in normal circumstances. If you are trying to raise your score or when you are attempting to take out debt, then you should be very conscious of where your credit score is but no need to check it weekly.

You want to be careful about the types of inquiries both you and others are making. There is a significant difference in a "**HARD INQUIRY**" versus a "**SOFT INQUIRY.**"

- Hard Inquiry: an inquiry that pertains to a lending decision such as applying for a mortgage, auto, student, business, or personal loan, or for a credit card. These inquiries will need your approval and will then show up on your credit report. One or two a year will not damage your score too much, but several hard inquiries at once or several throughout the year will have a negative impact on your score. This is because the constant request for more credit makes you seem like you need more to make your plan work and the likelihood of the lender getting their money back is lower.

- Soft Inquiry: an inquiry or investigation into who you are and not necessarily a request for more credit. This can be through employer background checks, a company who you are buying a good or service from, getting pre-approved for a loan, or you are checking your own credit score. These soft inquiries can be done without your permission and may not even show up on your credit report.

Money Vehicle does want to alert you to a common misunderstanding around checking your own credit report or credit score, in that people think it will negatively impact their credit score. The good news is that your credit score will not be impacted by you checking your score or transactions. When you review your credit score you are not asking for more credit or debt, so it is not considered a hard inquiry.

WHO ARE THESE "BUREAUS," ANYWAY?

A **CREDIT BUREAU** is also known as a "Credit Reporting Agency," and is a company that collects information about people's financial transactions. This information is then passed through the bureau's proprietary algorithm to create credit reports and credit scores. The bureau can then sell this information to banks, mortgage lenders, and credit companies to validate if the lender should trust this new applicant.

The three main credit bureaus are: **EXPERIAN**, **EQUIFAX**, and **TRANSUNION**. Each of these credit bureaus will gather information on you and create their own report.

WHAT, EXACTLY, ARE THESE BUREAUS GATHERING?

Credit bureaus will have your personal information such as your name, date of birth, social security number, past and current addresses, and any employment history. Then the credit bureaus will keep tabs on any money you owe or have owed, how long you have been using credit, your late and missed payments, how much of your credit you are using, and things like bankruptcies.

The bureaus will also keep records of any inquiries depending on soft or hard as we just learned. Normal day-to-today activities such as deposits and withdrawals from your checking account are not accounted for because it is dealing strictly with your money.

These bureaus receive the information directly from the banks, credit companies, or mortgage lenders you are working with to create Credit reports that are a snapshot of how you handle credit. Utilities, phone companies, or monthly bills can also provide information around how you are paying your bills. Situations like bankruptcies are reported on public records.

The goal in gathering all this data is to find out how you handle the trust (credit) being given you and measure if you are using it wisely or unwisely. For example, if you are going to rent an apartment, your landlord could look at these reports to answer what outstanding debt you have, how have you been making payments, and if you have broken the trust of others in the past.

All your information is then passed through each credit bureau and then passed onto a third party to create your overall credit score.

WAIT, THE SAME COMPANY DOES NOT PRODUCE THE REPORT AND SCORE?

No, that would be too easy. The credit bureau will pass their information onto a credit scoring company of which there are two main scores, **FICO SCORE** and **VANTAGE SCORE.** We introduced the "Fair, Isaac, and Company" earlier, but you will become more comfortable with this "FICO" scoring system.

Another system to be aware of is the Vantage Score. The claim and objective of both companies is to predict which consumer will pay their credit obligation back late or never at all.

FICO was built by a mathematician and an engineer in 1956, but it wasn't until 1989 that the first scoring models were introduced to lenders and contracted to solve the credit scoring issue. Today, FICO claims to be used by 90% of the top lenders in making decisions about you!

Vantage was founded by the three main credit bureaus – Equifax, Experian, and TransUnion – in 2006. Both companies collect data from the same three bureaus but then use their own proprietary calculations to predict the likelihood of repaying borrowed money.

To qualify for a score is a little more tedious with FICO than with Vantage. FICO requires you to have some form of credit line for at least six months and have transacted in the past six months. Vantage simply requires you to have evidence of some form of credit line, regardless of the length in time.

Today, both systems are calculated on the same 300-850 scoring scale. Where the higher the score the more trust you will receive from the lending company and the easier the process will be. But your scores may be different from FICO to Vantage Score because they use different methods to calculate your score.

SO, DOES CHECKING MY ACCOUNT HAVE ANYTHING TO DO WITH MY CREDIT SCORE?

Not exactly. It is true that your checking account deals with your money and will not be a primary driver of information for your credit report, there are a few situations that can impact your score.

 For instance, one example is if you were to overdraw on your account and fail to deposit money to make the account whole, your bank may turn you into a collection agency which would be listed on your credit report.

 Another example is when you first sign up for a checking account, the bank will run a soft inquiry. As you know now, this will not impact your score. However, the bank can run a hard inquiry if you sign up for "Overdraft Protection."

Banks advertise the benefits of this feature but fail to mention the relationship that has been formed. Overdraft protection is signing up for a line of credit and with that it will require a hard inquiry as well as being listed on your credit report.

I NEED TO KEEP AN EYE ON MY MONEY BUCKETS AND HANDLE ANY ISSUES WITH ACCOUNT RIGHT AWAY?

Yes! It is paramount that you understand where your money is going and where there are issues. As you saw in the checking account example, your credit score will not be impacted until credit is issued, or a collection agency is notified.

When you look at late fees, the penalty is typically $25 or $35 if not your first offense. But it is not until there are several late charges of a failure to pay the penalty that the creditor will "charge off" the account. This is when a creditor claims that the debt is unlikely to be collected and writes it off as a loss. This is extremely damaging to your credit score and can remain on your report for up to seven years!

CREDIT SCORES AND CURFEWS!

We have established that your credit score will become your financial reputation, a benchmark that people will use to decide if they trust you with their money or a variety of other financial circumstances. We have not discussed how this score is calculated.

Unfortunately, you do not start with a positive score. Oddly enough the fact you may have a "clean slate" when it comes to credit will be a disadvantage. Credit companies do not want to see a clean slate, they want someone with a track record and until you begin to build up yours, you will be at a disadvantage.

This begs the question of how credit companies calculate your score. To answer this, we will ask a question that has been asked by almost every teenager in the world: Can I get my curfew extended until midnight?

This question revolves around one measure: TRUST.

With this connection of trust, we will see how your parents and the credit company will ask the same five questions to decide if they will extend you more trust.

Adrian turned in assignment three, some extra work, and feels good about the final. So good that he is going to try and get a later curfew this weekend for the big party at Monique's house.

Adrian is excited and again hopeful, but he approaches his mom with some hesitation. "Mom, I am pretty sure I did enough to move my grade up in algebra."

"Glad to hear it and proud, although I do not think you should have been scrambling at the last minute," responds his mother. Adrian winces a bit at that response because he knows his mom is already on high alert. But with the biggest party of the year on the horizon, he pushes his luck: "Yeah, I will be more prepared next time. So, mom, this weekend is Monique's party. Any chance I could extend my curfew out until midnight?"

Adrian's mom responds without emotion and almost as if Adrian had not even asked a question: "When was the last time you broke curfew?"

FIRST QUESTION DETERMINING YOUR CREDIT SCORE:

 When was the last time you missed a payment?

Questioning when you broke curfew and when you missed a payment are establishing that they have trusted you in the past and questioning if you have broken that trust before, or how recently. Your track record in credit is called **PAYMENT HISTORY.**

In any relationship, you build trust by keeping true to what you said you were going to do. If you said you would be home by 11:00 or said you would make your monthly credit payment and then went on to break that promise, it would leave a mark. Your payment history is the biggest impactor of your final credit score at 35%.

Adrian knows this is a pivotal factor in his mom's decision but is happy to report "Mom, I haven't missed curfew in a long time! Ever since that crazy squirrel fire, but that wasn't my fault and since then I have always made it in on time."

Adrian's mom reluctantly admits that was not something Adrian could control, but quickly pivots to "last week, you came in at 10:59 when your curfew was at 11:00. I know you made it in on time, but I do not like that you were pushing the limit."

SECOND QUESTION DETERMINING YOUR CREDIT SCORE:

 How much of your credit line have you been using?

Pushing the limit on your curfew or your credit card limit is risky business. Do not be confused about your credit companies' intentions. They do want you to use your card and they do want to charge you that extra high interest payment, but they also want to make sure you will be able to make your payments. If you continue to max out your cards, the chances of the lender getting their money back goes down.

This concept is called **CREDIT UTILIZATION,** what percent of your credit line are you using or "utilizing." Someone using the full capacity of their credit is a red flag that you are not handling their finances well and should not be trusted with more credit.

It is effective to utilize your credit, meaning you should put purchases on your card, but as we have discussed before paying off the balance in full is the best option. If you are unable to zero out your credit each month, then attempt to have your credit utilization under 30% of the entire line. The less of your credit line you utilize the higher your credit score will be.

For example, if you have a $1,000 credit card limit you would want to keep your utilization under $300. Your credit utilization will make up 30% of your credit score.

FINANCIAL TIP:

Aim for 0%, with monthly payoffs. But if you must have a balance, remain under 30% of your credit utilization.

Adrian can see he is going to need to go on the aggressive here and changes his strategy. "Yes, but mom, I made it in before 11:00. And I am getting to be too old to have my curfew at 11:00, nothing fun happens before 11:00!"

Adrian's mom smiles and responds "Too old? You will always be my baby. But how long has your curfew been at 11:00 anyway?"

THIRD QUESTION DETERMINING YOUR CREDIT SCORE:

 How long have you had credit?

Establishing how long you have been at this curfew or credit limit will begin to show your maturity. The longer you have been at a current phase builds up your track record and will encourage the idea of pushing into the next. This is why young people are at a disadvantage with credit scores, their name simply does not have a track record.

Starting your credit history today will start this clock and immediately start to positively impact your score. Then of course you must continue U.S.E.ing credit the right way. Your **CREDIT HISTORY** will make up 15% of your credit score.

Adrian begins to plead as he sees his window closing. "Mom, I have been at 11:00 since I was like 8 years old! C'mon mom, tonight is the biggest birthday party of the year. Everyone is going to be there, and the party goes until 12:00. Pleaseeeee!"

This does not land as well as Adrian had hoped, his mom says "I don't care how big the party is, there is no reason you need to be out after 11:00. Besides, didn't you ask your father for a curfew extension last week? What are you just going around asking everybody for a later curfew now?"

FOURTH QUESTION DETERMINING YOUR CREDIT SCORE:

 Have you been shopping and asking around for more credit?

Persistence is a skill; nuisance is a tell.

The look of desperation is never a welcomed trait, no matter in your personal or financial life. When looking at your credit, companies do not want to see that you have been asking anyone in town for a loan. This look of desperation is a red flag and raises questions about your current situation. Why do you need this so bad right now? Again, the credit company will question the likelihood of getting their payments.

Money Vehicle is NOT saying you shouldn't shop your rates and offer around but like with everything in this program you need to do it with a strategy. When you are ready to take out a credit card, car loan, or student debt you should plan on sending your applications within a close time horizon. When you submit for a new loan every month, companies will simply be annoyed. The number of hard credit inquiries will make up 10% of your credit score.

FINANCIAL TIP:

When looking to take out a new loan, submit your inquiries in groups. Applying for an auto loan with 3 different lenders but all in the same week. Even if it is a HARD Inquiry and there is a consideration for a loan, submitting the request in batches will prevent damage to your Credit Score.

One last hope Adrian now lays it all out and hopes he can flip his mom by playing the cool card. "I know, I know; I did ask last week but tonight is the BIG party. Everybody at practice was talking about it, it would be so cool of you to let me stay out late."

Adrian's mom lays down the law "You think I care what everyone else is talking about? Practice? Let's talk about practice for a minute. Have you been practicing your Algebra score, have you got your grade in that class up since last we spoke? Or what about family dinner last night, you had to miss that for some odd reason. Feels like you have a little too much going on. I don't think you can handle a later curfew with everything that you are currently juggling."

FIFTH QUESTION DETERMINING YOUR CREDIT SCORE:

 Do you currently have multiple lines of credit or debt?

Your ability to juggle all the things in life simply shows responsibility. This can be school and band practice or a credit card and student loan, staying on top of it all is something both your parents and credit company want to see. This last measurement feels like a conflict of interest in our opinion, you will be rewarded for having more debt. However odd it may sound; it is true that having multiple lines of debt can positively impact your score.

For example, having one or two credit cards, a car payment, and a mortgage payment is a lot for credit companies to verify their trust in you. Would be foolish not to mention one more time that you must U.S.E. all these the correct way. The mix of credit you have will make up 10% of your credit score.

3 REASONS: NOT TO CANCEL THAT OLD CREDIT CARD

WAIT!! Before you cancel that old card, consider how it will impact your FICO score:

1. 30% OF FICO SCORE= DEBT OWED TO CREDIT LIMIT

Canceling your old credit cards, even though you don't want to use them anymore will decrease your total credit limit. Now, even though you are being more frugal and spending less, this action will decrease your total credit limit and make the ration of how much you are using go up, even if you aren't using more.

2. 15% OF FICO SCORE = LENGTH OF CREDIT HISTORY

What is the first question asked when you enter a job interview? "Do you have any experience?" Experience is the catch 22 of the corporate world, you need it to get a job and you can't get it until you have a job. This is oddly like applying for credit.

It takes a lifetime to build a reputation, and that is exactly the stance credit companies take. Credit companies want to see how long you have been making payments, building up your credit, and being responsible. From the credit company's eyes, if you cancel the older of the two cards your reputation has been cut from 7 years down to only 3. Reducing the length of credit history and negatively impacting your FICO score.

3. 10% OF FICO SCORE = MIX OF LOAN AND CARD TYPES

The credit company wants to see that you are responsible enough to manage more than one type of debt. Down the road you will get points in your score for having an auto loan or a home mortgage. For now, holding onto two credit cards and proving you can handle the responsibility of different lines of credit and different payment dates, will have a positive impact on your FICO score.

WHEN WOULD I CALL TO CANCEL MY OLD CREDIT CARD?

If your old card has some sort of annual fee attached to it, there is no need to pay $50 for a few points in your FICO score.

WHAT IS THE BEST PLAN OF ACTION?

Go into the drawer, get out a pair of scissors and cut up your old credit card. This way you won't be tempted to use it, but you will maintain all the positive effects on your FICO score mentioned. Then when you do want to use the card again, you simply call and get a new card mailed. Instead of applying for an entirely new card, which also can have a negative impact on your score.

NEXT STEPS:

- Take out the credit cards in your wallet and compare.
- Ask: Which has the longest history, which has fees attached, and which do I see myself using going forward?
- Go get some scissors!

CREDIT MYTHS WE MUST GET RID OF:

 1. IF I MAKE MY PAYMENTS ON TIME, I AM GOOD TO GO!

Yes, making your payments on time is a big piece of your credit score, but simply making a payment is not the only measurement. How big of a balance you have in relation to how much of your credit line is being used will also impact your score. Aim to U.S.E. under 30% of your credit lines.

2. CARRYING A BALANCE WILL BOOST MY SCORE!

According to the **CONSUMER FINANCIAL PROTECTION BUREAU (CFPB)** the rumor that debt helps your credit score is not only incorrect, but it is the opposite! The best way to improve your credit score is treating your credit like a debit and paying off your balance in full each month. Looking directly at Credit Utilization as a factor, you see that using less means a higher score.

 ## 3. PAYING WITH MY DEBIT CARD BUT USING THE "CREDIT" OPTION WILL HELP.

This election will slow down the transaction process but because you are still dealing with your debit card and your money, it will never be accounted for in your credit report. If your intention is to build your credit, then open a Secured Credit Card, become an authorized user, or open a traditional credit card.

 ## 4. GETTING MULTIPLE QUOTES FOR A CREDIT LINE WILL HURT YOUR SCORE.

We have discussed multiple inquiries being a negative, but the credit system does not want to dissuade conscious consumers from shopping around. The system will recognize multiple inquiries within a close period of time and bundle them together as a single inquiry. The time period is typically within 14 days but some debt like mortgages is even longer, up to 45 days.

 MONEY VEHICLE TIP:

Know what kind of loan you are looking for and when you are ready, get multiple quotes in the same week.

CREDIT SCORE BREAKDOWN

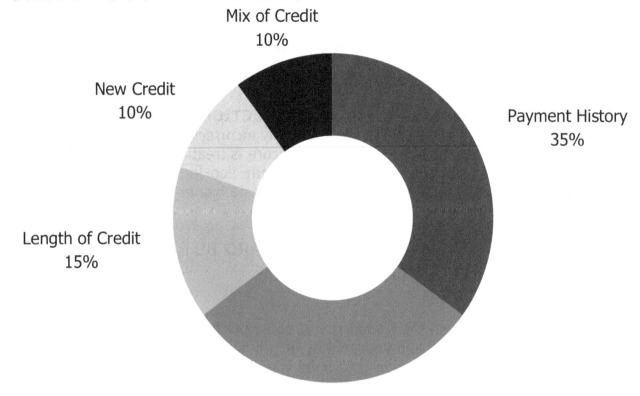

Mix of Credit
10%

New Credit
10%

Payment History
35%

Length of Credit
15%

Credit Utilization
30%

35%	**Payment History: Have you missed a payment lately?**
30%	**Credit Card Utilization: How much of your limit are you using?**
15%	**Credit History: How long have you had credit?**
10%	**New Credit: How often are you applying for more credit?**
10%	**Mix of Credit: How many different types of credit do you have?**

SECTION 5.4

RECAP

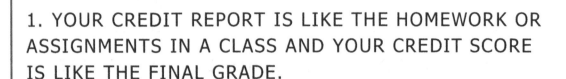

1. YOUR CREDIT REPORT IS LIKE THE HOMEWORK OR ASSIGNMENTS IN A CLASS AND YOUR CREDIT SCORE IS LIKE THE FINAL GRADE.

2. YOUR CREDIT SCORE BECOMES YOUR FINANCIAL REPUTATION.

3. YOUR FINANCIAL REPUTATION WILL IMPACT MANY ASPECTS OF YOUR FINANCIAL PLAN FROM GETTING A LOAN TO GETTING AN APARTMENT.

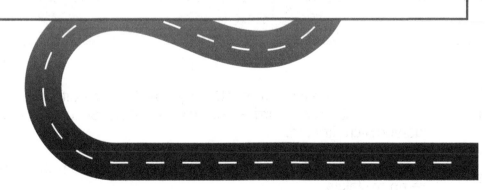

REVIEW

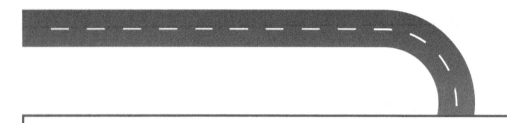

THE RULE: BUILD YOUR FINANCIAL REPUTATION

Start your credit history! Now you know that your debit card sends money over from your bank and your credit card sends credit from a third party. When you U.S.E. a credit card, you U.S.E. someone else's money and they will charge you interest on the balance. If you pay the M.A.D. you will fall into the credit trap where each purchase will end up costing more than you originally thought. Treating your credit card like a debit card will begin to build your Credit Score. This Credit Score will become your financial reputation and impact many aspects of your plan so U.S.E. credit wisely!

ACTION

Start building your financial reputation by opening a credit card.
- Get your 1st credit card – Authorized user, Secured Credit Card, or traditional credit card.
- Automate your credit payment each month.
- Look up your credit report at Annualcreditreport.com and confirm there are no mistakes.

OWNER'S MANUAL
FOR YOUR MONEY VEHICLE:

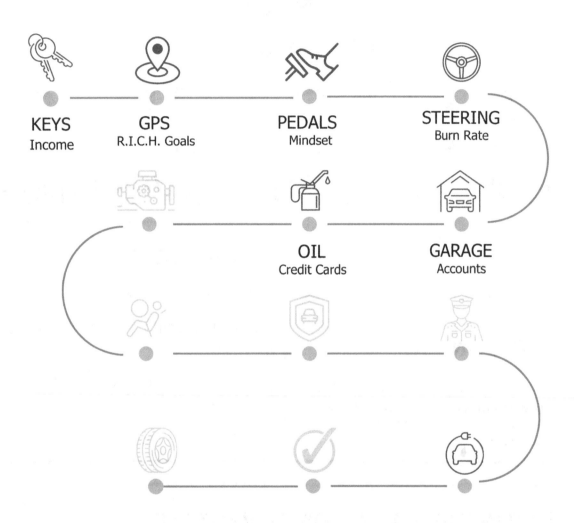

KEYS
Income

GPS
R.I.C.H. Goals

PEDALS
Mindset

STEERING
Burn Rate

OIL
Credit Cards

GARAGE
Accounts

INVESTING

CHAPTER 6

HOW DO I START INVESTING?

ACTION

Act like an Invest-OR, find a platform you trust and make your first investment using Be Average = Index

OVERVIEW

6.1: Investing Basics

6.2: Investing's Long-Term Free Lunch

6.3: The Difference Between Stocks and Bonds

6.4: Be Average = Index

DRIVING YOUR MONEY VEHICLE

Finally, we get to start talking about moving Your Money Vehicle forward and how the engine works. Everyone loves talking about the engine—the power it exudes and the thrilling roar it gives when you hit the gas. No question about it, the engine roar on your Money Vehicle is investments. They are the power that will drive your journey forward, but you will need to U.S.E. them at the right speed and lane for your plan.

SECTION 6.1
INVESTING BASICS

TERMS

CAPITALISM: an economic system where a country's trade or industry is controlled by private owners for profit.

CAPITALIST: someone who participates in the buying and selling of goods for a profit.

'DO' - INVESTING PRINCIPLE: Do follow the Golden Rule or you will not be able to invest.

'RE' - INVESTING PRINCIPLE: Return and risk are positively correlated, meaning the higher the risk the higher the potential return.

POSITIVE CORRELATION: when changes in one item will be the same changes in a second item, or put simpler – when Stock A goes up due to an event, so will Stock B.

RULE OF 72: mathematical formula that shows how long it will take for your money to double through investing.

'ME' - INVESTING PRINCIPLE: -You will need to remove your emotions through having an investment strategy.

RISK TOLERANCE: the ability to predict the risk involved in your actions and measure the emotional impact you are willing to bear.

WHAT IS THE FIRST THING YOU THINK OF WHEN YOU HEAR THE WORD CAPITALISM?

When thinking of **CAPITALISM**, many of us envision high and mighty businesspeople who care only about themselves. While that may be an accurate depiction of some capitalists, the true definition of a **CAPITALIST** is simply 'someone who participates in the buying and selling of goods for a profit'.

WHY ARE WE DISCUSSING CAPITALISM IN A FINANCIAL LITERACY CLASS?

Well, because you not only want to be a capitalist, but you also want to be a good capitalist. Together, we are embarking on this financial journey because you want to better Understand, Strategize, and Efficiently U.S.E. money in The Market. The market is where all publicly traded companies are held and transacted upon.

The Capitalistic system is the basis of investing, and if you do not believe there will be a profit in the market, then you should not bother investing in it. So, for now, and to help introduce you to the fundamentals of investing, let's all agree that over a long-term time horizon, the market will produce a profit, and capitalism will create wealth.

19

Now, for a brief musical break, let's look at the lyrics of "Do-Re-Mi" from Rogers and Hammerstein's 1959 classic, The Sound of Music.

> Let's start at the very beginning.
> A very good place to start.
> When you read you begin with A-B-C
> When you sing you begin with Do-Re-Mi.

Oddly enough, when you invest, you begin with Do-Re-Mi as well—or DO, RE, ME, to be exact.

DO

FOLLOW THE GOLDEN RULE.

The first step in any investment portfolio is living by the Golden Rule! If you spend more than you make, you will never have anything to save, let alone invest.

To begin investing, you will need to understand your earned income and your burn rate to see how much you can afford to put towards your 'Future You' bucket. You must start with this "DO" investment principle because making $100,000 does not matter to your investments if you are spending $100,000.

Remember you will start by saving your Corona Cushion before you can put money at risk in the investment world. But once you have your Golden Rule set and Corona Cushion in place, you are able to take on the risks of the market.

RE

RETURN HAS RISK.

The moment someone tells you that you could make money on something is the same moment they are telling you that you could be putting your money at risk of losing it. It doesn't matter what the investment is—the more money you can make, the more money you can lose!

What you need to see though is that without risk, there would be no return. If something was 100% safe to invest in, why would they pay you to do it? The risk and possibility of losing money is what creates the return potential.

Sure, there are some risks that you can reduce and even eliminate, but there is no such thing as an investment return without an investment risk! Risk and return are **POSITIVELY CORRELATED,** which is when changes in one item will be the same change in a second item. Put simpler – if Stock A has a high-risk profile, it should also have a high reward potential.

When you look at investments that have a potential return of 5% verse investments with a potential return of 20%, you should immediately see there is a bigger risk in the investment with a bigger return potential

ME

EMOTIONS

Ben Graham, the individual who taught Warren Buffett how to invest is known for stating 'The investor's chief problem and even their worst enemy, is likely to be themselves.'

Think about this for a moment, why or how can you and your emotions derail your financial plan?

- Feeling embarrassed by a decision you made.
- Fearing missing an opportunity.
- Overreacting to market changes.
- Becoming overconfident in your abilities.

You can identify the risk of investing with emotions when you think about what you want to invest in and what you want to stop investing in. If you had an option to invest in Company A or Company B and all you knew about them is that Company A was up 10% from last year and Company B was down 5% from last year, which do you emotionally want to buy, and which do you emotionally want to avoid?

You can quickly see the natural emotion in investing is to Buy High & Sell Low. This means you would want to buy companies who are doing well and therefore at a higher price point. While at the same time avoid or sell companies that are doing poorly and therefore at a lower price point.

This is an introduction to your individual **RISK TOLERANCE**, which is the ability to predict the risk involved in your actions and measure the emotional impact you are willing to bear.

Imagine you are driving on the freeway and the speed limit is 65 miles per hour. How you can view your risk tolerance is:

- Someone who is driving 60 mph: wants to avoid risk
- Someone who is driving 65 mph: low risk tolerance
- Someone who is driving 70 mph: moderate tolerance
- Someone who is driving 80 mph: high risk tolerance

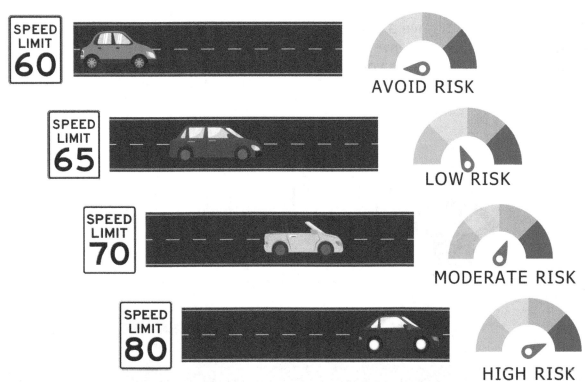

Your tolerance for risk will change throughout your life based on experience, planning, and overall comfortability with investing. For now, understand that with investing there is risk and only you can judge how much risk you want to take on.

Money Vehicle wants you to build an investment strategy that will remove your emotions from your plan and rely on the habits you have formed throughout the program. This is not an easy task, gaining control of our emotions, but it will be essential in driving Your Money Vehicle.

With a strategy in place and a long-term time horizon, you should be able to Buy Low Today & Sell Higher Tomorrow.

It is essential to understand the basics of investing 'Do, Re, Me', because today's investment world is more complex than ever. Oddly enough, even as the investing world gets more and more complicated, the individual investor is gaining more and more access to it. Which makes your emotions and decisions that much closer as well.

Build a strategy and have a plan that will remove your emotions. But no matter how you begin to invest, all plans should begin with the end in mind— R.I.C.H. goals. Focusing on your goals will allow you to set a plan in place and not let short-term emotions distract from your long-term priorities.

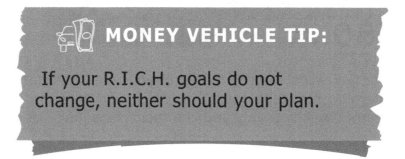

🚗💵 **MONEY VEHICLE TIP:**

If your R.I.C.H. goals do not change, neither should your plan.

SECTION 6.1
RECAP

1.DO: FOLLOW THE GOLDEN RULE, OR YOU WILL NOT HAVE ANYTHING TO INVEST.

2. RE: RETURN HAS RISK, THERE IS NO RETURN WITHOUT RISK.

3. MI: REMOVE ME EMOTIONS, THE CHIEF PROBLEM FOR THE INDIVIDUAL INVESTOR.

SECTION 6.2
INVESTING'S LONG-TERM FREE LUNCH

TERMS

DIVERSIFICATION: a risk management technique that mixes a wide variety of investments within a portfolio. Deemed a 'free lunch' because it can reduce your risk without reducing your returns.

INVERSELY CORRELATED: when changes in one item will be the opposite changes in a second item or put simpler – when Stock A goes up due to an event, Stock B will go down.

CONCENTRATION: the opposite of diversification where you invest in a small number or even a singular investment, creating more risk and the potential for more return.

FEDERAL SECURITIES ACT OF 1933: federal act that requires companies to disclose all any 'material' or important information related to a security investment.

SEC: federal agency responsible for regulating the securities industry, enforcing securities laws, and protecting you, the investor.

FINRA: created to regulate brokerage firms and registered advisors by creating a database of hundreds of thousands of firms and individuals is called BrokerCheck allowing investors to research their background and disciplinary actions.

DO YOU AGREE WITH THIS STATEMENT?:

 It is safer buying one company than trying to buy a lot of different companies.

It's a statement that challenges your familiarity with a concept called **DIVERSIFICATION**. Diversification is a risk management technique that mixes a wide variety of investments within a portfolio...yeah, I'm bored too.

LET'S SWITCH IT UP AND EXPLAIN IT LIKE MONEY VEHICLE, USING AN ANALOGY:

When I get home from work, I love taking my daughters to the park. Not only does it give my wife a much-needed break, but it also allows me to be the world's best dad—at least in my girls' eyes.

Our park trips always come down to a pivotal moment when one of them turns to me and says, "Dad, can I have a snack?"

Reaching into my pocket, I feel proud that I remembered to grab a granola bar before we left. Then, almost without seeing the bar, my daughter says, "I don't want that, I want fruit snacks."

After getting through a few failed park trips, and over the 'my kids-are-spoiled-these-days' disgruntlement, I began searching for a solution to the problem. My wife, a pro at keeping these things in line, gave me some advice: diversify!

Instead of arriving at the park with only one solution to the snack problem, she packs an entire backpack full of bars, fruit snacks, apples, and even some emergency lollipops.

Now, when we're at the park, and I get the question, "Can I have a snack?" I get to smile and say, "What would you like?"

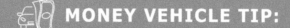

MONEY VEHICLE TIP:

The objective of diversification is to prevent any one event from ruining your entire plan.

If the park story made you say, "Why is this guy talking about his kids?" then maybe you have heard the age-old saying, "Don't put all your eggs in one basket!"

Think about it: if all your eggs are in one basket, one person can come by, knock the basket over, and break all your eggs with a single swipe of their hand. However, if you divide your eggs among several baskets, that person can still knock over one of your baskets, but because you diversified into other baskets, the damage is limited to only the eggs in that one basket that was knocked over.

Diversification is achieved in the investment world by having different types of investments that are **INVERSELY CORRELATED** to different events. Inversely correlated simply means that these investments react to the same event differently, typically heading in opposite directions.

IF MY MONEY IS INVERSELY CORRELATED, HOW WILL I MAKE MONEY?

Your investments will not always be moving in opposite directions. What you want to do is build a portfolio that is prepared for negative events like high inflation or low economic growth, but where your investments react differently to them.

- **Investment A** reacts positively to inflation but negatively to low economic growth.
- **Investment B** reacts negatively to inflation but positively to low economic growth.
- **If you diversify with Investments A & B**, then both scenarios will see your investments go up and down at the same time.

Responding inversely to negative events is what provides the plan protection through hard times. Avoiding losing lots of money during poor investment periods is key to diversification and then during positive investment periods your plan will generate a profit.

WHY HAS DIVERSIFICATION BEEN CALLED INVESTING'S FREE LUNCH?

The idea of 'free' is that you get something for nothing. With diversification in your plan, you can get the benefit of reducing your short-term risk, without giving up your long-term investment returns.

Diversification is coined 'investing free lunch' because it gives protection without taking anything away.

WAIT A MINUTE, I THOUGHT YOU SAID, "RETURN IS RISK."

Good memory from 6.1. Yes, diversification will reduce your risk, and therefore, reduce your potential short-term investment return.

The opposite of diversification is **CONCENTRATION**—that is, only investing in a single company. In the short-term, concentration can create larger investment returns, because it produces more risk. In the long-term money can be created and lost with concentration.

Jeff Bezos isn't one of the richest people in the world because he diversified, but because his wealth multiplied with a single company's value—Amazon. Mr. Bezos is also aware of this risk, in fact he is quoted saying 'One day Amazon will fail, but it is our job to delay it as long as possible'.   That means even one of the largest companies in the world is always aware that it is at risk of going down.

For the average investor, diversification gives protection in the short-term and still allows for solid, long-term investment return potential. Remember back in Ch. 2.3 when we learned how an Invest-OR looks at money through a long-term time horizon? That is what is needed for diversification to work.

FREE LUNCH: THE ABILITY TO GIVE SOMETHING LIKE PROTECTION IN THE SHORT-TERM, WHILE NOT TAKING AWAY LONG-TERM RETURNS

AGAIN, DO YOU AGREE WITH THIS STATEMENT:

It is safer buying one company than trying to buy a lot of different companies.

Your answer now will include the concepts of diversification and concentration, where one has a higher return potential in the short run, but as an Invest-OR that is not what you are concerned with!

IS THERE ANYONE OUT THERE HELPING ME PROTECT MY PLAN?

As we look at diversification to protect your plan, we should also introduce a few others out there looking to protect your plan – **SEC** & **FINRA**.

THE FEDERAL SECURITIES ACT OF 1933

This federal law was a response to the stock market crash of 1929 and the Great Depression that followed. The purpose of this act is to require companies to disclose all 'material' or important information related to a security investment. This is meant to protect you, the investor from fraud and deception but only works if you know what to look for in your investments.

To achieve this level of protection, the act requires any company who wants to offer a security or asset to the public to register with the SEC. With this registration the company must disclose their financial condition, company operations, management, and any relevant risks.

SECURITIES AND EXCHANGE COMMISSION (SEC)

This federal agency is responsible for regulating the securities industry, enforcing securities laws, and protecting you, the investor. Created in 1934 as part of the Federal Securities Act. The main divisions of the SEC are Corporation Finance, Trading and Markets, Investment Management, and Enforcement. But the SEC will also be the ones who oversee financial professionals, holding the power to bring lawsuits against the individual or the company they represent for violating securities law.

The SEC enters the mainstream media when they investigate major scandals like Enron, Bernie Madoff, or most recently with the crypto exchange FTX scandal.

SECTION 6.2
RECAP

FINANCIAL INDUSTRY REGULATORY AUTHORITY (FINRA)

Created in 2007 to oversee and regulate brokerage firms and registered advisors. This database of hundreds of thousands of firms and individuals is called BrokerCheck and allows investors to research the background and disciplinary actions of those within the list. FINRA is responsible for enforcing federal securities laws and FINRA rules, as well as providing education resources to you the investor. While the SEC oversees FINRA, FINRA is funded by its members.

1. DIVERSIFICATION: HAVING A WIDE VARIETY OF INVESTMENTS AND NOT CONCENTRATING ALL YOUR EGGS IN ONE BASKET.

2. 'FREE LUNCH': DIVERSIFICATION CAN MAINTAIN LONG-TERM UPSIDE WHILE REDUCING THE SHORT-TERM DOWNSIDE IN INVESTMENTS.

3. A DIVERSIFIED PORTFOLIO WILL HAVE INVERSELY RELATED INVESTMENTS, THAT ARE DESIGNED TO REACT DIFFERENTLY TO THE SAME EVENT.

SECTION 6.3
THE DIFFERENCE BETWEEN STOCKS AND BONDS

TERMS

BOND: investment that makes you a lender. The loan amount will be paid back plus interest on the bond's maturity date.

STOCK: investment that makes you a partner. The growth of the company is intended to pay the investor overtime.

MATURITY DATE: the length of time the loan is set for before needing to be paid back.

INVESTMENT GRADE BONDS: bonds with a high credit rating which means less risk and therefore lower return, issued by corporations who are looking to raise money.

MUNICIPAL BONDS (ALSO KNOWN AS MUNIS): bonds issued by states, cities, or counties to raise money for government projects. These are lower risk and sometimes can have a tax advantage to investing in them.

HIGH YIELD BONDS (ALSO KNOWN AS JUNK BONDS): bonds that do not meet the investment grade by rating agencies and therefore carry a higher risk of default. Because the risk is higher, these bonds will pay a higher interest rate in return.

US TREASURIES BONDS: bonds issues by the U.S. Treasury Department and carry the full faith of the United States government which means they are a very safe investment. Treasuries go by different names depending on the length of time the bond is issued for before it matures.
- **Treasury Bills:** matures in less than a year (Safest)
- **Treasury Notes:** matures between 1 and 10 years
- **Treasury Bonds:** matures between 10 and 30 years

TERMS

INFLATION PROTECTION BONDS:
- **TIPS:** Type of bond intended to protect against inflation. The interest rate will have the current inflation rate incorporated into the interest rate.
- **iBond:** Type of bond intended to protect against inflation. The interest rate will have a component that is fixed and a component that adjusts with the Consumer Price Index. Theoretically, the total interest rate will rise as inflation rises.

CAPITALIZATION 'CAP': how much money a company is worth in their market. Cap is an abbreviation for market capitalization.

SMALL CAP: market value between $250 Million and $2 Billion.

MID CAP: market value between $2 Billion and $10 Billion.

LARGE CAP: market value above $10 Billion.

GROWTH STOCK: company that you feel the price does not reflect the growth potential.

VALUE STOCK: a company that you feel the price is below the actual value.

With the Do, Re, Me and diversification principles setting the foundation of your investment strategy, it is time we discuss what you can start to invest in. To do this, we want to explain an analogy where two students are trying to start a business, lemonade stands, and need some money to get started.

Jon and Charles each stand in front of their respective mothers with the same question:

 Mom, can I have five dollars to start a lemonade stand?

At school earlier that day, the boys had challenged one another to see who could raise enough money to buy the new iPhone. Their idea is if they could get some money from their mom to start a lemonade stand, then they could earn the money needed to get the phone.

With the five-dollar investments, the two boys are seeking ingredients to open lemonade stands the following weekend, and although they had asked the same question, they received different responses.

JON'S MOM (BOND)

"Absolutely. I will let you borrow the five dollars, but I want you to pay me one dollar every week for five weeks, and then, in addition to that, I want you to pay me the five dollars back after the five weeks."

CHARLES' MOM (STOCK)

"Absolutely. I will give you the five dollars, but I want to be 50/50 partners. Every week, we will split the profits or losses down the middle, and you don't have to worry about paying me the five dollars back."

Jon and Charles each received the five dollars to start their lemonade stand businesses, but how they raised the money was by taking on different relationships.

Jon's mom became a lender when she let Jon borrow the money for his business. Jon will pay his mother interest for the privilege of using her money and then after the set time, he will need to return the money he borrowed. This relationship is like a **BOND**, where one party lends money to another party and is paid interest on the principal until it is returned (Section 2.1).

Charles' mom became a partner when she invested the money in Charles' business. Charles will share the profits of the company with his mother for the privilege of using her money. This relationship is like a **STOCK**, where you pay to own a piece of the business and take part in the rise or fall of it.

WHY WOULD JON'S MOTHER WANT TO BE A LENDER?

As an investor, she will receive a consistent stream of income and has a lower risk of losing her money.

WHY WOULD CHARLES' MOTHER WANT TO BE A PARTNER?

As an investor, she has a greater upside in being a part owner, and she believes that this reward outweighs the higher risk she has of losing her money.

After a few weeks, it is amazing to see that both lemonade stands make the same amount of income, but which investor (mom) comes out ahead and which boy ends up closer to getting his iPhone?

	COMPANY INCOME	JON'S MOM (BOND)	CHARLES' MOM (STOCK)
WEEK 1	-$4	$1	-$2
WEEK 2	$0	$1	$0

WEEK 1:

Jon didn't make any money, in fact he lost money in week one, but he still owes the $1 interest to his mom. The agreement was to pay this $1 in interest every week, no matter how Jon did. Charles, on the other hand, didn't owe his mom any interest and because they lost money in week one, he split the losses 50/50 with his partner.

WEEK 2:

Jon is better off now that he didn't lose money on top of the $1 interest payment, but not making any income is hurting with those payments still needing to be made. Charles and his mom are disappointed with the second week without making money, but at least they do not owe anyone any interest.

After weeks one and two it is transparent where the advantage in owning bonds comes in with guaranteed income to the investor. Jon's mom doesn't really care if he makes or loses money, as long as she gets paid her interest. She also is a big fan of not sharing in the losses Jon has experienced early on.

	COMPANY INCOME	JON'S MOM (BOND)	CHARLES' MOM (STOCK)
WEEK 3	$4	$1	$2
WEEK 4	$6	$1	$3

WEEK 3:

Finally, some money rolls in and after being hit hard at first both boys are excited as week three ends. Jon's mom (bond) still receives her $1 in interest, but now Jon gets to keep the extra $3 he earned. Charles on the other hand sees his (stock) $4 income and splits it in two, giving his mom $2.

WEEK 4:

Two weeks in a row the boys make money! Jon's mom gets her $1 in interest and then Jon keeps $5—booyah. Charles likes seeing the income go up but must again hand over half, $3 to his mom.

After weeks three and four it is transparent where the advantage in owning stocks comes in with the shared upside of the company. As Charles' business keeps earning money, his mom gets to see her risk of being a partner payoff and enjoy the bigger payouts.

	COMPANY INCOME	JON'S MOM (BOND)	CHARLES' MOM (STOCK)
WEEK 5	$6	$1 ($5 returned)	$3

WEEK 5:

Jon knows his time is up and he needs to pay his mom the last $1 in interest and then the $5 he borrowed from her. On the bright side, this is the end of their relationship, money was loaned, then returned, and now they are done. Charles on the other hand has a partner that is not going anywhere, they shared in the risk at the start and now are along for the ride.

After week five there is a benefit to both the bond and stock. Jon's mom can take her $5 she loaned out plus now she has $5 more of interest and do with it as she pleases. Charles' mom on the other hand sees a growing business and more income coming that she gets to be a part of.

	COMPANY INCOME	JON'S MOM (BOND)	CHARLES' MOM (STOCK)
WEEK 6	$4	$0	$2
TOTAL INCOME	$16	$5 BOND INTEREST	($8-$5) = $3 STOCK PROFITS

WEEK 6:

We see the bond relationship with Jon's mom drop off and now he is on his own. Charles will still move forward with his 50/50 partner.

SO, WHICH INVESTOR (MOM) CAME OUT AHEAD?

Jon's mom after five weeks: Loaned $5 and got her $5 back. Each week she made $1, totaling $5 income plus the $5 she started with which equals $10 total.

Charles' mom after five weeks: Invested $5 to be a partner. She had an income of $8 for the first six weeks, totaling $3 income after her investment of $5.

Jon's mom after six weeks: Made more money and now has $10 to loan out for the next bond.

Charles' mom after six weeks: Will continue to share in the profits as the company goes forward and therefore has more future upside.

WHO MADE MORE BETWEEN JON AND CHARLES AFTER SIX WEEKS?

Jon gave out a bond—early on it was hard not making money while still having interest payments, but when the company took off, so did Jon's income, and even after the $5 is repaid, Jon's income totals $11.

Charles gave out stock—he got to keep the $5 his mom invested, as well as share the income, totaling $13. So, Charles is currently ahead, but looking forward, Jon will take all the income home and Charles will have to split with his partner.

HOW DO BONDS AND STOCKS GET VALUED?

Bonds are valued based on the interest rate the loan is sent out at and the length of time before its **MATURITY DATE**. If a $10,000 bond is set for 3 years at 4% interest rate, the 4% interest rate is how the bond is valued. A risk factor in bonds is the 'term' or length of time until maturity. The longer the term is, the more risk involved, the shorter the term, the sooner it will be cash back in your pocket and the less risk.

Now when investors expect the Federal Funds Rate to go up, driving all interest rates higher, the price of existing bonds goes down – Future Price Up, Current Price Down. People will see the ability to get the same $10,000 bond but at a 5% interest rate and want to purchase that instead.

Stocks are valued based on the public perception of the company as it represents future. Notice how we say 'public perception' of the future, that is a massively important piece of this investment puzzle. Where bonds have a very clear evaluation, interest rates and stocks are more subjective valuations meaning there is emotion involved. The main indicator of a stock's value will be the companies' ability to create and grow profits. If there is a stock valued at $10 and people think the company is going to produce more profit, then someone will be willing to buy that stock at $11.

In general, you can see larger more established companies as less risky because the public perception is stronger. Smaller, start-up companies are riskier because the public's perception is still questionable.

OK, WHICH TYPE OF BOND OR STOCK DO I WANT TO GO BUY?

Money Vehicle is not here to give you investment advice, but we do see the importance in knowing what types of investments there are in the market today. This will be a brief introduction to these types of investments and in future courses we can dive deeper into investment strategy as well as portfolio allocation, but we will also provide a clear path to start investing in Section 6.4.

TYPES OF BONDS

- **INVESTMENT GRADE:** bonds with a high credit rating which means less risk and therefore lower return, issued by corporations who are looking to raise money.
- **MUNICIPAL (ALSO KNOWN AS 'MUNIS'):** bonds issued by states, cities, or counties to raise money for government projects. These are lower risk and sometimes can have a tax advantage to investing in them.
- **HIGH-YIELD, (ALSO KNOWN AS 'JUNK BONDS'):** bonds that do not meet the investment grade by rating agencies and therefore carry a higher risk of default. Because the risk is higher, these bonds will pay a higher interest rate in return.
- **U.S. TREASURIES:** bonds issues by the U.S. Treasury Department and carry the full faith of the United States government which means they are a very safe investment. Treasuries go by different names depending on the length of time the bond is issued for before it matures.
  - Treasury Bills: matures in less than a year (Safest)
  - Treasury Notes: matures between 1 and 10 years
  - Treasury Bonds: matures between 10 and 30 years
- **INFLATION PROTECTION BONDS:**
  - TIPS: Type of bond intended to protect against inflation. The interest rate will have the current inflation rate incorporated into the interest rate.
  - iBond: Type of bond intended to protect against inflation. The interest rate will have a component that is fixed and a component that adjusts with the Consumer Price Index. Theoretically, the total interest rate will rise as inflation rises.

 # TYPES OF STOCKS

'Cap' is an abbreviation for market **CAPITALIZATION** which means the size of the company.
- **SMALL CAP:** market value between $250 Million and $2 Billion, due to their relative size these companies are seen as riskier than the Mid or Large Cap.
- **MID CAP:** market value between $2 Billion and $10 Billion.
- **LARGE CAP:** market value above $10 Billion, due to their relative size these companies are seen as less risk than the Mid or Small Cap.
- **GROWTH STOCK:** company that you feel the price does not reflect the growth potential.
- **VALUE STOCK:** a company that you feel the price is below the actual value.

GROWTH VERSE VALUE STOCK

Imagine you are sitting in the 'War Room' for the NFL draft and can select your team's next quarterback. Your two options are:

- Option 1: Seasoned Veteran who got injured last year but is a proven player. Because he is a bit older and coming off an injury you can get him in the free agent market far below what he has been previously paid.
- Option 2: The hyped up and anticipated rookie 1st round pick. You are unsure where his career will go, but the potential is off the charts.

Which do you choose? Well, these two options are a lot like value and growth stocks. The veteran player at a discount represents the value stocks and the rookie player with high potential represents the growth stocks. The choice is yours.

ACT LIKE AN INVEST-OR

The 'Re' principle in investing states the higher the risk, the higher the potential reward. As a young Invest-OR, you should begin to be comfortable taking on risks, remember you have the time horizon needed to earn the potential reward.

When you look at these two investment options, you can see how the level of risk differs in each of their return offerings.

BOND

Jon's mom had a guaranteed income and therefore less risk, which means less potential reward.

STOCK

Charles' mom had no guarantee and therefore higher risk which means more potential reward.

Jon and Charles are both so pleased with the success of their lemonade stands that they begin to wonder how they can expand their investment into more lemonade stands around the city. This concept will be addressed in Chapter 6.4.

SECTION 6.3
RECAP

1. BONDS ARE DEBT AND MAKE YOU A LENDER. BONDS HAVE LOWER RISK, AND YOU WILL BE PAID INTEREST UNTIL YOUR PRINCIPAL LOAN IS RETURNED.

2. STOCKS ARE EQUITY AND MAKE YOU A PARTNER. BONDS HAVE A HIGHER RISK, AND YOU WILL BE PAID THROUGH THE GROWTH OF THE COMPANY.

3. UNDERSTAND THE TYPE OF BOND OR STOCK YOU ARE CHOOSING TO INVEST IN AND MAKE SURE YOU ARE COMFORTABLE WITH THE RISK.

SECTION 6.4

BE AVERAGE = INDEX

TERMS

MUTUAL FUND: an investment vehicle in which a group of investors pool money together to invest in diversified holdings under the guidance of a professional manager.

INVESTMENT MANAGER (ALSO KNOWN AS MONEY MANAGER): a financial professional who chooses where to invest a fund's cash for a management fee.

STOCK MARKET INDEX: a measurement that tracks every company within a section of the stock market or the entire market at large to provide a comparison for market performance.

MARKET SECTOR: a part of the economy that represents a group larger than an industry.

INDEX FUND: like a mutual fund, this is an investment vehicle in which a group of investors pool money together to invest. The difference comes with what they invest in, with an index fund there is no choosing investment by a manager, the investment is simply made in the entire index.

BE AVERAGE - INDEX: Money Vehicle investment philosophy sharing the power and simplicity of investing in index funds.

CUSTODIAN: a financial institution that can hold your investment securities such as stocks, bonds, or other digital assets.

STOCK EXCHANGES: a market where investment securities are bought and sold.

NYSE: The New York Stock Exchange is the world's largest stock exchange by market capitalization, or size of companies on it, and is in Manhattan, New York. This exchange is a broad group of industries including industrial, utility, transportation, and financial corporations.

NASDAQ: National Association of Securities Dealers Automated Quotations, was the world's first electronic market exchange. This exchange is focused on the technology sector – Apple, Google, Microsoft, Amazon, and Meta.

10-K REPORT: a comprehensive report filed annually by a publicly-traded company about its financial performance and is required by the U.S. Securities and Exchange Commission (SEC)

Jon and Charles huddle up one day after school and empathize about the pain of having all their lemons in one stand. Having each been in the business for a year now, they both see that some weeks are great, and some weeks are not —like when the baseball game is rained out and they have no customers, that means they have no income. They realize the risk of having only one stand is too great!

The boys begin to ponder how they could diversify (Chapter 6.2) their investments—either by branching out into owning different types of stands or by owning more than just one lemonade stand each. Since they don't know much about other types of food stands, they decide that the best idea is to take their original idea further and open multiple lemonade stands.

MAP OF STITCHVILLE

Looking at a map of town, Jon sees the five blocks that make up Stitchville as the territory he can expand. Between Main Street and Fourth Avenue, there is already a lemonade stand on each block owned by something called Mutual Fund Lemonade.

He believes the ones on Second and Fourth Avenues will find the most clients, because there is a playground on Second and a soccer field on Fourth. Jon seeks out Mutual Fund Lemonade, which owns a portion of all the lemonade stands on Second and Fourth Avenues, with the hope that they will let him diversify his investment by buying into their company.

A **MUTUAL FUND** is an investment vehicle in which a group of investors pool money together to have a professional money manager purchase a selection of stocks, bonds, or other investments.

The fund is then managed by a professional **MONEY MANAGER** who, for a fee, chooses where to invest to create a return for the fund's investors. This mutual fund vehicle can be an efficient way to get introduced to the investment world in a diversified way for a small fee.

Charles, on the other hand, believes the lemonade business is going to rise but doesn't think he can predict which stands kids will go to after they are done playing or which block holds an advantage. He wants to buy a piece of every lemonade stand in Stitchville. A company called Sweet and Sour Index owns precisely what he is looking for, a small share of each of the ten stands throughout Stitchville.

 A **STOCK MARKET INDEX** is a measurement that tracks every company within a section of the stock market. That means if you look at any part of the economy, known as a **MARKET SECTOR** of the market, you would be able to group that entire part of the economy into an index.

 For example, sectors of the stock market could be Energy, Health Care, Industrial, or Technology.

Now if you understand what the market index is, the grouping of an entire part of the economy together, you are probably wondering how it can benefit you as an individual investor? Well, this is where investing has taken giant leaps to help individuals like you and me to have success investing our money.

In 1976, Jack Bogle who was the founder of Vanguard,[22] created an idea where you as an individual investor could stop trying to pick which one stock would go up and start investing in all the stocks in a market index. With this new tool, the individual investor would no longer look at what the market returned overall and attempt to beat its return, but instead would just accept the return of the overall market. This new idea was called an index fund.

 An **INDEX FUND** is an investment vehicle in which a group of investors pool their money together to purchase a variety of stocks, bonds, or other investments that fall within a specific market index.

With index funds there is no money manager needed as there is no selection process for the investments. Simply put, you invest in everything that falls in the index chosen.

 For example, the S&P 500 is an index fund owning shares of the 500 largest companies in the United States, or the top companies market index.

So, Jon can own a part of the lemonade stands on Second and Fourth in a mutual fund, or Charles can own a part of all the stands in Stitchville in an index fund.

WHICH IS A SAFER INVESTMENT — MUTUAL FUND OR INDEX FUND, AND WHICH HAS MORE UPSIDE?

In choosing a smaller group of lemonade stands (or investments), Jon has some diversification in Mutual Fund Lemonade. But Jon also has some concentration risk in owning specific stands and not all. If more people go to his stands, then Jon benefits, if more people go to the stands on First and Third avenues then Jon loses.

Jon believes he knows where the market will return the greatest reward and by concentrating his investments in those areas, he is taking on more risk than Charles. This is the same assumption that a money manager makes, they believe they know where in the market will return the greatest reward and concentrate there.

MUTUAL FUND OR **INDEX FUND**

In choosing to invest in all the lemonade stands or indexing the entire Stitchville market, Charles is practicing maximum diversification. Charles is accepting a smaller risk by owning a piece of every stand.

Charles does not believe he can predict where the market will return the greatest reward, so he simply bets on the market at large. This is the same assumption that an index investor makes, they believe there is no way to know where in the market will return the greatest reward and choose to invest in the index.

I THOUGHT YOU SAID DIVERSIFICATION DID NOT LOWER YOUR CHANCE OF RETURNS.

Seriously, you are catching on and thinking like an Invest-OR!

Over a long-time horizon, it has been proven that diversification does not lower your chance of returns. In fact, of the actively managed mutual funds that concentrate predicting where returns will come, 80% do underperform the S&P 500 Index. However, in the short-term, diversification can lower your upside if the concentrated area (the stands on Second and Fourth Avenues) does exceptionally well.

Owning a piece of everything means you will receive some of the upside from every area, but not all the upside from one concentrated area. Concentration on one stock, or even one group of stocks, has a higher potential upside, but also a much higher potential downside, risk.

The key is that diversification will significantly lower your downside. When things go bad in concentration, they go bad, possibly even to $0. But in an index fund, when things go bad, there are so many companies in the index that some of them will be making money and therefore cushion the down. Over time, avoiding the big losses and still receiving most of the upside will show you why index funds are a great way for students to start investing.

Example: Investing in Company A can see a huge upside of 30% in one year, while investing in Index B may only receive a 10% upside in the same year. The next year Company A is down -20% whereas Index B is only down -5%.

	COMPANY A	INDEX B
INITIAL INVESTMENT	$100	$100
YEAR 1	$130	$110
YEAR 2	$104	$104.50

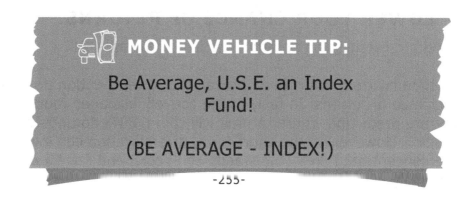

MONEY VEHICLE TIP:

Be Average, U.S.E. an Index Fund!

(BE AVERAGE - INDEX!)

HOW IS A MUTUAL FUND DIFFERENT FROM AN INDEX FUND?

All index funds are mutual funds, but not all mutual funds are index funds. Where they differ is in their investment selection, management style, and fee structure.

	MUTUAL FUND	INDEX FUND
INVESTMENT SELECTION	MANAGER PICKS INVESTMENTS	ALL INVESTMENTS IN THE INDEX
MANAGEMENT STYLE	ACTIVE EVALUATION & TRADING	IF REMAIN IN THE INDEX, REMAIN INVESTED
FEE STRUCTURE	PAY PROFESSIONAL TO MANAGE	SMALL FEE TO OWN THE FUND
DIVERSIFICATION	YES	BEST

MUTUAL FUND   OR   **INDEX FUND**

WAYS TO CHOOSE YOUR INVESTMENTS AND RISK MANAGEMENT

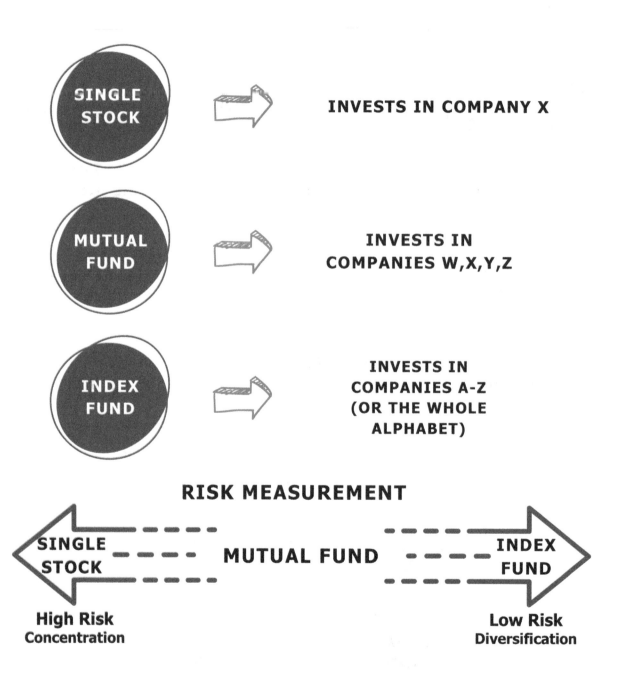

SINGLE STOCK → INVESTS IN COMPANY X

MUTUAL FUND → INVESTS IN COMPANIES W,X,Y,Z

INDEX FUND → INVESTS IN COMPANIES A-Z (OR THE WHOLE ALPHABET)

RISK MEASUREMENT

← SINGLE STOCK — MUTUAL FUND — INDEX FUND →

High Risk
Concentration

Low Risk
Diversification

HOW DO I START INVESTING?

Your first step in investing will be finding a **CUSTODIAN**. This custodian will be a financial institution that is able to hold investment securities such as stocks, bonds, or other digital assets. This custodian will provide safekeeping of your investments to prevent them from being stolen or lost, like a bank account (Chapter 4).

The custodian will not make decisions on what or when you should make investments, that is the job of you or a money manager. The custodian is meant to 'custody' or look after your money.

WHERE ARE STOCKS TRADED?

The last thing we need to discuss is where all these stocks and index funds are being traded. These are called **STOCK EXCHANGES** and they serve two primary purposes.

- First, stock exchanges allow companies to publicly list their business to the public and raise money from interested investors. This is what people mean when they say they 'took the company public'.

- Second is that stock exchanges provide a central marketplace for investors to buy and sell stock.

THE MOST COMMON STOCK EXCHANGES YOU WILL ENCOUNTER IN THE UNITED STATES ARE:

- **NYSE:** The New York Stock Exchange is the world's largest stock exchange by market capitalization, or size of companies on it, and is in Manhattan, New York. This exchange is a broad group of industries including industrial, utility, transportation, and financial corporations.

- **NASDAQ:** National Association of Securities Dealers Automated Quotations, was the world's first electronic market exchange. This exchange is focused on the technology sector – Apple, Google, Microsoft, Amazon, and Meta.

WHAT ABOUT DAY-TRADING?

Well, we have made it this far and this is a good question because many of you are marketed to believe you can find success with this endeavor. Money Vehicle's response to 'day-trading' is three-fold:

1. **Expertise**: There are literally buildings full of people in New York and all over the world spending hours upon hours trying to figure out which stock will move. If you have not read a 10-K REPORT on the company or their competitors, do you really believe you know more than these experts?

2. **Repeatable**: The hardest part about trading every day is repeating success. You must be right THREE times. You must be right when you buy, must be right when you sell, and then must be right again when you buy the next thing. This process occurs each day! How long do you think you can repeat that successfully?

3. **Mindset**: Throughout Money Vehicle we try to give you an investor mindset which means you see things long-term. For this we will use a quote from Warren Buffett to reflect how he sees the stocks he buys, "I buy everything with the assumption they could close the market for 5 years and it would still be a good purchase."

When approached about day trading and trying to gamble on stocks, remember this quote:

Time IN the market is far more important than TIMING the market!

SECTION 6.4
RECAP

1. MUTUAL FUND: GROUP OF INVESTORS POOLING THEIR MONEY TOGETHER AND PAYING A MANAGER TO SELECT STOCKS.

2. INDEX FUND: GROUP OF INVESTORS POOLING THEIR MONEY TOGETHER AND BUYING A PORTION (OR ALL) OF A MARKET FOR A SMALL FEE.

3. BE AVERAGE = INDEX IS THE MONEY VEHICLE INVESTMENT PHILOSOPHY THAT EMPOWERS STUDENTS TO MAKE THEIR FIRST INVESTMENT IN AN INDEX FUND.

REVIEW

THE RULE: ACT LIKE AN INVEST-OR

Before you make an investment, you must understand why you are buying and what you are buying. Investing begins with DO—Follow the Golden Rule; RE—Return equals' risk; ME—My emotional control. What you buy begins with the two major ways to participate in the market: lender (bond) or owner (stock). Both have specific characteristics that make them the right decision for different scenarios and time horizons. Next, you need to decide how you want to buy into the investment world. It is up to you to buy a single investment, a mix of investments, or an entire index. Remember that concentration comes with a higher upside and a (much) higher downside. Diversification, when done thoughtfully, can give you solid long-term returns while also limiting your potential downside; hence it is a 'free lunch.' Money Vehicle investment philosophy Be Average – Index, is simple yet many do not understand its meaning. Now you know why in investing all you must do is take the average return.

ACTION

Act like an Invest-OR, find a platform you trust and make your first investment using Be Average = Index.
- Decide how much you want to put to work in your Future Bucket.
- Open a Brokerage Account at a custodian.
- Choose your first investment using Be Average!

OWNER'S MANUAL
FOR YOUR MONEY VEHICLE:

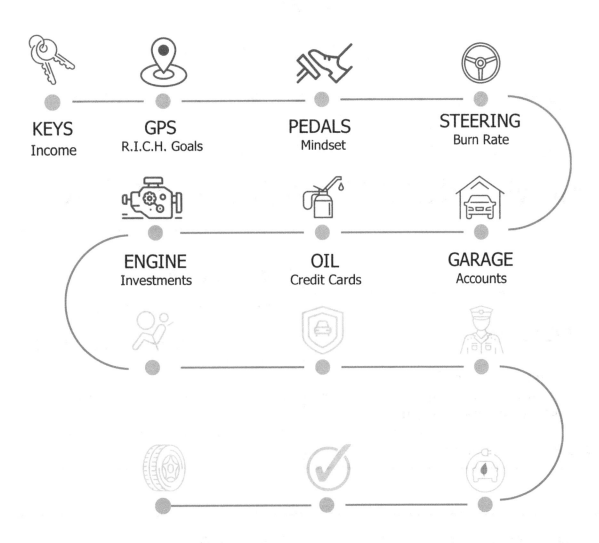

KEYS
Income

GPS
R.I.C.H. Goals

PEDALS
Mindset

STEERING
Burn Rate

ENGINE
Investments

OIL
Credit Cards

GARAGE
Accounts

INSURANCE
CHAPTER 7
HOW SHOULD I MANAGE RISK?

OVERVIEW

7.1: Four Ways to Handle Risk

7.2: Cost to Own and Cost to Use Insurance

7.3: Basics of Auto Insurance

7.4: Other Types of Insurance

ACTION

Transfer your risk through an insurance policy and lower your cost by increasing our deductible, bundling, or shopping around.

DRIVING YOUR MONEY VEHICLE

Okay, so now you are humming along with the engine (investments), and you begin to think, what happens if I get in an accident? Your car has safety measures built into it, such as an airbag that will transfer these types of risk. On your Money Vehicle, these features of protection are your insurance policies, and they will be your first line of defense in the case something major happens.

SECTION 7.1
FOUR WAYS TO HANDLE RISK

TERMS

RISK MANAGEMENT: the ability to forecast certain dangers and prepare a strategy to avoid that risk.

INSURANCE: an arrangement where a company provides a guarantee of compensation for specified loss, damage, illness, or death in return for payment of a premium.

TOO VALUABLE TO LOSE: Money Vehicle phrase that is used to measure and identify what you should insure.

Why do people put on sunscreen? Why do people study for a test? Why do people put on seatbelts?

People take these actions because there is a risk if they do not, and they believe these actions will lower the chance or impact of that risk. There is no way to escape risk in life; we are made very aware that it lies around every corner. The answer to dealing with risk becomes how you respond to these two questions:

- What is the likelihood that the event will occur—low or high?
- What is the level of damage it would cause—low or high?

How you answer those two questions about risk will influence how you handle each type of risk that occurs in your life.

For example, how you handle a risk that has a high likelihood to occur is different than how you handle a risk that has a low likelihood to occur. Looking at these simple questions and the risks in your life, we can develop 4 ways to handle 4 different types of risk.

TYPES OF RISK SCENARIOS:

Low/Low ➡ Likelihood is **low** and potential damage is **low**

High/Low ➡ Likelihood is **high** and potential damage is **low**

High/High ➡ Likelihood is **high** and potential damage is **high**

Low/High ➡ Likelihood is **low** and potential damage is **high**

As you begin to look throughout your life and eventually your financial plan, you will begin to measure risks in these 4 scenarios. Next step is developing strategies on how to handle different types of risk. **RISK MANAGEMENT** is the ability to forecast certain dangers and prepare a strategy to avoid that risk. The risk management strategies you will use are – Retain, Reduce, Avoid, and Transfer.

Let's look at an example of each risk scenario and the strategy on how to manage it as you are getting behind the wheel of your car.

Get a Flat Tire: The chances that you will get a flat tire driving home tonight are low, and the only damage would be that you have a flat tire, which you'd then have to replace with a spare tire. This risk is low likelihood and low potential damage and is the type of risk you retain or handle yourself by changing your tire.

Retain a risk when likelihood is low, and damage is low.

Run out of Gas: When you're driving around it is inevitable that you will run out of gas eventually, and the damage will be an empty gas tank, which you'll then have to fill. This risk is high likelihood and low potential damage so you would reduce the risk by keeping your gas tank full.

Reduce a risk when likelihood is high, and damage is low.

Get a DUI: We have all seen the commercials that say something like, "If you drive drunk, you will be caught!" Beyond the idea of getting caught, the damages in this risk both social and financial are very high! The risk is high likelihood and high potential damage so you would handle it by avoiding it all together. Almost all risks that can result in the death of you or someone else will fall into this avoidance technique.

Avoid a risk when likelihood is high, and damage is high.

Get in an Accident: Accidents happen, there's no doubt about it, but if you practice safe driving, the likelihood of having an accident is low. However, when accidents do occur, the damage can be very high. This type of risk, one you cannot avoid and that is too costly to retain, is the risk you transfer to someone else. This transfer of risk is called INSURANCE.

Transfer a risk when likelihood is low, and damage is high.

Looking at your life, you can begin to see how each risk scenario will be treated in a different way. This chapter is going to focus on the idea of transferring risk through insurance policies. Money Vehicle wants you to see the things in your life that are too valuable for you to lose.

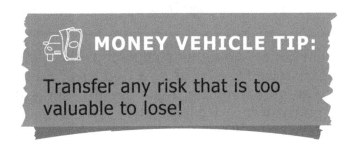

MONEY VEHICLE TIP:

Transfer any risk that is too valuable to lose!

At first you may think I am still young and do not have things valuable enough to get insurance on. Stop and think though about your income, your health, your car, or even the money you have in your Today Account. All those things are valuable to you and their risk can be transferred.

 Example from Chapter 4: FDIC & NCUA insurance on your deposits.

But insurance can not only protect something you own, but it can also transfer the risk of damage you may cause or just be responsible for. When you think about parking next to a nice car, you are not concerned with scratching your vehicle, you are concerned with scratching their vehicle. That concern is transferred to your insurance policy.

CHECK OUT THESE FUN FACTS ABOUT THINGS WORTH INSURING:

NFL Player Troy Polamalu took out insurance on his hair because he had a contract with Head and Shoulders shampoo.

Pop icon Miley Cyrus has made a name for herself in many ways, one of which is by sticking her tongue out in photos. This look has garnered so much attention that Cyrus took out a one-million-dollar insurance policy to protect her tongue!

Superstar Mariah Carey had an ad campaign with Gillette Razor in which she was bestowed the "Legs of a Goddess." Between that campaign and Carey's career, her team deemed her legs valuable enough to insure them for $1 billion!

Looking at the list of celebrities who transferred the risk connected to their body, you can see that they viewed each of their features as too valuable to lose! To handle the risk of losing these features, they transferred it to an insurance company.

As you prepare Your Money Vehicle and your financial plan, begin to ask yourself:

What is too valuable to lose?

SECTION 7.1
RECAP

1. MEASURE THE LIKELIHOOD AND DAMAGE OF THE RISK.

2. RISKS THAT IS LOW LIKELIHOOD AND HIGH DAMAGE SHOULD BE TRANSFERRED THROUGH AN INSURANCE POLICY.

3. ANYTHING THAT YOU DEEM IS 'TOO VALUABLE TO LOSE' SHOULD BE COVERED BY INSURANCE.

SECTION 7.2
COST TO USE AND COST TO OWN INSURANCE

TERMS

PREMIUM: the cost to own an insurance policy, this cost is due no matter if the policy is used.

DEDUCTIBLE: the cost to U.S.E. an insurance policy, this cost only occurs in the event the policy is used.

SELF-INSURANCE: maintaining a Corona Cushion or an account to cover possible losses instead of buying an insurance policy.

CO-INSURANCE: the percentage of insurance costs you will pay after the deductible has been met.

CO-PAY: a fixed dollar amount you will pay each time you use a specific health care service such as a trip to the doctor or refilling prescription.

HAZARDS TO YOUR WEALTH: items that can cause damage to your financial plan such as car accidents, physical illnesses, and even inflation.

"$1,000 for the loan and storage? I didn't even take Happy Days out last month!"

The same thought goes through Darrel's mind every month that he doesn't get to use his beloved boat, Happy Days. But when a sunny summer afternoon comes around and he's on Happy Days, floating out in the middle of the lake, with music playing and chips dipping, it's clear to Darrel—even after gassing it up and purchasing supplies for the day—that the cost to own and the cost to use Happy Days is worth every penny.

Okay, so you may not own a boat, neither do I, and most people don't, but hopefully you can see the connection in this story. Darrel must pay for the boat even when he does not use it. No matter if he gets to go out on it or not, the storage rent and the interest on his loan is still due. Then when he does get to use Happy Days, he has other costs like the gas and guacamole.

Maybe a stretch, but you see there are two costs, the cost to own and the cost to use.

People have a very similar understanding of paying for risk-management strategies, such as insurance policies. You must pay to own the policy even if you don't use it and you must pay to use the policy. but just like with a boat, on the days you do use them, you are happy you have them.

NOW CAN YOU SEE THE SIMILARITIES:

	BOAT COSTS	INSURANCE COSTS
COST TO OWN	PURCHASE LOAN STORAGE	PREMIUM
COST TO USE	GAS FOOD	DEDUCTIBLE

WHAT ARE THE COSTS TO OWN AND USE THE POLICY?

The cost to own an insurance policy is referred to as a **PREMIUM** and will be due each month, regardless of use.

The cost to use an insurance policy is referred to as a **DEDUCTIBLE** and will be due each time you use your policy.

When months and months pass during which you do not file a claim or need to use your insurance, you may begin to question why you even pay for the policy. But now you see that the risk is being transferred to the insurance company each time you make the monthly premium payment.

In our story when Darrel got a sunny day, he was able to use the boat. Well, in the case of insurance it will be a stormy day, in the form of an accident, when you use your policy. During such a stormy day, you will see that the cost of owning the policy is worth every penny.

An accident occurs and even though you have paid your premiums, the insurance company will require you to also pay a deductible. This is the amount that you need to pay to use the policy before the insurance protection will take over.

 Example: If your plan has a $1,000 deductible, you will pay the first $1,000 of costs in the accident and then the insurance company will start to pay.

WAIT A MINUTE I PAID THE PREMIUM AND NOW I PAY AGAIN WITH A DEDUCTIBLE, INSURANCE DOESN'T SEEM LIKE SUCH A GREAT DEAL.

Remember, insurance is meant to cover things that are too valuable to lose. This means it is intended to cover costs that are a high potential damage, not little costs. When you transfer the risk in an insurance policy, you are transferring the risk of tens of thousands of dollars.

You transfer the possibility of high risk (an accident causing $10,000+ worth of damage) for a low risk (the premium—the cost to own your policy—plus the cost of the deductible—the cost to use your policy).

 Example: You pay $100 a month for your premium and are frustrated that you haven't even had an accident for 6 months but are still paying the premium! That is $600 wasted, right?

Wrong! Then it happens, you didn't see the person backing out and rear end them, causing $10,000 of damage. Now you will need to pay the $500 deductible, but you begin to see the benefit when you look at the math.

Cost to you = $600 premium + $500 deductible = $1,100

Cost you saved with insurance = $10,000 - $1,100 = $8,900

Paying for insurance does not feel 'worth it' until there is an accident, remember our fire extinguisher? Once you use your policy you will be very happy you have one. Just imagine for a moment if the damage in an accident was $100,000!

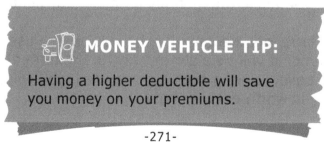

MONEY VEHICLE TIP:

Having a higher deductible will save you money on your premiums.

IS THERE ANY WAY TO REDUCE MY MONTHLY PREMIUM PAYMENTS?

Yes, now that you know inverse relationships, know that premiums and deductibles are inversely related. That means if you increase your deductible, your premium will go down. But before you do that, understand by increasing your deductible you are increasing the amount of money you will need to pay out of pocket in the event of an accident. Increasing your deductible is a form of **SELF-INSURANCE** where you maintain a Corona Cushion or an account to cover possible losses instead of buying an insurance policy. Take this action if you are confident, you will not get in many accidents and would rather have a lower cost to own your policy than a lower cost to U.S.E. your policy.

ARE THERE OTHER INSURANCE COSTS I SHOULD BE AWARE OF?

There will be plenty more terms and costs in insurance, but Money Vehicle wants you to become confident in the basics with your auto insurance first. We will discuss more costs for other types of insurance in 7.4. For now, two other costs you will be sure to come across in your medical insurance are **CO-INSURANCE** and **CO-PAY.**

Co-insurance: the percentage of insurance costs you will pay after the deductible has been met.

 Example: Your policy says you have an 80/20 coinsurance, this means that after the $250 deductible, your plan will cover 80% of the costs and you will be responsible for 20% of the costs.

CO-PAY: a fixed dollar amount you will pay each time you use a specific health care service such as a trip to the doctor or refilling prescription.

 Example: You need to refill a prescription medicine and go to the pharmacy, the cost is not however much the medicine costs, instead it is a $20 co-pay to refill.

Insurance is not an exciting subject; in fact, it is preparing for the worst. But insurance will remove hazards to your wealth by transferring those hazards to an insurance company. Understanding why you need insurance, along with how the premium and deductible work, will lead to less confusion when your insurance bill arrives.

SECTION 7.2

RECAP

1. COST TO OWN INSURANCE IS A PREMIUM AND COST TO U.S.E. INSURANCE IS A DEDUCTIBLE.

2. THERE IS AN INVERSE RELATIONSHIP BETWEEN PREMIUMS AND DEDUCTIBLES, WHICH MEANS THE HIGHER YOUR DEDUCTIBLE, THE LOWER YOUR PREMIUM.

3. YOU PAY FOR INSURANCE THROUGH PREMIUMS AND DEDUCTIBLES, BUT THIS PAYMENT REMOVES HAZARDS TO YOUR WEALTH!

SECTION 7.3
BASICS OF AUTO INSURANCE

TERMS

AUTO INSURANCE: the primary purpose of this type of insurance is to provide financial protection against damage to the vehicle or bodily injury to the passengers in the case of an accident.

BODILY INJURY: in case the accident results in people being hurt.

PROPERTY DAMAGE: in case the accident results in other's property being damaged.

UNINSURED MOTORIST: in case the accident involves another vehicle owner who is illegally driving around without insurance or if their insurance coverage is very low.

COLLISION: covers damage to your car that is caused by a collision or an accident.

COMPREHENSIVE: covers damage to your car that is caused by something other than a collision, such as weather or theft.

RISK CLASS: your insurance provider will place you in a category that they feel is a good assessment of your driving risk and then charge you based on this class.

DECLARATION PAGE: the first page of your policy will specify exactly who is insured, the policy period, the policy coverage components, and the policy limits.

VIN (VEHICLE IDENTIFICATION NUMBER): how the insurance company will identify which vehicle is being covered is through this identification number in your declaration pages.

ENDORSEMENTS, (ALSO KNOWN AS RIDERS): additional policy terms added to your policy.

Sitting behind the steering wheel feels so right! Once he's passed his driver's test, Adrian is ready to get out on the open road and never ask his mom or dad for a ride again. The world is his playground! Until he realizes there is another requirement for driving on the road: **AUTO INSURANCE.**

 Auto Insurance: the primary purpose of this type of insurance is to provide financial protection against damage to the vehicle or bodily injury to the passengers in the case of an accident.

Buying auto insurance is just like having a fire extinguisher— when you need it, you are happy you bought it.

 When you buy a fire extinguisher, you hope to never have to use it, but when you are sitting in your living room as those cookies are baking in the oven and begin to smell smoke, you are glad you have that extinguisher nearby. Same with your insurance policy!

Since 1927, auto insurance [25]has been mandatory to drive on roads. Why? Well, the government came to understand that the financial responsibility of an accident was too much for the individual driver to retain, so it decided to mandate the transfer of that responsibility or risk (7.1).

Meaning that, legally, each person must carry a minimum amount of insurance to drive. The only state that does not require auto-insurance is New Hampshire but you must prove that you can cover the cost of an accident yourself or self-insure. The coverage types and amounts differ from state to state, however there is a common set of coverages that we will introduce here using an example of Washington State.

The three required components of Washington State minimum auto-insurance requirements are:

BODILY INJURY	In case the accident results in people being hurt.
PROPERTY DAMAGE	In case the accident results in other's property being damaged.
UNINSURED MOTORIST	In case the accident involves another vehicle owner who is illegally driving around without insurance or if their insurance coverage is very low.

WHAT IS THE MINIMUM INSURANCE COVERAGE AMOUNT?

The minimum coverage is the lowest level of protection you must have through your insurance policy and still be following the law. The amounts will differ from state to state, and we will research your state in your Owner's Manual, but you will see the minimums listed as a series of three numbers: 25/50/10.

These three numbers mean that at a minimum, in a state like Washington, you must carry:

- $25,000 Bodily Injury per person OR $25,000 coverage for Uninsured or Underinsured accidents
- $50,000 Bodily Injury in total per accident, if more than one victim
- $10,000 Property Damage per accident

WANT TO FIND OUT YOUR STATE REQUIREMENTS:

www.nerdwallet.com/article/insurance/minimum-car-insurance-requirements

---

WHAT HAPPENS IF I GO OVER THE COVERAGE AMOUNT?

If your policy covers up to $25,000 and the damages in an accident are $30,000 then the amount over your policy ($30,000 - $25,000 = $5,000) will transfer back onto you. This is why you will need to increase your coverage amount as your income and assets grow.

Revisiting your policy limits on an annual basis will allow you to confirm the policy limit is still in line with your current income and assets.

 Example:
- $25,000 is a minimum to start.
- But once you have investments or a home beyond that, you can increase to $100,000 or more.

Some people have coverage up to $500,000. But you will not need that much for a while.

WHAT HAPPENS IF I GET HURT OR MY CAR IS DAMAGED IN AN ACCIDENT THAT I CAUSED?

You saw the underlying message in these minimum requirements, they are meant to protect others on the road and not necessarily meant to cover you.

In the event you are injured, this becomes a situation for your health insurance (7.4) and is not covered by your auto insurer.

In the event your car is damaged, under the minimum requirements, your policy does NOT cover your vehicle. There are other options where you can pay for coverage on your vehicle, such as:

- **COLLISION**: Covers damage to your car that is caused by a collision or an accident.
- **COMPREHENSIVE**: Covers damage to your car that is caused by something other than a collision, such as weather or theft.

Insurance is all about measuring risk. When you look at covering the risk of your car being damaged, you should measure how much it would take to repair or replace your current car with the cost of this extra collision or comprehensive coverage.

 Example: If your car is older and has a lot of miles with a total value of $10,000, you do not need to pay thousands of dollars for extra coverage.

HOW WILL THE INSURANCE COMPANY DECIDE WHAT TO CHARGE ME?

Now that you know what will be covered and that you pay to own and use the policy, this is an obvious next question. The company places you in an **INSURANCE RISK CLASS** (sort of like a category) that they feel is a good assessment of your driving risk. The insurance company is a business and is in this to make money, so they will need to charge more in premiums for those they feel will get in more accidents and in doing so cost the insurance company money.

This class begins with groupings around your age, gender, and even education level. Then the class will be defined by your driving record (tickets), how many claims you have filed (accidents), what type of car you drive (minivan, SUV, luxury), and where you live (California, Kansas, New York). The less risky the class you are placed in, the less expensive your insurance will be.
The most expensive insurance risk class is new drivers and even more so for new male drivers.

WHAT DECIDES YOUR INSURANCE RISK CLASS:

AGE	TICKETS
GENDER	ACCIDENTS
EDUCATION	LOCATION

WHAT IF I HAVE A DEDUCTIBLE OF $300, AND I'M IN AN ACCIDENT WITH $350 WORTH OF DAMAGE?

In this case, you would want to measure the impact of filing a claim versus the $350 coming out of your pocket today. When you file a claim, not only does it go on your record, but it also causes your future premiums to rise, since you will then move into a riskier class. Not to mention that filing the claim will only save you $50 after you have paid the deductible.

WHAT IF MY FRIEND BORROWED MY CAR AND GOT IN AN ACCIDENT?

This is a very important lesson for new drivers as it is often misunderstood. Car insurance follows the car, not the driver. When you take out auto-insurance, the policy is connected to the vehicle, not the driver. Whoever is responsible for the vehicle and is paying the premiums will be connected to any accidents that vehicle is in. So, next time your friend asks to borrow your car, remember if they get in an accident, they are not responsible – You Are!

HOW WOULD I FIND OUT HOW MUCH COVERAGE I HAVE?

Your insurance **DECLARATION PAGE** is the first page of your policy and will specify exactly who is insured, the policy period, the policy coverage components, and the policy limits. You can find this either by asking whomever you get insurance through or by logging onto their website and looking in the documents section for "Declaration Page." It is a good recommendation to review the Declaration Pages before your policy goes through and once your policy is approved.

(1)

INSURANCE COMPANY

POLICY NUMBER: 123-45-678
POLICY EFFECTIVE DATE: JAN 1 2023

SUMMARY

NAMED INSURED AND ADDRESS
JANE DOE **(2)**
1234 HAPPY LANE
CITY, TEXAS 00000

YOUR AGENT
A. GENT
(123) 456-7890

POLICY NUMBER **(3)**
123-45-678

(4) **POLICY PERIOD**
EFFECTIVE JAN. 2023 TO JUN 1, 2023

DRIVER(S) LISTED
JANE DOE **(5)**
JOHN DOE

DRIVER(S) EXCLUDED
NONE

DESCRIPTION OF VEHICLE(S) **ANNUAL MILEAGE** **ID. NUMBER (VIN)** **(6)**

1.'08 FORD EXPLORER   5,000   AB123C456D78E9F00

COVERAGE

COVERAGE **(7)**	LIMITS **(8)**	DEDUCTIBLE **(9)**	PREMIUM **(10)**
LIABILITY			
BODILY INJURY	EA. PER $100,000		
	EA. ACC $300,000		$100.05
PROPERTY DAMAGE	EA. ACC $100,000		$101.10
COMPREHENSIVE	ACTUAL CASH VALUE	$500.00	$50.10
COLLISION	ACTUAL CASH VALUE	$500.00	$100.20
UM/UIM			
BODILY INJURY	EA. PER $100,000		
	EA. ACC $300,000	$250.00	$35.05
PROPERTY DAMAGE	EA. ACC $100,000		$25.55
TOTAL PREMIUM			**$412.05**

YOUR POLICY DOCUMENTS

AUTO POLICY
AU100-01

ENDORSEMENTS
 (11) AB1234
CD5678
EF0000

<u>KEY</u>

1. What insurance company is the policy with.
2. Who will be paying the premium and deductible.
3. What is your Policy identification number.
4. What are the dates the policy is in effect.
5. Who is insured under the policy.
6. What is the car Information - make, model, and VIN (Vehicle Identification Number)
7. What are the details of the coverage components.
8. What are the details of the coverage limits.
9. How much does the deductible cost.
10. How much does the premium cost.
11. Endorsements, also known as 'Riders', are additional policy terms added to your policy.

LET'S WORK THROUGH SOME EXAMPLES OF HOW AN AUTO INSURANCE POLICY CAN PROTECT YOUR PLAN:

Let's say Kim is driving around in her Ford Escape with coverage for 25/50/10. Her premium payment is $50 a month and the deductible is $250.

SCENARIO A

Kim is a safe driver, goes 6 months without an accident. What is the total cost?

RESULT

Kim would have paid 6 months of premium payments totaling $300 ($50 x 6 = $300) but no accident means no deductible.

TOTAL COST

Premium of $300

SCENARIO B

After 6 months driving around Kim is in an accident where the other car has two people. The 1st person has $15,000 of bodily injuries and the 2nd person has $23,000 of bodily injuries. What is the total cost?

RESULT

- Kim would have paid 6 months of premium payments totaling $300 ($50 x 6 = $300) and now that there is an accident, she needs to pay her deductible.
- She must review her declaration pages to see how much of the accident will be covered by her and how much by her insurance policy.
- Bodily Injury Person 1: $15,000 with the $25,000 coverage per person, Kim's insurance policy will completely cover these damages and there will be no more cost to Kim after the $250 deductible.
- Bodily Injury Person 2: $23,000 with the $25,000 coverage per person, Kim's insurance policy will completely cover these damages.

TOTAL COST

Premium of $300 + one-time Deductible of $250 = $550

SCENARIO C

After 6 months driving around Kim is in an accident where the other car has two people, the 1st person has $23,000 of bodily injuries and the 2nd person has $35,000 of bodily injuries. What is the total cost?

RESULT

- Kim would have paid 6 months of premium payments totaling $300 ($50 x 6 = $300) and now that there is an accident, she needs to pay her deductible.
- She must review her declaration pages to see how much of the accident will be covered by her and how much by her insurance policy. With the $25,000 coverage per person and $50,000 per accident, Kim's insurance policy will cover these damages up to those amounts.
- Bodily Injury Person 1: $23,000 will be covered under the $25,000 limit after the $250 deductible.
- Bodily Injury Person 2: $35,000 goes over the $25,000 per person coverage by $10,000. The $25,000 will still be covered by the insurance company, but now the overage of $10,000 will be on Kim to pay. Since Kim has already paid her deductible of $250 for this accident, she will not be charged that again.

TOTAL COST

Premium of $300 + Deductible of $250 + $10,000 over coverage = $10,550

SCENARIO D

After 6 months driving around Kim is in an accident where the other car has five people, each having $15,000 of bodily injuries and the car has $15,000 of damages. What is the total cost?

RESULT

- Kim would have paid 6 months of premium payments totaling $300 ($50 x 6 = $300) and now that there is an accident, she needs to pay her deductible.
- She must review her declaration pages to see how much of the accident will be covered by her and how much by her insurance policy. With the $25,000 coverage per person and $50,000 per accident, Kim's insurance policy will cover these damages up to those amounts.
- Bodily Injury: Each Person 1 - 5 will be covered under the $25,000 limit per person, but now we must evaluate the total accident cost as well. With five people having $15,000 of damage each the total accident bodily injury is $75,000 (5 x $15,000 = $75,000). Her policy only covers up to $50,000 per accident and after the $250 deductible, Kim would be responsible for the overage of $25,000.
- Property Damage: The other car also experienced $15,000 of damage and Kim is only covered up to $10,000 of property damage. Kim would be responsible for the $5,000 over her coverage.

TOTAL COST

Premium of $300 + Deductible of $250 + $25,000 over bodily injury coverage + $5,000 over property damage = $30,550

HOW MUCH IS THE INSURANCE POLICY ACTUALLY SAVING ME IN THESE SCENARIOS?

A

Total accident cost $0 – Total cost to you $300

Total Saved none, you owe $300

B

Total accident cost $38,000 – Total cost to you $550

Total Saved $37,450

C

Total accident cost $58,000 – Total cost to you $10,550

Total Saved $47,450

D

Total accident cost $90,000 – Total cost to you $30,550

Total Saved $59,450

WAYS TO SAVE MONEY ON AUTO-INSURANCE

Shop around

There are a lot of deals and discounts out there to be grabbed, so keep an eye out. Be sure to compare insurance company cost and ask your friends and family about their insurance companies' prices and services.

Combine

Combine policies with your home or renter's policy.

Pay in lump sums

Pay in one or two lump sum amounts. Although it may be appealing to choose an installment plan because it is easier to manage the smaller payments versus one large payment, the company will charge you service fees for their efforts each month.

Choose a higher deductible

Choosing to cover more out of pocket in the case of an accident will lower your premium—but be cautious. If you are in an accident, you will have to pay that high deductible.

Drive safely

Showing the insurance company that you can be trusted—which means no tickets and no accidents—will reduce your premiums.

SECTION 7.3
RECAP

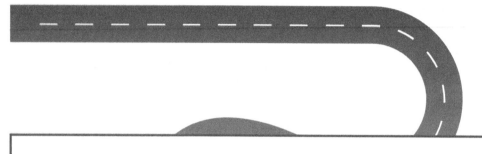

1. THREE REQUIREMENTS OF AUTO INSURANCE COVERAGE ARE: BODILY DAMAGE, PROPERTY DAMAGE, UNDER/UNINSURED DAMAGE.

2. OPTIONAL COVERAGE TO PROTECT YOUR CAR: COLLISION AND COMPREHENSIVE.

3. WAYS TO SAVE ON INSURANCE: SHOP AROUND, COMBINE POLICY WITH OTHER INSURANCE, PAY A LUMP SUM, INCREASE YOUR DEDUCTIBLE, OR JUST DRIVE SAFELY.

SECTION 7.4

OTHER TYPES OF INSURANCE

What is too valuable for you to lose outside of just your car?

That is a question only you can answer, but when you begin to see other types of insurance policies you begin to identify things that people view as hazards they need to transfer.

Here is an overview of these 'other' types of insurance that will transfer Hazards to Your Wealth:

 HEALTH INSURANCE:

COVERAGE	Your medical bills, not your income.
DO YOU NEED HEALTH INSURANCE?	Yes, these hospital bills add up very quickly and can derail your financial plan.

1 IN 5 PEOPLE WITH MEDICAL BILLS END UP IN BANKRUPTCY [26]

This is what will protect you in a car accident that is your fault. You can also qualify for preventative care because insurance companies know it is less expensive to cover preventative care than a major incident but check with your provider.

Medical Insurance is a key benefit for being an employee of a company. The costs for this coverage is very high, so when you can access them through your employer, you will save a lot of money. The American Medical Association reports that medical costs are rising each year 4-5%, so try to stay healthy and always be covered.

 # HOMEOWNERS OR RENTER'S INSURANCE

HOME COVERAGE	The physical structure of your home, the cost of the belongings within your home, and the liability of guests visiting your home.
RENTER'S COVERAGE	NOT the physical structure because you do not own it but will cover your belongings and your liability of guests.
DO YOU NEED HOMEOWNERS INSURANCE?	• No, if you do not own a home. • Yes, if you own a home.
DO YOU NEED RENTER'S INSURANCE?	• No, if your landlord does not require it and you are not concerned with the value of your belonging. • Yes, if your landlord requires it or if you want to protect your plan from an unforeseen hazard.

DISABILITY INSURANCE

COVERAGE	Replaces your income in the event you cannot work from a disability.
DO YOU NEED DISABILITY INSURANCE?	• No, if you are not reliant on your income. • Yes, if you want to protect your income.

We know many of our financial plans are dependent on our income, the keys to Your Money Vehicle. While Health insurance is very important, those bills can add up, it does not replace your income if you can't go to work. That is where the value in Disability Insurance comes in. This will replace a portion of your income if you are unable to go to work.

You are your greatest asset today, make sure and transfer this hazard of losing your income outright. Sure, you can 'self-insure' a few months with your Corona Cushion, but peace of mind that your income will not be interrupted is a big one.

1 IN 4 PEOPLE WILL HAVE A MAJOR EVEN IMPACT THEIR LIFE.[27]

DISABILITY INSURANCE

COVERAGE	Provides a windfall for those you leave behind and are dependent on you.
DO YOU NEED LIFE INSURANCE?	• No, if no one else is dependent on you. • Yes, if you have people who depend on your income, or if you have large debts you want to pay off to not pass to your dependents, or if you have a R.I.C.H. Goal you were not able to accomplish but will do so with this windfall.

DISABILITY INSURANCE

COVERAGE	Replaces your income in the event you cannot work from a disability.
DO YOU NEED DISABILITY INSURANCE?	• No, if you are not reliant on your income. • Yes, if you want to protect your income.

We know many of our financial plans are dependent on our income, the keys to Your Money Vehicle. While Health insurance is very important, those bills can add up, it does not replace your income if you can't go to work. That is where the value in Disability Insurance comes in. This will replace a portion of your income if you are unable to go to work.

You are your greatest asset today, make sure and transfer this hazard of losing your income outright. Sure, you can 'self-insure' a few months with your Corona Cushion, but peace of mind that your income will not be interrupted is a big one.

 # LIFE INSURANCE

COVERAGE	Provides a windfall for those you leave behind and are dependent on you.
DO YOU NEED LIFE INSURANCE?	• No, if no one else is dependent on you. • Yes, if you have people who depend on your income, or if you have large debts you want to pay off to not pass to your dependents, or if you have a R.I.C.H. Goal you were not able to accomplish but will do so with this windfall.

1 IN 4 PEOPLE WILL HAVE A MAJOR EVEN IMPACT THEIR LIFE. [4]

UMBRELLA INSURANCE

COVERAGE	Provides wealth protection beyond the limits of your underlying insurance plan.
DO YOU NEED UMBRELLA INSURANCE?	Not until you have a high Net Worth beyond the limits of your current insurance policies.

PET INSURANCE

COVERAGE	Provides a windfall for those you leave behind and are dependent on you.
DO YOU NEED LIFE INSURANCE?	• No, if no one else is dependent on you. • Yes, if you have people who depend on your income, or if you have large debts you want to pay off to not pass to your dependents, or if you have a R.I.C.H. Goal you were not able to accomplish but will do so with this windfall.

SECTION 7.4
RECAP

1. HEALTH INSURANCE WILL COVER MEDICAL BILLS, BUT NOT YOUR INCOME.

2. DISABILITY INSURANCE WILL COVER YOUR LOST INCOME IN THE EVENT YOU CAN'T WORK.

3. DEPENDING ON YOUR LIVING SITUATION, HOMEOWNERS OR RENTER'S INSURANCE CAN PROVIDE PEACE OF MIND.

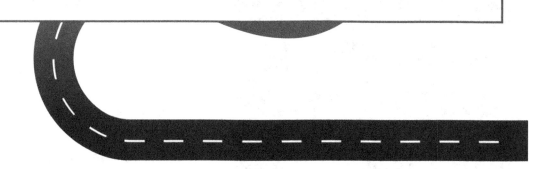

REVIEW

THE RULE: TRANSFER HAZARDS TO YOUR WEALTH

There will always be risk in life. How you deal with that risk will be determined by your answers to the following questions: is this risk likely to occur, and how much damage could this risk cause? Anything that is too valuable to lose or too risky to bear must be transferred to an insurance company or avoided entirely. Like a fire extinguisher, there are times when paying for insurance policies may feel like a waste of money, however, on those occasions when your policy kicks into place, it will be more than worth it. You need Auto Insurance because most drivers cannot afford to pay the damages out of pocket and it is a requirement to protect the other people on the road. Insurance policies are meant to transfer the Hazards to your Wealth.

ACTION

Transfer your risk through an insurance policy and lower your cost by increasing our deductible, bundling, or shopping around.

- List out items that are 'too valuable to lose' and get insurance to cover them.
- Review your declaration pages to see how much protection you have.
- Annually review the costs and coverage of your insurance policies.

OWNER'S MANUAL
FOR YOUR MONEY VEHICLE:

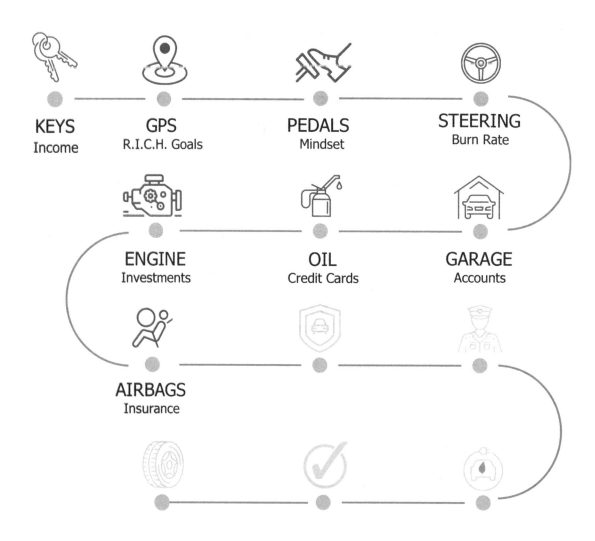

KEYS
Income

GPS
R.I.C.H. Goals

PEDALS
Mindset

STEERING
Burn Rate

ENGINE
Investments

OIL
Credit Cards

GARAGE
Accounts

AIRBAGS
Insurance

CHAPTER 8

HOW DO I PROTECT MYSELF ONLINE?

ACTION

Setup your first line of cyber defense with a strong password that has 8+ characters and is not predictable based on your information.

OVERVIEW

8.1: From The Bank Line To Online

8.2: The New Phishing Hole

8.3: Fight The Hackers

DRIVING YOUR MONEY VEHICLE

Okay, so, an insurance policy will transfer the risk, if it happens, but how can you prevent some risks from even happening at all? In the Money Vehicle world, a car jacker is called a cyber security threat. This is where your car alarm comes into play, because someone trying to break into your car can be stopped by a good alarm.

SECTION 8.1
FROM THE BANK LINE TO ONLINE

TERMS

CYBERSECURITY: every aspect of your defense to fight the hackers.

MALWARE: software that is designed to disrupt, damage, or gain unauthorized access to a computer.

RANSOMWARE: a type of Malware that gains access to your operating system, then locks you out of your own system, holding your own computer ransom until you pay for its release.

SOCIAL ENGINEERING: the use of deception to manipulate an individual into giving personal information away.

PHISHING: sending fraudulent messages that imitate a real company in the hope of being given personal information.

PRETEXT: creating a story based on bits of information that the attacker has gathered to earn trust and manipulate an individual to share personal information.

TROJAN HORSE: leaving a piece of infected hardware, like a USB drive, some place public and waiting for someone to pick it up and try to use it, providing access to your system.

FINANCIAL FUNNY MIRROR: the lens people see the world of social media through, never a clear picture but always warped into how the content creator wants you to see them.

Somewhere, off in a foreign country, hackers are wearing hooded sweatshirts pounding away on keyboards in an abandoned building—or that's what most people imagine when they hear about cyberattacks or data breaches. But the reality is that cyberattacks occur every day.

In fact, a study done at the University of Maryland quantified that there is a cybersecurity attack every thirty-nine seconds! 28 Reality is you do not have to be a hooded sweatshirt computer wizard to attack people online these days and most attacks are often perpetrated by amateurs operating out of their own living rooms.

39 SECONDS

CYBERATTACKS HAPPEN EVERY 39 SECONDS!

In the past the main concern with people stealing your money was someone going into the actual bank and taking out cash in the vault. But gone are the days of bank robbers or train heists and remember there is A LOT more money in circulation than in a bank vault. Today you rarely even see the person committing the crime, and in many cases, you don't even know there was a crime committed until it is too late.

Be on alert because you are being targeted. According to Cybersecurity Ventures, approximately $8 trillion is expected to be spent globally on cybersecurity defense in 2023 and it is estimated that businesses will lose over $10 TRILLION dollars in 2025.   With over five billion people using the internet, cybersecurity experts say that the global ransomware damage will continue to grow each year.

Stop—think about the concern if $6 trillion is being spent to defend it.

CYBERSECURITY has been called a problem with no solution because the only way to stop it completely is by not using the internet. In fact, it is also one of the fastest growing professions in the world and according to the Information Systems Audit and Control Association (ISACA), 70% of organizations report a labor shortage for their security team. Leaving the grid is not an option we are willing to accept, and you cannot fill one of those job openings just yet, so we must better understand the risks and how we can best protect ourselves today.

For starters, let's go over two major types of cybersecurity threats.

1. MALWARE, OR MALICIOUS SOFTWARE

Back in the beginning of cyberattacks, people created software with malicious intent - **MALWARE**. Some of it was meant for anarchy and some for ransom, but it was all meant to disrupt the operations on your computer.

This old type of attack begins by downloading a WORM onto your computer. The worm is a self-replicating algorithm that seeks out vulnerabilities in your operating system and infects them. The worm then spreads to as many systems as it can breach, until you detect the virus. Typically, the victim will notice a slowing in their computer's speed or that their computer has become incapable of completing certain tasks.

Once hackers realized that they could get into operating systems, they began to release RANSOMWARE. This type of malware gains access to your operating system, then locks you out. The program will hold your own computer ransom until you pay for its release.

What's scary about malware is that it can infect your computer system without any human intervention. However, security stepped up and antivirus programs improved. As these defense measurements improved, it forced hackers to adapt their attack, enter the next evolution of cyberattacks.

2. SOCIAL ENGINEERING

This form of attack relies on the mental manipulation of its victims to divulge their personal information. Instead of hacking into your system, this attack attempts to trick you into handing over information or access to your computer.

Malware can be completed without your knowledge or intervention. **SOCIAL ENGINEERING** depends on deceiving YOU into lowering your guard and giving the attacker access or information. 95% (ninety-five percent) of 30 cybersecurity breaches are not caused by a failure in the IT department but occur from human error!

YOU LET THE HACKER IN WITH SOCIAL ENGINEERING!

Imagine walking into McDonald's and seeing a sign marked "Order to the Left." Usually, you walk straight up to the counter, but the sign has the McDonald's logo on it, and when you look over to the left side, there is a cashier waiting to take your order, so you go ahead.

After you place your order, the cashier says, "Your rewards program has been locked out, and I need your password."

Wait, why does McDonald's need my password, and why are the cashiers not where they usually are?

Here are some common types of social engineering attacks that you must become aware of:

1. PHISHING: sending fraudulent emails or messages misrepresenting as a trusted company to trick someone into revealing personal information. The attacker will send an email that appears to come from a legitimate business—for example, your bank or credit card company—requesting some type of verification. The message will seem like a warning and offer you the chance to fix the problem, but when you click to go to the next site, you are the phish who just bit down on the hook! Any information you give on this new site is information being used criminals.

For example: "Your Venmo account is about to be suspended. Click here to update your information and continue..."

2. PRETEXTING: The attacker will create a scenario based on information they have been able to gather about you that will entice you to disclose even more information.

For example: "You are late on your $31.54 bill from last month. Please enter..."

3. TROJAN HORSE: The history lesson here is to be careful what you let into your city; and in this case, your city is your computer. Attackers will leave a piece of infected hardware, like a USB drive, someplace like a public restroom, parking lot, or coffee shop with an enticing label. All the attacker must do is wait for someone to pick it up and try to use it.

For example: You find a USB drive sitting at a local coffee shop that says, "Kardashian beauty secrets" or "Fortnite secret codes."

This is exponentially more important today because we are living in the age of information and once you put information out there, you can never get it back. If any of the personal information that you post on social media ends up in the wrong hands, it can haunt you forever.

IT IS HARD LIVING IN THE VIRTUAL WORLD TODAY, NOT ONLY AM I BEING ATTACKED ONLINE, BUT ALSO IT SEEMS AS THOUGH EVERYONE IS DOING BETTER THAN ME! HOW CAN I DEAL WITH THAT?

Now you see the threat has changed. Have you also noticed something is beginning to smell phishy?

SECTION 8.1
RECAP

1. MALWARE: TRADITIONAL ATTACK WHERE A HACKER SNEAKS ONTO YOUR COMPUTER SYSTEM.

2. SOCIAL ENGINEERING: THE NEW ATTACK WHERE THE HACKER MANIPULATES YOU INTO GIVING YOUR PERSONAL INFORMATION DIRECTLY TO THEM.

3. THE BATTLE IS REAL; TRILLIONS OF DOLLARS ARE BEING SPENT TO FIGHT THESE CYBER-ATTACKS.

SECTION 8.2
THE NEW PHISHING HOLE

TERMS

TYPES OF PHISHING:
- **ACCOUNT ACTIVITY:** phishing attack where the hacker sends a message regarding your account being locked out or unusual sign ins.

- **MEMBERSHIP UPDATE:** phishing attack where the hacker sends a message regarding the restart or deactivation of your membership.

- **CREDENTIALS PHISH:** phishing attack where the hacker sends a message for you to log back into your account.

- **PACKAGING PHISH:** phishing attack where the hacker sends a message regarding a package being delivered.

- **UNEXPECTED MONEY PHISH:** phishing attack where the hacker sends a message regarding some unearned money being given to you.

VISHING: voicemail messages demanding you to take action.

SMISHING: SMS phishing text messages asking you to click here.

QUISHING: QR codes that lead to fraudulent resources.

'THINK BEFORE YOU CLICK': Money Vehicle's 5 Cybersecurity questions to ask yourself as you receive messages today, no matter if it looks like a known source or not.

-300-

MV Pay Stub

1) Paycheck ID No.
a) #452767

4) Personal Information
a) Name
b) Address

2) Payment Period (From)
a) 08/01/2023

Payment Period (To)
a) 08/31/2023

3) Payment Date
a)09/2/2023

5) Gross Income
a) $50,000

6) Witholdings
a) Federal
b) State
c) FICA
d) Unemployment

7) Deductions (Pre-Tax)
a) 401(k)
b) Insurance Premiums
c) FSA
d) HSA

8) Dedcutions (After-Tax)
a) Roth

WARNINGS

MESSAGES AND NOTES

10) Net Income

9) Employer Benefits
a) Tuition Reimbursement
b) Training
c) Paid Vacation

As students you are all competing for jobs that will provide your Desired Lifestyle. But not too long ago, companies realized that they are also competing for you!

The best companies need to attract the best talent and then provide a place of work that employees want to come back to. This realization was the origin of EMPLOYEE BENEFITS. These employee benefits are designed to maximize workplace productivity and help in retaining employees. Employee Benefits have become so desirable that you will see them marketed in a company's recruiting tactics.

Employee benefits are categorized into tangible and intangible benefits.

- TANGIBLE BENEFITS can be measured through dollar amounts.
- INTANGIBLE BENEFITS cannot be measured by a dollar amount but can still contribute to your overall job satisfaction.

As you begin to compare job offerings you will first compare the overall income being offered and then you will begin to value other benefits which are also included. If you do not see benefits that you desire, then the opportunity to begin negotiating for specific benefits becomes available to you in the recruiting process. This negotiation does not conclude once you are hired, in fact each year that you have a review of your work, you will be presented with another opportunity to negotiate your benefit package.

HOW WILL MY BENEFITS CHANGE WITH WHAT TYPE OF EMPLOYEE I AM?

If you are a **FULL-TIME EMPLOYEE,** typically working more than 35 hours a week for a company, you will have access to the benefits offered at the company. While there may be specific compensation benefits available to senior employees or executives, most benefits will be available to all full-time workers.

If you are a **PART-TIME WORKER**, typically working less than 35 hours a week at a company, you will be at the discretion of your employer to what benefits are available. This means the employer is not required to provide you with the same benefits as a full-time employee and can choose what benefits to provide and who to provide them with.

If you are a self-employed worker, you will be responsible for purchasing all benefits on your own.

WHAT ARE EXAMPLES OF TANGIBLE BENEFITS?

Tangible benefits are offered from your employer and can be measured by a dollar amount. These benefits come through providing healthcare resources, retirement programs, or opportunities for additional compensation.

 Healthcare: If a company has 50 employees, they are required by law to provide healthcare plans to full-time employees. Part-time employees may be able to receive benefits, but it is at the discretion of the employer. In companies with less than 50 employees it is at the discretion of the employer to offer healthcare.

a. GROUP HEALTH: the traditional way employers will provide health insurance to their employees is by offering a policy that includes everyone in the company. This grouping of employees together allows the company to receive better coverage at lower prices than individuals would receive because insurance risks go down as the number of employees in the policy goes up. Each employee will have the opportunity to choose if they want to join the group policy or find health insurance on their own. Two types of Group Health plans:
- **HEALTH MAINTENANCE ORGANIZATION (HMO):** Your company offers a list of providers that will be covered by the company insurance plan, and you must visit only providers on the list. HMO is typically a less expensive policy.
- **PREFERRED PROVIDER OPTION (PPO):** The employee can choose from a larger group of providers or be reimbursed for providers outside of the network. PPO plans are typically more expensive than HMO plans.

b. Tax advantaged healthcare accounts: these accounts are offered through your employer with the primary use for healthcare costs, however there will also be tax advantages for contributing to this type of account. Two types of tax-advantaged healthcare accounts you will see are:
- **FLEXIBLE SPENDING ACCOUNTS (FSA):** A tax advantaged healthcare account offered through your employer group health plan, where you contribute pre-tax dollars to be used for specific purposes. You must declare your contributions at the beginning of the year and are unable to change your contribution through the year.

*Caution with the FSA, any dollars you do not use in the account will be lost. That is right, if you don't use it, you lose it.

- **HEALTH SAVINGS ACCOUNTS (HSA):** A tax advantaged healthcare account that is connected to a high deductible insurance policy. You can contribute pre-tax dollars anytime throughout the year and any unused dollars can be rolled to the next year. There are higher contribution limits and even investment options with the dollars in this account. This type of account is also available to self-employed individuals if they are using a high deductible insurance policy.

ACCORDING TO THE AMERICAN HEALTH INSURANCE PLANS (AHIP) 50% OF WORKERS SAY THEIR HEALTH BENEFITS ARE A KEY FACTOR IN CHOOSING AND STAYING AT THEIR JOB.

Retirement: Employers want to provide their employees with a path to achieve financial success. This freedom comes from offering employee benefits to both encourage and fund this path to success. Two retirement benefits offered by employers are pensions and 401(k)'s.

a. Pension: This retirement benefit is earned through years of service and creates a guaranteed stream of income after the employee stops working at the company. Back in Chapter 1 we discussed how most pension systems are going extinct.

b. 401(k): This retirement benefit is a tax-advantaged account that allows employees to contribute and invest pre-tax dollars towards their retirement.
- Employer Match: To incentivize an employee to contribute to their retirement, a company will offer to match a percentage of the employee's contribution.

c. Individual Retirement Account: This type of tax-advantage account is not offered through an employer, instead it becomes the self-employed individual's way to prioritize their retirement and receive tax benefits.

Additional Compensation: Offering different avenues for employees to receive extra compensation that is not connected directly to their primary salary or wage.

a. HEALTH REIMBURSEMENT ACCOUNT (HRA): A type of employee benefit where a company offers an account with a certain amount of dollars available to reimburse the employee for healthcare related costs.

b. Tuition reimbursement: A type of benefit where a company will offer to reimburse an employee for going to receive a certification or higher education degree.

c. Professional Development or Career Training reimbursements: A type of benefit where a company will offer to reimburse types of classes or programs that will develop the employee into a more valuable worker.

d. EMPLOYEE STOCK OPTIONS (ESO): A type of benefit where a company will offer an employee the ability to purchase or earn ownership of the company. There are many forms of ESO that would require an entire chapter to cover, but for now just understand that this is the ability to become owner of stock in the company.

WHAT ARE EXAMPLES OF INTANGIBLE BENEFITS?

Intangible benefits are offered from your employer and while they cannot be measured by a dollar amount, they still provide value to your work experience. These intangible benefits come through perks in your work schedule, offering wellness programs, or the overall company culture.

 Work schedules: In today's world of work, there are benefits not only around what you do for work, but also around how you work. What time of day you want to work, where in the world you want to work from, and even how often you must work can be turned into benefits.

a. Holidays: When you look at the calendar, what are the national, industry, or company holidays that the company will recognize and take off. You may get Thanksgiving off, but what about President's Day? Government employees typically start with 10 recognized National Holidays.

b. PTO (PAID TIME OFF): A typical entry level salaried position will begin with two weeks (10 Days) of paid time off. These are days you can take off from work to go on vacation or schedule a visit to the doctor, but you will still receive your full year's salary. This can also be an area you decide to negotiate for more PTO but be careful of the message you are sending to your new employer, when right away you are requesting more time off. Remember, wage workers only get paid when they are clocking hours.

c. Flexible working environment: Not just what days you work, but when or where you work can be a benefit too. Are you expected to work from 9:00 am to 5:00 pm or can you log in when you like, are you expected to go into the office or can you be completely remote. Discuss and even negotiate your work environment to benefit your work life.

 Wellness programs: Corporate America is concerned with the stress level of their employees, both for the individual and the companies' sake. This creates the opportunity to provide WELLNESS PROGRAMS. Wellness programs are designed to improve and promote the health and fitness of an individual. Finding these offerings from your employer may not be what you originally thought of as benefits, but anything that increases your overall wellness is a benefit.

a. Childcare program: For working parents, the relief of from the question 'who will watch my kids' is almost priceless. Having a childcare offering at work or a partnership deal with a local daycare resource can reduce the stress of many parents. Yes, dog care can now be added to this consideration as well.

b. Physical Health program: There is a connection between your body and your mind, both must be exercised. Companies see the opportunity for you to invest in you as something that will benefit both parties. These benefits come through a gym at work, a gym membership, or reimbursable fitness activities.

c. Mental Health programs: We all deal with issues, but some more than others. Company programs can identify common and catastrophic issues that people need more support to overcome. Dealing with things like stress, anger, or addiction? You may find a lot of value in a company resource that can help you manage.

d. Nutrition program: Are you a morning person? If not, 'free coffee' may be the best benefit you can imagine. Many companies have done research on having coffee and snacks at work as both a benefit to their employees but also a way to increase productivity. Make sure you evaluate the free protein bars and espresso machine in the break room.

 Company Culture: The last intangible benefit to evaluate is the enigma or being of the company beyond what, when and who works there. Discussing the interactions between colleagues and the identification of the company from the outside world will be tough to put a dollar amount but valuable to know. This can be categorized as company culture and branding.

a. CULTURE: Company culture is how people within the company view what the companies' values are and how it operates. This will be the morale of the employees and overall satisfaction with working at this company.

b. BRAND: Company brand is how people outside the company view the companies' values and how it operates. This will be the recognition and prestige the company holds when added to your resume.

Your decision of where to go to work begins with what desired lifestyle you are trying to afford. Once your lifestyle is set, you can begin to evaluate which careers of work are able to afford this level of income. Once you have evaluated how much money you will need and the types of jobs that can provide that level of income, the next thing you will begin doing is weighing the benefits the company offers.

These benefits can be tangible or intangible and are intended to remove work stress. Your overall compensation and benefit package should bring satisfaction to your life. Evaluate and compare the extra dollars you can use, against the non-financial benefits that will bring value into your work life.

SECTION 11.1
RECAP

1. YOUR PAYSTUB IS AN ESTIMATED OVERVIEW OF WHAT IS HAPPENING WITH YOUR MONEY.

2. FOR A W2 WORKER, A PAYSTUB WILL SHOW YOUR SOCIETY AND FUTURE CHOICES AS WELL AS COMPANY BENEFITS. FOR A 1099 CONTRACTOR, YOUR PAYSTUB WILL SHOW GROSS INCOME AND YOU WILL BE RESPONSIBLE FOR THE REST.

3. COMPANY BENEFITS THAT HAVE A DOLLAR VALUE ARE TANGIBLE, FOR EXAMPLE HEALTHCARE, RETIREMENT, OR ADDITIONAL COMPENSATION. COMPANY BENEFITS THAT DO NOT HAVE A DOLLAR VALUE ARE INTANGIBLE, FOR EXAMPLE SCHEDULING, WELLNESS PROGRAMS, OR COMPANY CULTURE.

SECTION 11.2
GAME OF INCHES CHALLENGE

WHAT IS THE BIGGEST DIFFERENCE BETWEEN COLLEGE FOOTBALL AND PROFESSIONAL FOOTBALL?

People often ask me that question and it reminds me of a lesson I learned from a thirteen-year NFL veteran I met while running wind sprints on the Kansas City Chiefs.

This veteran would always finish our conditioning drills five yards farther than everyone else. We'd all run forty yards, he'd run forty-five yards; if we ran 100 yards, he would run 105 yards. At first, you joke about the older guy needing time to slow down, but then you start to wonder why he's doing it.

In the weight room, we would be required to rep a set of 10 and he would do 11 reps. He would also try to be the last person to go and add five pounds to the weight set up.

When it came to studying film, we would all be told to get 2 games on tape, and he would go get one more game on tape than everyone else.

One day, I had to ask, "What's up with the extra running and reps? Why do you think 5 pounds will make a difference?"

This Pro-Bowl veteran told me 'Every player in here is cheaper, faster, and healthier than me. The only reason I am still here after 13 years is because I come in each day and try to steal this.' He held up his fingers to show a small space in between his thumb and pointer fingers. Each day his focus was on getting an edge over everyone else by stealing an inch or a small advantage.

He went on to say, 'I steal an inch a day because an inch can lead to a yard, a yard to a first down, a first down to a score, a score to a win, and a win can take us to the Super Bowl!'

These little things, inches, are the biggest difference that separates a rookie from a veteran. A vet looks for and appreciates all those inches knowing that winning is a game of inches.

THE BIGGEST DIFFERENCE WAS VERY SMALL.

You can take this idea and begin to transfer it to how you see money.

As your routine around money begins to take shape, and you U.S.E. your Money Buckets, you will begin to see your Money Inches reveal themselves. This can occur when you do your vehicle 'tune-up' and review your paystub. Taking a moment to see how much is going where and then what you are doing with the rest. You will be able to find small changes to your habits and identify things that you can either start doing or stop doing that will add value to your plan.

RICH GOAL CHALLENGE:
STARTING TODAY, HOW MANY MONEY INCHES CAN YOU EARN, SAVE, AND CREATE THAT WILL BE ADDED UP ONE YEAR FROM TODAY?

$5,000	$1,000
$14 a day	$3 a day
$97 a week	$20 a week
$417 a month	$84 a month

WHAT DO 'MONEY INCHES' LOOK LIKE?

GOING OUT

⇨ Sticking with water at dinner

⇨ Finding a free activity

⇨ Stay in & stream a movie instead of going to the movies

⇨ Make a gift for a friend instead of buying one

BILLS

⇨ Turn off lights to keep your energy bill down

⇨ Cancel subscriptions you are not using

⇨ Plan out your grocery list and cook large amounts for leftovers

DEBT

⇨ Avoid interest on your credit card balance

⇨ Improve your credit score and get better offerings

⇨ Consolidate your debt into a lower APR

INVEST

⇨ 401(k) free money

⇨ Finding a Savings Account with better interest

SPENDING DECISIONS

⇨ Hold off for thirty days on purchasing something, then ask yourself if you need or even want it.

⇨ Instead of spending, transfer the dollars into your investment account.

SECTION 11.2
RECAP

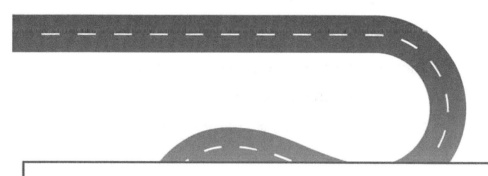

1. THE BIGGEST DIFFERENCE IN PROFESSIONALS WAS AN INCH.

2. YOU CAN FIND MONEY INCHES THROUGHOUT YOUR PLAN TO ADD EFFICIENCY AND VALUE.

3. BREAK DOWN YOUR R.I.C.H. GOAL INTO MONEY INCHES.

SECTION 11.3
THE ROAD TO FREEDOM

We have discussed everything from our goals to our accounts, broken down what you spend on and even categorized these expenses into your Money Buckets, but now it is time to share a perspective change on why you are working. Many see the focal point of work as retirement. Money Vehicle Chapter 1.1 discusses how you can no longer solely depend on pensions or social security for your financial plan. How you will 'retire' has changed and now what 'retire' means needs to change as well.

The good news is that you are not solely reliant on these old sources of income for your plan to work anymore. You have begun to set up multiple streams of income throughout Money Vehicle. These new sources of income can be seen from your Brokerage Account to your Roth Account, and through finding ways to create sources of income. This diversification (Chapter 6) of your income streams will provide you with the confidence that your strategy can sustain the challenges that life is going to throw at you.

Better news is that we are going to retire from the word retirement. You are no longer reliant on the 'old sources' of income, so you should no longer be setting the same old destination either. Your Money Vehicle is not driving to a date where you stop just working for money, because now that money works for you, you are already there.

You are now driving to a place where you stop making decisions based on money, a destination where you can see your values reflected in your financial choices, and a place where you feel freedom from financial stress. This is why we want Your Money Vehicle to be directed at Financial Freedom, and no longer retirement.

Money Vehicle hopes you feel more empowered to U.S.E. money on this road to freedom, but one last lesson we want to leave you with is around the best thing money can buy. To do this we will share one final story from Morgan Housel's Psychology of Money.

At a party thrown by a hedge fund billionaire one of the guests turns to Joseph Heller, a wildly successful author most known for writing Catch-22 and says, 'Is it crazy that the host made more money in a single day than you did off your entire Catch-22 sales?!'

Mr. Heller responds "Yes, but I have something he will never have."

The people around Mr. Heller confusedly begin to wonder what on earth he can have that a billionaire cannot buy?

After a moment Mr Heller says "ENOUGH."

This example is a symbolic way to conclude a program centered around money. Today people will do their best to show you how much money they have through social media or extravagant purchases. But seldom do you see people boast about having the simple elegance of enough.

This 'enough' comes when Your Money Vehicle enters a destination where you are free from the demands of others and the demands of money. This is again why we use the term, Financial Freedom. Money can buy many things and your financial plan will take you to many places, but you must keep in balance that the best thing money can buy is enough.

 THE BEST THING MONEY CAN BUY IS...ENOUGH!

JUST THE BEGINNING

The lessons in Your Money Vehicle were designed to empower your U.S.E. of money: Understand, Strategize and Efficiently use money! As you begin to speak the language of money you will be able to take advantage of the financial tools and information available to you in your day-to-day life.

Congratulations for investing in yourself and taking ownership of Your Money Vehicle. To test your knowledge and give you the sense of confidence you are looking for, we have created Certification for Money Vehicle Financial Literacy Level 1. This is a great resume builder and can be a good conversation piece in a job interview.

Please send your success stories and get Your Certification by sending a message to:

STUDENT@YOURMONEY VEHICLE.COM

But this is only the beginning. You have taken the first 10 steps in establishing Your Money Vehicle, but there is still much to learn and many places to go. Never stop finding ways to U.S.E. money!

ONE LAST REVIEW
OF YOUR OWNER'S MANUAL:

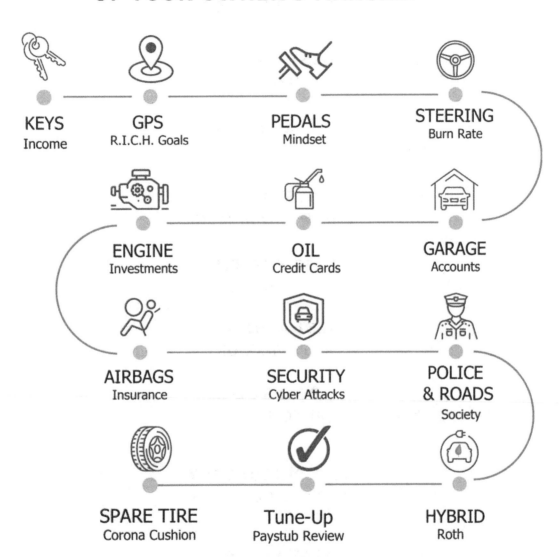

KEYS
Income

GPS
R.I.C.H. Goals

PEDALS
Mindset

STEERING
Burn Rate

ENGINE
Investments

OIL
Credit Cards

GARAGE
Accounts

AIRBAGS
Insurance

SECURITY
Cyber Attacks

**POLICE
& ROADS**
Society

SPARE TIRE
Corona Cushion

Tune-Up
Paystub Review

HYBRID
Roth

THE BEST OF MONEY VEHICLE

BEST LESSON:
OPPORTUNITY COST

BEST NUMBER:
BURN RATE

BEST ADVANTAGE:
TIME

BEST RULE:
EMPLOY YOUR MONEY

BEST SYSTEM:
MONEY BUCKETS

BEST VEHICLE:
ROTH ACCOUNT

BEST TOOL:
AUTOMATIONS

BEST PHILOSOPHY:
BE AVERAGE = INDEX

BEST RETURN:
401(K) FREE MONEY

BEST TAKEAWAY:
FREEDOM IS HAVING
ENOUGH!

REVIEW

THE RULE: FIND AN INCH

The hardest part of driving Your Money Vehicle is the start, so take pride in the fact you have begun and do not be overwhelmed by some of the bumps you will hit. Take time to check in on your plan when reviewing your paystub, review the benefits being offered, and confirm that your choices are still leading to your R.I.C.H. Goals. Through it all, your goal is to find what Freedom means to you and to one day have enough. The road to get there may be long, but if you can look at the next mile and see that it is just a bunch of inches, you will be there in no time!

ACTION

- Each day, find one money inch that you can take.
- Find an inch in your paystub.
- Find an inch in your benefits.
- Find an inch in your spending.

CERTIFICATION

MONEY VEHICLE CERTIFICATION

Congratulations! Working through this program has developed your financial literacy skills and we want to reward you with a Certification proving your growth.

GLOSSARY

10-K REPORT: a comprehensive report filed annually by a publicly-traded company about its financial performance and is required by the U.S. Securities and Exchange Commission (SEC). [CH. 6]

1099 CONTRACTOR: you work for yourself; you pay taxes and benefits for yourself. [CH. 9]

1099 DIV: tax document relating to any dividends you were paid. [CH. 9]

1099 INT: tax document relating to any interest you were paid. [CH. 9]

1099 K: tax document relating to any third-party income payments you were paid, for example PayPal, Venmo, Upwork. [CH. 9]

1099 NEC 'NON-EMPLOYEE COMPENSATION': tax document sent at the end of the year, summarizing what you were paid as a contractor. [CH. 9]

401(k): an employer sponsored 'defined contribution' personal pension account that is provided by a company you work for as a W2 employee, with a tax advantage for retirement savings. [CH. 10]

ACCESSIBILITY: ability to withdraw money from a specific account. [CH. 4]

ACCOUNT CLOSURE FEE: a fee charged by financial institutions for opening and closing an account within a designated period of time. [CH. 4]

ACCOUNT STATEMENTS: monthly reports of what occurred in your account and can be delivered physically or virtually. [CH. 4]

ACCREDITED INVESTOR: the SEC defines this investor as someone who EITHER has a gross income of $200,000 in each of last two years ($300,000 with spouse) OR has a Net Worth over $1,000,000. [CH. 10]

ACT LIKE AN INVESTOR: Money Vehicle term meaning you will not just become educated in money but will implement your learnings into actions. [INTRO]

AFTER TAX CONTRIBUTIONS: dollars that are placed into an account after they have been taxed. [CH. 10]

ALERTS: a resource provided by financial institutions to tell you important messages about your account. [CH. 4]

AMERICAN OPPORTUNITY TAX CREDIT: a tax deduction relating to educational expenses such as tuition, books, and even some transportation costs. [CH. 9]

AMORTIZE (AMORTIZATION SCHEDULE): means to gradually write off or payback the cost of an asset over time. The Amortization Schedule will show you exactly how much is being paid in each installment and how much of that installment is going towards principal or interest. [CH. 2]

ANNUAL FEE: a yearly cost a credit company will charge you to have a specific credit card. [CH. 5]

ANNUAL PERCENTAGE RATE (APR): the interest rate the credit company will charge you on a yearly (annual) basis, 365 days. [CH. 5]

ANNUAL PERCENTAGE YIELD (APY): the total amount of interest paid on an account based on the interest rate and frequency of compounding over a 365-day period. [CH. 4]

ANTIVIRUS SOFTWARE: a program designed to detect and remove viruses and other malware from your computer. [CH. 8]

ASSET: something that puts money into your pocket. [INTRO]

ATM (AUTOMATED TELLER MACHINE): a machine that allows you to withdraw cash without going up to the bank teller. [CH. 4]

AUTHORIZED USER: for minors wanting to use credit, this is a way to connect your name onto someone else's account and begin to build your credit. [CH. 5]

AUTO INSURANCE: the primary purpose of this type of insurance is to provide financial protection against damage to the vehicle or bodily injury to the passengers in the case of an accident. [CH. 7]

AUTONOMY: the freedom to choose, to decide what you believe will be best for your plan. [CH. 1]

BALANCING A CHECKBOOK: a traditional way to review how much money was in your account by looking at the deposits and withdrawals you tracked in your checkbook. With virtual banking, this has become less of a practice but still a good concept to understand. [CH. 4]

BANK: a for-profit financial institution that will accept deposits from the public. [CH. 4]

BANK ACCOUNT NUMBER: number sequence that identifies your account at a financial institution. [CH. 9]

BANK ROUTING NUMBER: number sequence that identifies your financial institution. [CH. 9]

BE A PRO: Money Vehicle mindset that brings employability through finding confidence, building trust, and adding value. [INTRO]

BE AVERAGE - INDEX: Money Vehicle investment philosophy sharing the power and simplicity of investing in index funds. [CH. 6]

BODILY INJURY: in case the accident results in people being hurt. [CH. 7]

BOND: investment that makes you a lender. The loan amount will be paid back plus interest on the bond's maturity date. [CH. 6]

BRAND: company brand is how people outside the company view the companies' values and how it operates. [OUTRO]

BRETTON WOODS AGREEMENT: an agreement stating you can exchange an ounce of gold for $35 cash. [INTRO]

BUDGET: an estimate of income and expenses for a specific period of time. This term has had a limiting mindset attached to it and that is why Money Vehicle does not use it. [CH. 3]

BUREAU OF LABOR STATISTICS (BLS): the government agency responsible for measuring inflation. [INTRO]

BURN RATE: the amount of money you spend to support your lifestyle each month. This will be your Past and Present choices. [CH. 1]

BUSINESS DEBT: when money is owed for purchases used by a company. [CH. 2]

CAPITAL GAIN: the amount your investment has gained in value and will be subject to tax. [CH. 9]

CAPITAL LOSS: the amount your investment has lost in value and will be able to reduce taxable gains. [CH. 9]

CAPITALISM: an economic system where a country's trade or industry is controlled by private owners for profit. [CH. 6]

CAPITALIST: someone who participates in the buying and selling of goods for a profit. [CH. 6]

CAPITALIZATION 'CAP': how much money a company is worth in their market. Cap is an abbreviation for market capitalization. [CH. 6]

CASH ADVANCE: allows you to withdraw cash from your credit limit and the moment you pull the cash out, interest begins to accrue on your balance with no grace period. [CH. 5]

CASH MANAGEMENT: a management of income and expenses before money even arrives. This term is more empowering to a growth mindset. [CH. 3]

CERTIFICATE OF DEPOSIT (CD) OR SHARE CERTIFICATES: a type of savings account at a financial institution that can be used to protect money and earn a higher interest rate than a traditional savings account, but your cash will not be liquid. [CH. 4]

CERTIFIED PUBLIC ACCOUNTANT (CPA): a professional license to provide accounting services to the public. [CH. 9]

CHARGED OFF: if you have missed payments for six (6) months, the credit company will write off your debt as uncollectible and negatively impacts your credit score. You are still liable for this debt; it will just transfer to a debt collector or bankruptcy. [CH. 5]

CHECKING ACCOUNT (ALSO KNOWN AS TODAY ACCOUNTS): intended for use on purchases and activities that you do today. With a checking account, you can pay for lunch, buy those shoes, or just take out cash to have. [CH. 4]

CO-INSURANCE: the percentage of insurance costs you will pay after the deductible has been met. [CH. 7]

CO-PAY: a fixed dollar amount you will pay each time you use a specific health care service such as a trip to the doctor or refilling prescription. [CH. 7]

COCKINESS: an external voice that tells others how good you are. [INTRO]

COLLATERAL: something pledged as security in a loan that will be forfeited if the borrower does not pay. [CH. 2]

COLLISION: covers damage to your car that is caused by a collision or an accident. [CH. 7]

COMPOUND INTEREST: the 8th wonder of the world and occurs when you receive interest payments based on the principal amount you plus the interest that has already been created. [CH. 2]

COMPREHENSIVE: covers damage to your car that is caused by something other than a collision, such as weather or theft. [CH. 7]

CONCENTRATION: the opposite of diversification where you invest in a small number or even a singular investment, creating more risk and the potential for more return. [CH. 6]

CONFIDENCE: an internal voice that tells you how good you are. This can come from getting an education about your job both in and out of traditional school. [INTRO]

CONTRIBUTION (SEEDS): dollars you place into the Roth account. [CH. 10]

CONSUMER CREDIT PROTECTION ACT OF 1968: a statute that mandates that the total cost and calculation of a loan be disclosed, along with any fees. [INTRO]

CONSUMER DEBT: when money is owed for purchases used by an individual or family. [CH. 2]

CONSUMER FINANCIAL PROTECTION BUREAU (CFPB): a government agency dedicated to making sure you are treated fairly by banks, lenders, and other financial institutions as well as enforce consumer protection laws. [INTRO]

CONSUMER PRICE INDEX (CPI): CPI is a theoretical basket of over 80,000 goods and services that consumers will purchase, and this basket can be used to compare prices of those purchases from one year to another year. [INTRO]

CORONA CUSHION (EMERGENCY FUND): a cushion of money that provides your plan with a little protection from the unexpected such as illness, accidents, or loss of job. Aiming for 3-6 months of your Burn Rate. [CH. 4]

CREATED INCOME: money that worked for you and represents secondary income sources. [INTRO]

CREDIT BUREAU: a company that collects information relating to your credit and makes the information available to financial institutions. [CH. 5]

CREDIT CARD: a payment card that borrows credit from a third party. [CH. 5]

CREDIT HISTORY: a measurement in your Credit Score based on how long you have been using credit. [CH. 5]

CREDIT LIMIT: the amount of credit that is available on your credit card. [CH. 5]

CREDIT REPORT: a list of every credit-related action you have taken in a period of time. [CH. 5]

CREDIT SCORE: a single number derived from the transactions in your Credit Report that will provide a comparative benchmark between lenders. [CH. 5]

CREDIT TRAP: when something you purchase ends up costing more than the original price due to interest paid on credit card. [CH. 5]

CREDIT UNION: a not-for-profit financial institution that will accept deposits from the public. [CH. 4]

CREDIT UTILIZATION: a measurement in your Credit Score based on how much of your credit limit you are using. [CH. 5]

CUE: the trigger— the thing that tells your body and mind to start. [CH. 3]

CULTURE: Company culture is how people within the company view what the companies' values are and how it operates. [OUTRO]

CUSTODIAN: a financial institution that can hold your investment securities such as stocks, bonds, or other digital assets. [CH. 6]

CYBERSECURITY: every aspect of your defense to fight the hackers. [CH. 8]

DAILY RATE: the interest rate the credit company will charge you on a daily basis, 1 day or the APR divided by 365. [CH. 5]

DEBIT CARD: a payment card that can be used to pull cash from your account. [CH. 5]

DEBT: when money is owed. [CH. 2]

DECLARATION PAGE: the first page of your policy will specify exactly who is insured, the policy period, the policy coverage components, and the policy limits. [CH. 7]

DEDUCTIBLE: the cost to U.S.E. an insurance policy, this cost only occurs in the event the policy is used. [CH. 7]

DEFINED CONTRIBUTION: an account where contributions are made regularly by employer and employee, with a limit of how much you can contribute. [CH. 10]

DEPENDENTS: a tax election you will make around who you are responsible for taking care of. You must also confirm if your parents claim you as dependent. [CH. 9]

DESIRED LIFESTYLE: the life that you are building a plan to support in your future. [INTRO]

DIVERSIFICATION: a risk management technique that mixes a wide variety of investments within a portfolio. Deemed a 'Free lunch' because it can reduce your risk without reducing your returns. [CH. 6]

DIVIDEND: a sum of money that is paid out regularly to shareholders of a certain stock. [CH. 9]

'DO' INVESTING PRINCIPLE: Do follow the Golden Rule or you will not be able to invest. [CH. 6]

E-COMMERCE: buying or selling things online. [INTRO]

E-FILE: ability to sign and file your taxes electronically and not have to physically mail it in. [CH. 9]

EARNED INCOME: money you went to work for and represents your primary income. [INTRO]

EARNINGS (FRUIT): dollars created while the money is invested in the Roth account. [CH. 10]

ECONOMIC CONTRACTION: the economy is shrinking. [CH. 2]

ECONOMIC EXPANSION: the economy is growing. [CH. 2]

EFFECTIVE TAX RATE (ETR): the average tax rate you pay on earned income. [CH. 9]

EFFICIENT: the third step in how to U.S.E. money and means you are finding ways to add value to your plan. This is achieving the maximum productivity with minimum wasted effort and will be found by bringing energy to your job. [INTRO]

ELECTRONIC FUNDS TRANSFER ACT: debit card allows only 2 days to report fraudulent activity, before you are liable for up to $500. [CH. 5]

EMERGENCY FUND: Money Vehicle wants to update this to something more relevant and tangible for you as a student, see Corona Cushion. [CH. 4]

EMPLOYEE BENEFITS: any compensation provided by your employer that is in addition to your wage or salary and intended to increase your overall satisfaction and productivity. [OUTRO]

EMPLOYEE STOCK OPTIONS (ESO): a type of benefit where a company will offer an employee the ability to purchase or earn ownership of the company. [OUTRO]

EMPLOYER MATCH 'FREE MONEY': your employer can contribute more into your retirement plan account based on your contributions. Called a match because you contribute and then they will, called 'free' because this benefit does not cost you anything. [CH. 10]

ENDORSEMENTS, (ALSO KNOWN AS RIDERS): additional policy terms added to your policy. [CH. 7]

ENTREPRENEUR: someone who creates a business that can function without them. [INTRO]

EQUAL CREDIT OPPORTUNITY ACT OF 1974: a statute that aims to require banks, credit card companies, and any other lenders to make credit equally available to all creditworthy customers. [INTRO]

EQUIFAX: member of the 'big three' credit reporting agencies. [CH. 5]

EXPENSE RATIO: the fee you pay to own the mutual fund or index fund. [CH. 10]

EXPERIAN: member of the 'big three' credit reporting agencies.[CH.5]

FAIR CREDIT & REPORTING ACT: Federal legislation to promote the accuracy, fairness, and privacy of consumer information captured by consumer reporting agencies. [CH. 5]

FAIR CREDIT REPORTING ACT OF 1970: a statute that aims to promote accuracy, fairness, and privacy of consumer information obtained by a reporting agency. [INTRO]

FAIR DEBT COLLECTION PRACTICES ACT OF 1977: a statute that aims to eliminate abusive practice in the collection of consumer debt. [INTRO]

FAIR CREDIT BILLING ACT: protects information gathered by credit bureaus and removes liability for fraudulent transactions. [CH. 5]

FANNIE MAE & FREDDIE MAC: mortgage companies created and backed by the United States Government to purchase mortgages in a secondary market, neither institution issues their own mortgages. [CH. 5]

FEDERAL DEPOSIT INSURANCE CORPORATION (FDIC): created by the Banking Act of 1933, this is a United States government corporation providing insurance on deposits to American commercial banks. [CH. 4]

FEDERAL FUNDS RATE: this is the benchmark interest rate that financial institutions will lend their money reserves held at the FED to one another. [CH. 2]

FEDERAL OPEN MARKET COMMITTEE (FOMC): the branch of the FED who is responsible for managing the money supply and attempting to achieve the FOMC mandate. That mandate is a goal of 2% inflation annually, and to keep unemployment low. [INTRO]

FED REGULATION D: created from the Securities Act of 1933 this imposes a reserve requirement on certain deposits and specifies how the institution classifies different deposits. [CH. 4]

FEDERAL RESERVE (COMMONLY CALLED THE FED OR FED): a central bank for the United States that was created by the Federal Reserve Act back in 1913 as a response to financial panics occurring in the United States. [INTRO]

FEDERAL SECURITIES ACT OF 1933: federal act that requires companies to disclose all any 'material' or important information related to a security investment. [CH. 6]

FEDERAL TRADE COMMISSION (FTC): Established in 1914 to administer and protect fair competition in the marketplace. [CH. 5]

FEDERAL INCOME TAX: the progressive tax paid to the Federal Government from your earned income. [CH. 9]

FEES: a payment made to an institution for a service. [CH.4]

FIAT SYSTEM: an economic system where the currency is backed by an intangible concept such as confidence or trust in the country's economy. [INTRO]

FICA TAX (FEDERAL INSURANCE CONTRIBUTIONS ACT): the tax deducted from your paycheck to go toward paying Social Security and Medicare Taxes. The amounts will be based on your income level and your employer will pay half of the cost. [CH. 9]

FICO: Fair Isaac Corporation is perhaps the best-known company that calculates personal credit scores. [CH. 5]

FICO SCORE: a numerical analysis created by the FICO company to represent an individual's creditworthiness or financial reputation. [CH. 5]

FIDUCIARY: someone who is legally obligated to put your financial interest above their own. [INTRO]

FIGHT THE HACKERS: Money Vehicle's approach to defending yourself in the online cyber war. [CH. 8]

Made in the USA
Monee, IL
03 November 2023

45606315R00236